I AM THAT

Talks On The Isha Upanishad

I AM THAT

Talks On The Isha Upanishad

I AM THAT

Talks On The Isha Upanishad

by

Osho

JAICO PUBLISHING HOUSE
Mumbai Delhi Bangalore Kolkata
Hyderabad Chennai Ahmedabad Bhopal

Published by Jaico Publishing House
121 Mahatma Gandhi Road
Mumbai - 400 001
jaicopub@vsnl.com
www.jaicobooks.com

Copyright © 2008 Osho International Foundation.
All rights reserved
First Publication Copyright © 1981, Osho International Foundation.
Copyright ©-all revisions 1953-2008 Osho International Foundation.
All rights reserved
OSHO is a registered trademark of
Osho International Foundation, used under license.
www.osho.com

I AM THAT: TALKS ON THE ISHA UPANISHAD
ISBN 978-81-7992-747-2

First Jaico Impression: 2008
Second Jaico Impression: 2008

No part of this book may be reproduced or utilized in
any form or by any means, electronic or
mechanical including photocopying, recording or by any
information storage and retrieval system,
without permission in writing from the publishers.

Printed by
Rashmi Graphics
#3, Amrutwel CHS Ltd., C.S. #50/74
Ganesh Galli, Lalbaug, Mumbai-400 012
E-mail: tiwarijp@vsnl.net

Contents

1.	Beyond The Changing	1
2.	Living In Your Own Light	25
3.	By Following Nobody Knows	47
4.	Surrender Is Of The Heart	70
5.	Bound In Deep Togetherness	96
6.	Absolute Lobe, Absolute Freedom	121
7.	Each Moment — Miracles !	143
8.	Knowing Nothing About Everything	164
9.	Both And More	185
10.	The Eternal Religion	209
11.	No Mind At All	234
12.	A Mystery To Be Lived	258
13.	Prayer Simply Happens	279
14.	Without Women — No Buddhas	306
15.	Everybody Has His Uniqueness	331
16.	It Is Already The Best	349

Beyond The Changing

Aum
That Is The Whole.
This Is The Whole.
From Wholeness Emerges Wholeness.
Wholeness Coming From Wholeness,
Wholeness Still Remains.
At The Heart Of This Phenomenal World,
Within All Its Changing Forms,
Dwells The Unchanging Lord.
So, Go Beyond The Changing,
And, Enjoying The Inner,
Cease To Take For Yourself
What To Others Are Riches.
Continuing To Act In The World,
One May Aspire To Be One Hundred.
Thus, And Only Thus, Can A Man Be Free
From The Binding Influence Of Action.
Unillumined Indeed Are Those Worlds Clouded
By The Blinding Darkness Of Ignorance.
Into This Death Sink All Those Who Slay The Self.

Aum

Purnamadah
Purnamidam
Purnat Purnamudachyate
Purnasya Purnamadaya
Purnameva Vashishyate.

Aum

That Is The Whole.
This Is The Whole.
From Wholeness Emerges Wholeness.
Wholeness Coming From Wholeness,
Wholeness Still Remains.

We are entering today into one of the most enchanting and mysterious worlds — that of the Upanishads. The days of the Upanishads were the highest as far as the spiritual quest is concerned. Never before and never afterwards has human consciousness achieved such Himalayan heights.

The days of the Upanishads were really golden, for many reasons. The most important of them is contained in this seed mantra:

Aum
Purnamadah
Purnamidam
Purnat Purnamudachyate
Purnasya Purnamadaya
Purnameva Vashishyate

The emphasis of the Upanishads is on wholeness. Remember, it is not on perfection but on wholeness. The moment one becomes interested in being perfect, the ego enters in. The ego is a perfectionist — the desire of the ego is to be perfect — and perfection drives humanity towards insanity.

Wholeness is totally different; its flavor is different. Perfection is in the future: it is a desire. Wholeness is herenow: it is a revelation. Perfection has to be achieved, and of course every achievement takes time; it has to be gradual. You have to sacrifice the present for the future, the today for the tomorrow. And the tomorrow never comes; what comes is always today.

Existence knows nothing of future and nothing of past; it knows only the present. Now is the only time and here the only space. The moment you go astray from now and here you are going to end into some kind of madness. You will fall into fragments; your life will become a hell. You will be torn apart: the past will pull a part of you towards itself and the future the other part. You will become schizophrenic, split, divided. Your life will be only a deep anguish, a trembling, an anxiety, a tension. You will not know anything of bliss, you will not know anything of ecstasy because the past exists not.

And people go on living in the memories which are only footprints left on the sand; or they project a life into the future, which is also as non-existential as the past. One is no more, the other is not yet, and between the two one loses the real, the present, the now.

Wholeness is of the now. If you can be simply here, then this very moment the revelation! Then it is not gradual, it is sudden, it is an explosion!

The word upanishad is tremendously important. It simply means sitting down close to a Master; it is a communion. The Master is living in wholeness; he is living herenow, he is pulsating herenow. His life has a music, his life has a joy, a silence of immense depth. His life is full of light.

Just to sit silently by the side of a Master is enough, because the presence of a Master is infectious, the presence of the Master is overwhelming. His silence starts reaching to your very heart. His presence becomes a magnetic pull on you: it pulls you out of the mud of the past and the future. It brings you into the present.

Upanishad is a communion, not a communication. A communication is head-to-head and a communion is heart-to-heart. This is one of the greatest secrets of spiritual life, and nowhere else, at no other time, it was understood so deeply as in the days of the Upanishads.

The Upanishads were born about five thousand years before. A secret communion, a transmission beyond the scriptures, a communion beyond the words... this is what Upanishad is — you sitting silently, not just listening to my words but listening to my presence too. The words are only excuses to hang the silence upon. The silence is the real content, the word is only a container. If you become too much interested in the word you miss the spirit.

So don't be too much interested in the word. Listen to the heartbeat of the word. When a Master speaks, those words are coming from his innermost core. They are full of his color, of his light. They carry some of the perfume of his being. If you are open and vulnerable, receptive, welcoming, they will penetrate into your heart and a process is triggered.

What Carl Gustav Jung calls synchronicity explains exactly what happens between a Master and a disciple. It is not the same as what happens between a teacher and a student. Between teacher and a student there is a communication; some information is transferred by the teacher to the student, but no transformation — only information. The teacher himself is not transformed, he himself has not arrived. He is repeating words from other teachers, he may be even repeating words from other Masters, but he has not known himself; his words are borrowed. He may be very scholarly, he may be very well-informed, but that is not the real thing. Information is not the real thing — transformation. And unless one is transformed he cannot trigger the process of transformation in others.

Carl Gustav Jung calls this synchronicity. The Master cannot cause your enlightenment. It is not a scientific process, it is far more poetic. It is not a law like the law of cause and effect; it is far more liquid, far more loose, far more flexible. The Master cannot cause the enlightenment to happen in you, but he can trigger the process, and that too only if you allow, not against your will. Nothing can be done to you unless you are totally receptive. This can happen only in a love affair.

Between the teacher and the student there is a business: between the Master and the disciple there is a love affair. The disciple is surrendered; that is the meaning of "sitting down". He is surrendered, he has put his ego aside. He is simply open, in tremendous trust. Of course, doubt will hinder the process.

Doubt is perfectly good when you are collecting information: the more you doubt, the more information you will be able to collect, because each doubt will create questions in you and questions are needed to find answers. But each answer will be doubted again in its own turn, creating more questions, and so on, so forth.

But with a Master doubt is a hindrance. It is not of asking a question, it is a quest of the soul; it is enquiry of the heart, it is not intellectual curiosity. It is not curiosity, it is far more important — it is a question of life and death.

When one is tired of all questions and all answers, when one is fed up with all philosophy, only then one comes to a Master. When one has accumulated much information and still remains ignorant, and all that information does not create any light within his soul, then he comes to a Master, to sit by his side. There are no questions any more; he knows now one thing. that all questions are futile. He has tried and he has seen the whole futility of it. Now he sits in silence, open, available, receptive, like a womb.

The disciple becomes feminine, and only in those feminine moments the Master, without any effort on his part, starts overflooding the disciple. It happens naturally. The disciple is not doing anything, the Master is not doing anything — it is not a question of doing at all. The Master is being himself and the disciple is open.

When your nose is not closed by cold and you pass by the side of a flower, suddenly the fragrance is felt. The flower is not doing anything in particular; it is natural for the flower to release its fragrance. If you are open to receive it you will receive it.

The word Upanishad means coming to a Master, and one comes to a Master only when one is tired of teachers, tired of teachings, tired of dogmas, creeds, philosophies, theologies, religions. Then one comes to a Master.

And the way to come to a Master is surrender. Not that your being is surrendered — only the ego, the false idea that you are somebody, somebody special. The moment you put the idea of the ego aside, the doors are open — for the wind, for the rain, for the sun — and the Master's presence will start entering in you, creating a new dance in your life, giving you a new sense of poetry, mystery, music.

It is synchronicity. The Master is beating in a certain rhythm, he is dancing on a certain plane. If you are ready, the same dance starts happening in you — in the beginning only a little bit, but that's enough, that little bit is enough. In the beginning only dewdrops, but soon they become oceanic.

Once you have tasted the joy of being open you cannot be closed again. First you may open only a window or a door, and then you open all your windows and all the doors.

And a moment comes in the life of a disciple when not only windows and doors are opened, even the walls disappear! He is utterly open, available multidimensionally. This is the meaning of the word Upanishad.

The Upanishads are written in Sanskrit; Sanskrit is the oldest language on the earth. The very word sanskrit means transformed, adorned, crowned, decorated, refined — but remember the word "transformed" The language itself was transformed because so many people attained to the ultimate, and because they were using the language, something of their joy penetrated into it, something of their poetry entered into the very cells, the very fiber of the language. Even the language became transformed, illuminated. It was bound to happen. Just as it is happening today in the West, languages are becoming more and more scientific, accurate, mathematical, precise. They have to be because science is giving them its color, its shape, its form. If science is growing, then of course the language in which the science will be expressed will have to be scientific.

The same happened five thousand years before in India with Sanskrit. So many people became enlightened and they were all speaking Sanskrit; their enlightenment entered into it with all its music, with all its poetry, with all its celebration. Sanskrit became luminous Sanskrit is the most poetic and musical language in existence.

A poetic language is just the opposite of a scientific language. In scientific language every word has to be very precise in meaning; it has to have only one meaning. In a poetic language the word has to be liquid, flowing, dynamic, not static, allowing many meanings, many possibilities. The word has to be not precise at all; the more imprecise it is the better, because then it will be able to express all kinds of nuances.

Hence the Sanskrit sutras can be defined in many ways, can be commented upon in many ways — they allow much playfulness. For example, there are eight hundred roots in Sanskrit and out of those eight hundred roots thousands of words have been derived, just as out of one root a tree grows and many branches and thousands of leaves and hundreds of flowers. Each single root becomes a vast tree with great foliage.

For example, the root Ram can mean first "to be calm", second "to rest", third "to delight in", fourth "cause delight to", fifth "to make love", sixth "to join", seventh "to make happy", eighth "to be blissful", ninth "to play", tenth "to be peaceful", eleventh "to stand still", twelfth "to stop, to come to a full stop", and thirteenth "God, divine, the absolute". And these are only few of the meanings of the root. Sometimes the meanings are related to each other, sometimes not; sometimes even they are contradictory to each other. Hence the language has a multidimensional quality to it. You can play with those words and through that play you can express the inexpressible; the inexpressible can be hinted.

The Sanskrit language is called devavani — the divine language. And it certainly is divine in the sense because it is the most poetic and the most musical language. Each word has a music around it, a certain aroma.

How it happened? It happened because so many people used it who were full of inner harmony. Of course those words became luminous: they were used by people who were enlightened.

Something of their light filtered to the words, reached to the words; something of their silence entered the very grammar, the very language they were using.

The script in which Sanskrit is written is called devanagari; devanagari means "dwelling-place of the gods", and so certainly it is. Each word has become divine, just because it has been used by people who had known God or godliness.

This Upanishad in which we are entering today is the smallest — it can be written on a postcard — and yet it is the greatest document in existence. There is no document of such luminosity, of such profoundness anywhere in the whole history of humanity. The name of the Upanishad is Isha Upanishad.

The world of the Upanishads is very close to my approach. In fact, what I am doing here is giving a rebirth to the spirit of the Upanishads. It has disappeared even from India, and it has not been on the scene at least for three thousand years. There is a gap of three thousand years, and in these three thousand years India has destroyed its own achievement.

The first thing is that Upanishads are not anti-life, they are not for renouncing life. Their approach is whole: life has to be lived in its totality. They don't teach escapism. They want you to live in the world, but in such a way that you remain above the world, in a certain sense transcendental to the world, living in the world and yet not being of it. But they don't teach you that life has to be renounced, that you have to escape from life, that life is ugly or life is sin. They rejoice in life! It is a gift of God; it is the manifest form of God.

This fundamental has to be remembered. Upanishads say that the world is the manifest form of God and the God is the unmanifest form of the world, and every manifest phenomenon has an unmanifest noumenon inside it.

When you see a flower, the flower is only the manifest form of something inside it, its essence, which is unmanifest, which is its soul, its very being. You cannot catch hold of it, you cannot find it by dissecting the flower. For that you need a poetic approach, not the scientific approach. The scientific approach analyzes; the poetic perspective is totally different. The science will never find any beauty in the flower because beauty belongs to the unmanifest form. Science will dissect the manifest form and will find all kinds of substances the flower is made of but will miss its soul.

Each and everything has both, the body and the soul. The body is the world and the soul is God, but the body is not against the soul, the world is not against the God. The world manifests God, expresses God. God is silence and the world is the song of that silence. And the same is true about you. Every person has both: the manifest, the bodymind structure, and the unmanifest, your consciousness.

Religion consists in discovering the unmanifest in the manifest. It is not a question of escaping anywhere; it is exploring your innermost depths. It is exploring the silent center, the center of the cyclone. And it is always there; any moment you can find it. It is not something that has to be found somewhere else, in the Himalayas or in a monastery. It is within You! You can discover it in the Himalayas, you can discover it in the marketplace.

The Upanishads say that to choose between the absolute and the relative is wrong. Any choice will make you partial; you will not be whole. And without whole there is no bliss, without whole there is no holiness; without whole you are always going to be a little bit lopsided, insane. When you are whole you are healthy because you are total.

The relative means the world, the changing, phenomenal world, and the absolute means the unchanging center of the changing world. Find the unchanging in the changing. And it is there so there is no question; just you have to know the technique of discovering it. That technique is meditation.

Meditation simply means becoming attuned to the unmanifest. The body is there, you can see it; the mind is there, you can see it too. If you close your eyes you will see the mind with all its activity, with all its working. Thoughts are passing, desires are arising, memories surfacing, and the whole activity of the mind will be there; you can watch it.

One thing is certain: the watcher is not the mind. The one who is conscious of the activities of the mind is not part of the mind. The watcher is separate, the witness is separate. To become aware of this witness is to have found the essential, the central, the absolute, the unchanging.

The body changes: once you were a child, then a young man or a young woman, then old age... One day you were in the mother's womb, then you were born, then one day again you die and disappear into the womb of existence. The body goes on changing, continuously changing.

The mind goes on changing. In the morning you are happy, in the afternoon you are angry, in the evening you are sad. Moods, emotions, feelings, go on changing; thoughts go on changing. The wheel goes on moving around you. This is the cyclone; the phenomenal world is the cyclone. It is never the same, not even for two consecutive moments.

But something is always the same, always, never changes — it is the witness. To find that witness is to find God.

Hence Upanishads don't teach you worship, they teach you meditation. And meditation can be done anywhere because the question is to know the witness. If you go into a monastery the same method will have to be applied there; if you go into the mountains the same method has to be applied there. You can be in the home, in the family, in the marketplace — the same method.

In fact, in the world it is easier to see the changing. When you go to the desert it will be more difficult to see the changing because in the desert almost nothing seems to change, or the change is so subtle that it is not visible. But in the marketplace, sitting by the side of a road, you can see the change continuously, the traffic on the road changing; it is never the same.

Living in the monastery is living in a static world, in a dormant world. It is living like a frog in a pond, in a well, enclosed. To live in the ocean will make you more aware of the changes.

It is good to be in the world: that is the message of the Upanishads. The Upanishadic seers were not ascetic. Of course they renounced many things, but the renunciation came not through effort, it came through understanding, it came through meditation. They renounced the ego because they saw that it is just a manufactured entity by the mind. It has no reality, no substance in it; it is pure shadow, and to waste your life with it is stupid. To say that they renounced is not right; it will be better to say that because they became so aware it withered away on its own accord.

They became non-possessive. It is not that they did not possess things, but they became non-possessive. They used things. They were not beggars. They lived joyously, enjoying everything that was available to them, but they were not possessive, they were not clingers. That is true renunciation: living in the world and yet remaining absolutely non-possessive. They loved, but they were not jealous. They loved totally but without any ego trip, without any idea to dominate the other.

This is what I am trying to do here, and there are fools in India who think I am against Indian culture. Of course I am against what has happened in these three thousand years — that is not true culture, that is a deviation, that is ugly. That has made India poor, that has kept India a slave for twenty-two centuries; that has made India so starved, unhealthy, unhygienic, for the simple reason if you teach people that life is not good to live — it is only worth renouncing, it has no value, the only value it has is to renounce it, the only virtue is to be anti-life — naturally life is going to suffer.

But this is not the message of the Upanishads, and the Upanishads are the very soul of this country, and not only of this country but of all the people who have been religious anywhere. They will find in Upanishads their very heart they will rejoice in Upanishads because Upanishads teach wholeness.

The relative has to be lived as the relative, knowingly that it is relative, knowingly that it is changing, and remembering continuously the unchanging. Abide in the unchanging and go on living in the changing. Remain centered in the unchanging, but allow the changing, beautiful world to move around you with all its seasons, with all its colors, with all its beauty, splendor. Enjoy that too, because it is the manifest form of God. This is a very holistic approach.

The first sutra:

*Aum
Purnamadah
Purnamidam
Purnat Purnamudachyate
Purnasya Purnamadaya
Purnameva Vashishyate
Aum*
That Is The Whole.

"That" means the ultimate, the absolute, the hidden aspect of reality, the invisible, the unmanifest. You can call it God truth, nirvana, Tao, Dhamma, Logos.

That Is The Whole
This Is The Whole Too.

And by "this" is meant the phenomenal world, the manifest world, the world that surrounds you. "That" means your center, "this" means your circumference. And both are whole, in fact both are one whole.

From Wholeness Emerges Wholeness.

From "that" emerges "this", and out of wholeness only wholeness can be born. You cannot dissect wholeness, you cannot divide wholeness. Out of wholeness only wholeness is born, so both are whole.

Wholeness Coming From Wholeness,
Wholeness Still Remains.

Although the wholeness comes from the whole it does not

Beyond The Changing

mean that the whole, the original whole, starts losing something. It loses nothing; it still remains the whole. This is a tremendously important statement. It will be good to try to understand it through your experience.

You love somebody; that does not mean that because you have given; on the contrary, it may be even more. It is not ordinary economics. In the ordinary economics if you give something, of course you will have less. If you have ten rupees with you and you give five to somebody you cannot still have ten rupees, and certainly you cannot have fifteen rupees; you will have only five rupees left. This is the ordinary economics, the economics of the outside world.

The inner world is totally different. You give love and you have still the same love or may be even more, because by giving, your love starts flowing. It may have been dormant, stagnant; by sharing it starts flowing. It is like you draw water from a well: the moment you draw water from a well, from the hidden springs more water starts coming to the well to fill the space. If you don't draw the water from the well the water will become dirty, it may even become poisonous. And the springs will not be used; they will become blocked. If you go on drawing water every day, more and more water will be flowing in the well and the springs will become bigger because they will be used more.

But people live in the outside economics even in their inner life. The wife becomes very much angry if she finds her husband just being friendly with another woman. The husband becomes aggressive, jealous. if he finds that his wife was having a good time with somebody else, just enjoying, laughing. This is sheer stupidity! It is not understanding the inner world and the inner meta-economics. He is still thinking in terms of money — that if his wife has laughed with somebody else that means she will be not able to laugh with him any more; so much laughter is lost! Now he is a loser, and of course that creates anger.

In fact, if the wife does not laugh with many people, does not enjoy friendship, is not loving, to many people, her love sources will die; she will not be able to love her husband either. She will forget how to love, her springs will go dry.

That's why you see husbands and wives looking so sad and bored with each other; it is bound to happen. They are going against a natural inner law: you have more the more you give. Giving does not destroy anything in you; in fact it is creative. The person who loves many people will be able to love his wife or her husband more totally.

But humanity has not understood this simple phenomenon even yet. We are still behaving in a very childish and stupid way.

It is as if your beloved asks you that, "You can breathe only when I am there and when I am not there stop breathing, because so much breath will be lost, so much life will be lost. And when you come home and you have been breathing in every place, everywhere, you will be almost dead! So when I am not with you, stop breathing!" And the husband insists also that, "When I am not at home you stop breathing, so that when we are together great breathing happens!" But both will die!

That's how we have killed love in the world, we have killed everything valuable, because our whole logic is stupid. It is good that the husband goes for a morning walk and breathes in the fresh air, jogs and runs on the seabeach, and enjoys the sun. And the wife also goes and enjoys the flowers and the trees and the grass. And when they come together they will be able to be more alive with each other, more loving to each other. They will be at their peak; they will be full of life-juices to share. But this has not happened yet.

My sannyasins have to remember it: jealousy kills love, possessiveness kills love. Be non jealous if you want great love to happen; if you want your life to grow multidimensionally it needs freedom. You need freedom and the person you love needs freedom. In freedom only there is expansion, growth.

The word that the Upanishads use for the absolute is Brahma; it comes from a Sanskrit root bri; bri means to grow, to expand.

Beyond The Changing

Hence for the universe the Sanskrit word is brahmand.

It is only in this century that Albert Einstein discovered the idea, the hypothesis that the universe is expanding. Five thousand years before Albert Einstein the Upanishads were saying the same thing: that the universe is continuously growing and expanding. The name they gave to the universe, brahmand, means that which goes on expanding, which is continuously growing. There is no end to that growth, no limit to that growth.

A sannyasin, a meditator, has to live his life in such a way that everything goes on growing, expanding, without any limit. Your love, your joy, your silence, your life — everything should be allowed to grow. And it can happen only if you allow the same to others.

But what we have been doing for thousands of years is just the opposite: we encroach on each other's territory, we destroy the space of everybody in the name of love, in the name of friendship. We use beautiful words to hide ugly realities.

If you really love a person you will allow all the space possible to the person; you will never encroach on his or her freedom. That is the only indication of your love, not those stupid love letters that you write! Any fool can do that — a computer can do far better than you do! A computer can write love letters, there is no problem in it. Your love can be proved only by one thing: how much freedom you are giving to the other — even the freedom to love others; that is the only indication of your love.

And the miracle is, the more we allow each other to love as many people as possible, you will find the person infinitely loving towards you, because love is not money, love is not a commodity. It is an inner energy which grows by sharing, which dies by not sharing.

Every Upanishad begins with a seed mantra. The seed mantra means it contains the whole Upanishad. If you can understand the seed mantra you have understood the whole Upanishad. The whole Upanishad is just the tree that grows out of the seed mantra.

This is a seed mantra:

Aum
Purnamadah
Purnamidam
Purnat Purnamudachyate
Purnasya Purnamadaya
Purnameva Vashishyate

In this small sutra the whole Upanishad is contained. What follows is just a growth out of this seed. This is the unmanifest part of it, then the whole Upanishad is the manifest part of it.

And each seed mantra is preceded by the mystic sound Aum; that contains even the seed mantra. If you understand Aum you have understood everything. Upanishads are written in such a beautiful way: first Aum... if you can understand that there is no need to go ahead. Aum means nothing; it is not a word, hence it is not written alphabetically, it is a symbol.

It contains three sounds: A, U, M. These are the basic sounds: A, U, M; all other sounds come out of these three sounds. This is the basic trinity of sounds, then the whole music of life grows out of this.

Aum means exactly what Zen people call "the sound of one hand clapping". Aum is the innermost music of your being. When all the thoughts and desires and memories have gone, have disappeared, and the mind is absolutely quiet and silent, there is no noise inside, you start hearing a tremendously beautiful music which does not consist of any meaning. It is pure music without any meaning, gives you great joy, fills you with celebration, makes you dance. You would like to shout "Alleluia!" But the music itself has no meaning; it is pure music, not polluted by any meaning.

Aum represents that inner music, that inner harmony, that inner humming sound which happens when your body, your mind, your soul are functioning together in deep accord, when the visible and the invisible, the manifest and the unmanifest are dancing together, when they are like two lovers in deep love-embrace merging, melting into each other, the manifest making love to the unmanifest, the unmanifest making love to the manifest when the manifest and the unmanifest are no more two but have become one.

This is represented in the Upanishads by the number hundred. The number hundred is used to symbolize the ultimate state of oneness. The two zeros in the number hundred represent "this" and "that", the manifest and the unmanifest, the phenomenal and the noumenal — two zeros. Both are whole, and when these both wholes become one, the number one in hundred represents that oneness.

One hundred is a symbolic number; it has a message. The two — the body and the soul, the world and God, the changing and the unchanging, the time and the timelessness, the matter and consciousness — are represented by the two zeros. When those two zeros become one, when they are not antagonistic to each other — as in these three thousand years the so-called religious people have done. They have destroyed this beautiful symbol; they have put those two zeros against each other. They have created a life-negativity; instead of affirming life they have condemned it as sin. When these two zeros merge in a love affair, into a deep lovers' embrace into each other, then oneness is born. That is represented by number one in hundred.

A full material existence with a full spiritual life: that is wholeness. And that's my message to you. Be a spiritual materialist — or a materialist spiritualist — because to me they are not separate. The inner aspect is spiritual, the outer aspect is material.

The religions have divided humanity into materialists and spiritualists. Now Soviet Russia, China and other communist countries think they are materialist. They are communist — they deny God, they deny consciousness, they deny soul, they deny the unmanifest; they believe only in matter. The word "matter" means that which can be measured; the "matter" comes from "meter" — that which can be measured. They don't believe in the immeasurable. But the immeasurable is there: whether you believe in or not does not matter. Your belief of disbelief makes no difference to reality. The immeasurable is there, and not only the mystics are saying it is so — now even the physicists are saying so, that the immeasurable is there.

The existence is immeasurable; it is so vast it cannot be measured. And the vastness is also expanding, every day becoming bigger and bigger. It is already infinite, and it goes on becoming more infinite! It is already perfect, and it goes on becoming more and more perfect, from one perfection to another perfection. It is never imperfect, so it is not a question of from imperfection to perfection. It is always perfect, it is always infinite, but it goes on expanding.

This is the paradox of modern physics. This has been a paradox to all the mystics, but they were not worried by it. That's why they are called mystics: they accept the paradox, they enjoy in the paradox. They love the paradoxical because they know truth can only be paradoxical. But modern physics is very much puzzled, because physics is rooted in logic and logic cannot accept paradox. Either it has to be "this" or "that" — it is always either/or.

Mysticism is never either/or, and if it is either/or then : it is not mysticism. Mysticism is Both/And!

All religious, so-called religious people are against me — Christians, Mohammedans, Hindus, Jains, Buddhists — for the simple reason because I am teaching wholeness. I am teaching to my sannyasins: be spiritual materialists — because both are! What we can do? It is not a question of our choice; it is already the case: the matter is there and the consciousness is there. Logicians are always choosing...

The so-called spiritualists of the world go on trying to prove that the world is illusory so that they can prove that only spirit exists, the world does not exist — it is maya, it is illusory, it is untrue, it is made of the same stuff as dreams are made of. And the materialist goes on doing the same from the other polarity. He says there is no consciousness; consciousness is an epiphenomenon. Karl Marx says that consciousness is a byproduct of matter and nothing more; it has no substance of its own. Matter is real and consciousness is only a shadow. It is the same logic!

Berkeley says: consciousness is real and matter is only a shadow, a thought, nothing else but a dream. But their logic is the same: both are afraid of accepting both, both are choosing one. They live in the world of either/or.

But the true mystic, the Upanishadic mystic, accepts both; he does not even call them two — they are one appearing as two. These two are aspects of one reality: the inner and the outer, the material and the spiritual.

So to me there is no problem: you be scientific and religious, you be materialistic and spiritualistic. Live in the world and live joyously, but also remain centered in your consciousness. This is bringing the Upanishads back. It is a resurrection!

> At The Heart All This Phenomenal World,
> Within All Its Changing Forms,
> Dwells The Unchanging Lord.

Everywhere God is present; all that is needed is the eyes to see. Then you will see him in the rocks and in the stars and in the birds and in the animals and in the people around you. But the first experience has to happen within you; only then you will be able to see him everywhere else.

> So, Go Beyond The Changing,
> And, Enjoying The Inner,
> Cease To Take For Yourself
> What To Others Are Riches.

The unchanging is the God and the changing is the world.
... Go Beyond The Changing...

Not against the changing, remember—beyond. Beyond is not

against. "Beyond" means Live in it, but live in such a way that you remain above it, like a lotus flower. It grows in the lake but goes beyond the lake. It lives in water, but the water cannot touch its velvety leaves. Even in the morning when dewdrops gather on the leaves or petals of the lotus they remain separate. The dewdrops are there on the leaves and you can see them, so beautiful in the morning sun, like pearls, but they are separate. The leaf remains absolutely dry; the dewdrops cannot make it wet.

That's the way of a sannyasin, that's the way of the Upanishads: living in the world and yet not being of it.

... Go Beyond The Changing,
And, Enjoying The Inner...

Don't enforce — enjoy the inner, and then you can understand my approach very easily. It is not a question of forcing. Meditation should not be enforced; you should not start a kind of regimentation, a violent discipline. You are not a soldier, you are a sannyasin!

A sannyasin simply enjoys the inner; he enjoys the outer also. He enjoys! He enjoys the outer and on the same wave of enjoyment he enters the inner — it is the same wave. It is like breathing: the breath comes in and the breath goes out. Do you think these are two separate breaths? It is the same breath that goes out and comes in and goes out and comes in... It is the same breath, it is the same process. The same breath comes in and goes out.

Enjoy the outer, ride on enjoyment, and enter in the inner also with the same joy, with the same dance. Don't create a division — there is none. All divisions are manufactured by the priests, the hypocrites, the moralists. They go on creating demarcations that: "This is outer and this is inner". There is no line which can demark what is outer and what is inner; they are part of one process, one whole.

Just as you come out of your house... When it is too cold in the morning you come out of the house to sit in the sun, to take a sunbath. And when it becomes too hot you get up and go in.

Beyond The Changing

There is no question of enforcing; just a little awareness that now it is too hot, so you move in, into the shade to the coolness of the house. And when it is too cold inside, just a little awareness and you come out.

Enjoy the outer and the inner in the same way, and go on moving, riding the same wave of enjoyment. And don't create any distinction —it is the same wave, same reality.

So, Go Beyond The Changing,

And, Enjoying The Inner...

Don't make it something very serious. Don't make a long face because you are meditating, because you are a sannyasin! Look at the pictures of your saints — such long faces that to live with these saints will be a hell! I don't think these saints can ever enter into heaven, or, wherever they will go they will create their hell. The hell is in their seriousness.

Once Buddha was asked, "What do you say happens when an enlightened person dies? Does he go to heaven?"

Buddha said, "Don't ask nonsense questions! Wherever the enlightened person is, there is heaven — wherever he is, it does not matter where — wherever he is... If he goes to the hell, the hell will be transformed. His presence carries its heaven around himself."

Heaven hangs around the Buddha, around the awakened person. You cannot send an enlightened person to hell — impossible; and you cannot send your so-called saints to heaven — impossible. The hell is so much engrained in their beings; wherever they are they will create boredom for themselves and for others.

Saints are not good company; even sinners are far better. I have lived with both, and, believe me, sinners are far better company than saints. Saints are utterly boring! Saints are very juicy just if they are saints in the sense of Upanishads, in the sense I call my sannyasins.

My sannyasins are saints, but not in the ordinary sense of being a Hindu saint or a Jain saint or a Christian saint. The Christian saint seems to be the worst — so boring that I can believe Friedrich Nietzsche that God is dead; he must have committed suicide! Surrounded by all these saints, what he can do, what else he can do? He must have committed suicide, feeling utterly bored. And this company is going to be there for eternity now! You cannot escape.

Upanishads are full of joy, full of flowers and fragrance.

... Enjoying The Inner — not enforcing it —
Cease To Take For Yourself
What To Others Are Riches.

And the Isha Upanishad is not saying that, renounce the world. It says:

... Cease To Take For Yourself...

Don't possess, don't become owners of persons or things; just use them as a gift of the universe. And when they are available, use them; when they are not available. Enjoy the freedom. When you have something, enjoy it; when you don't have it, enjoy not having it — that too has its own beauty.

If you have a palace to live in, enjoy! If you don't have, then enjoy a hut and the hut becomes a palace. It is the Enjoyment that makes the difference. Then live under a tree and enjoy it. Don't miss the tree and the flowers and the freedom and the birds and the air and the sun. And when you are in a palace don't miss it — enjoy the marble and the chandeliers...

Go on enjoying wherever you are, and don't possess anything. Nothing belongs to us. We come empty-handed in the world and we go empty-handed. The world is a gift, so enjoy while it is there. And remember, the universe always gives you that which you need.

A Sufi mystic used to say every day in his prayers, "Thank you, God, for all that you go on doing for me. How can I repay? I feel so grateful!"

Once it happened that he was traveling and for three days they were refused shelter because they were thought to be heretics, they were thought to be anti-religious, rebellious. They were not given food, not even water, and no shelter. For three days, hungry, thirsty...

And the third day when he was praying, again he was saying to God, "Thank you! How I can repay you? I feel so grateful!"

Now it was too much His disciples said, "It is time to say something!" They said, "Wait — just a moment! For what you are thanking? For three days we have been hungry, thirsty, no shelter, in the desert, at the mercy of wild animals. For what you are being thankful?"

And the Sufi laughed and he said, "You don't understand — this is what I must have needed for these three days! God always gives to me whatsoever I need. This must have been my need, otherwise he would not have given it to me. I am thankful for it. He always takes care. He does not bother what I desire; he always gives what he feels is right. I am thanking him... three days fasting, three days no shelter, three days the open sky with stars in the desert, sleeping in the desert, and no wild animal has attacked us. And why you are looking so sad? It must have been our real need!"

This is trust, and this is the joyful attitude. This is real sannyas!

Continuing To Act In The World,
One May Aspire To Be One Hundred.

Continue to act in the world, and now remember: one may aspire to be one hundred. It does not mean only a long life. Of course, that too it means, because Upanishadic seers were not against life; they wanted to live long and live joyously, so it was perfectly good — that meaning is perfectly right.

Aspire to live long and aspire to live deep, and aspire to live intensely and passionately — perfectly right! — but don't forget the symbol of one hundred. That is its true meaning, the higher meaning, the invisible meaning.

... One may aspire to be one hundred.

Even living and acting in the world you can become one. Those two zeros of this world and that, those two zeros of the body and the soul, those two zeros of the changing and the unchanging, can meet and merge into one even while you are acting in the world, so there is no need to renounce.

Thus, And Only Thus, Can A Man Be Free
From The Binding Influence Of Action.

Not by renouncing action but by acting in such awareness, in such deep meditativeness, one becomes free of action and its binding effects.

Unillumined Indeed Are Those Worlds Clouded
By The Blinding Darkness Of Ignorance.

Upanishads call people ignorant... if they are living in the half they are ignorant. The materialist is ignorant, the spiritualist is ignorant, because both are unaware of the whole. Only the one who knows the whole knows.

Into This Death Sink All Those Who Slay The Self.

And by dividing your being into two, is like slaying your very being, murdering yourself, killing yourself Don't cripple yourself, don't paralyze yourself. Accept your totality and live it joyously.

Aum
Purnamadah
Purnamidam
Purnat Purnamudachyate
Purnasya Purnamadaya
Purnameva Vashishyate

Aum

That Is The Whole.
This Is The Whole.
From Wholeness Emerges Wholeness.
Wholeness Coming From Wholeness,
Wholeness Still Remains.

Living In Your Own Light

Question 1

OSHO,
What is god?
— *Prem Sukavi*

God is not a person. That is one of the greatest misunderstandings, and it has prevailed so long that it has become almost a fact. Even if a lie is repeated continuously for centuries it is bound to appear as if it is a truth.

God is a presence, not a person. Hence all worshipping is sheer stupidity. Prayerfulness is needed, not prayer. There is nobody to pray to; there is no possibility of any dialogue between you and God. Dialogue is possible only between two persons, and God is not a person but a presence — like beauty, like joy.

God simply means godliness. It is because of this fact that Buddha denied the existence of God. He wanted to emphasize that God is a quality, an experience — like love. You cannot talk to love, you can live it. You need not create temples of love, you need not make statues of love, and bowing down to those statues will be just nonsense. And that's what has been happening in the churches, in the temples, in the mosques.

Man has lived under this impression of God as a person, and then two calamities have happened through it. One is the so-called religious man, who thinks God is somewhere above in the sky and you have to praise him. to persuade him to confer favors on you, to help you to fulfill your desires, to make your ambitions succeed, to give you the wealth of this world And of the other world. And this is sheer wastage of time and energy.

And on the opposite pole the people who saw the stupidity of it all became atheists; they started denying the existence of God. They were right in a sense, but they were also wrong. They started denying not only the personality of God, they started to deny even the experience of God.

The theist is wrong, the atheist is wrong, and man needs a new vision so that he can be freed from both the prisons.

God is the ultimate experience of silence, of beauty, of bliss, a state of inner celebration. Once you start looking at God as godliness there will be a radical change in your approach. Then prayer is no more valid; meditation becomes valid.

Martin Buber says prayer is a dialogue; then between you and God there is an "I-thou" relationship — the duality persists. Buddha is far closer to the truth: you simply drop all chattering of the mind, you slip out of the mind like a snake slipping out of the old skin. You become profoundly silent. There is no question of any dialogue, no question of any monologue either. Words have disappeared from your consciousness. There is no desire for which favors have to be asked, no ambition to be fulfilled. One is now and here. In that tranquility, in that calmness, you become aware of a luminous quality to existence. Then the trees and the mountains and the rivers and the people are all surrounded with a subtle aura. They are all radiating life, and it is one life in different forms. The flowering of one existence in millions of forms, in millions of flowers.

This experience is God. And it is everybody's birthright, because whether you know it or not you are already part of it. The only possibility is you may not recognize it or you may recognize it.

The difference between the enlightened person and the unenlightened person is not of quality — they both are absolutely alike. There is only one small difference: that the enlightened person is aware; he recognizes the ultimate pervading the whole, permeating the whole, vibrating, pulsating. He recognizes the heartbeat of the universe. He recognizes that the universe is not dead, it is alive.

This aliveness is God!

The unenlightened person is asleep, asleep and full of dreams. Those dreams function as a barrier; they don't allow him to see the truth of his own reality. And, of course, when you are not even aware of your own reality, how can you be aware of the reality of others? The first experience has to happen within you. Once you have seen the light within you will be able to see it everywhere.

God has to be freed from all concepts of personality. Personality is a prison. God has to be freed from any particular form; only then he can have all the forms. He has to be freed from any particular name so that all the names become his.

Then a person lives in prayer — he does not pray, he does not go to the temple, to the church. Wherever he sits he is prayerful, whatsoever he is doing is prayerful, and in that prayerfulness he creates his temple. He is always moving with his temple surrounding him. Wherever he sits the place becomes sacred, whatsoever he touches becomes gold. If he is silent then his silence is golden; if he speaks then his song is golden. If he is alone his aloneness is divine; if he relates then his relating is divine.

The basic, the most fundamental thing is to be aware of your own innermost core, because that is the secret of the whole existence. That's where the Upanishads are tremendously important. They don't talk about a God, they talk about godliness. They don t bother about prayer. their whole emphasis is on meditation.

Meditation has two parts: the beginning and the end. The beginning is called dhyana and the end is called samadhi. Dhyana is the seed, samadhi is the flowering. Dhyana means becoming aware of all workings of your mind, all the layers of your mind — your memories, your desires, your thoughts, dreams — becoming aware of all that goes on inside you.

Dhyana is awareness, and samadhi is when the awareness has become so deep, so profound, so total that it is like a fire and it consumes the whole mind and all its functionings. It consumes thoughts, desires, ambitions, hopes, dreams. It consumes the whole stuff the mind is full of.

Samadhi is the state when awareness is there, but there is nothing to be aware inside you; the witness is there, but there is nothing to be witnessed.

Begin with dhyana, with meditation, and end in samadhi, in ecstasy, and you will know what God is. It is not a hypothesis, it is an experience. You have to Live it — that is the only way to know it.

Question 2

OSHO,

Your discourse on the Isha Upanishad was so beautiful. I have heard it said that the Upanishads are commentaries on or extensions of the Vedas. Is this true? I bow to you.

— Anand Santamo

The Upanishads are not commentaries on the Vedas, neither are they extensions of the Vedas. Of course, Hindus go on insisting that they are commentaries or extensions of the Vedas, but that is a falsehood perpetuated by the priesthood for their own reasons.

In fact, Upanishads are rebellions against the Vedas. Another name for the Upanishads is vedanta. The priests have been saying that vedanta means the culmination of the Vedas; the word can be interpreted that way, but in fact it means the End of the Vedas and the beginning of something absolutely new. Vedas are very ordinary compared to the Upanishads.

The Upanishads say that there are two kinds of knowledge: the lower and the higher. The lower knowledge is the realm of the priesthood, the scholars, the pundits, and the higher knowledge is the world of the Buddhas, of the awakened ones. The priest is a businessman; his whole effort is to exploit people in the name of religion. He oppresses people, dominates people, and of course he goes on saying, "It is for your own sake." He makes people afraid of hell and greedy for heavenly joys. This is a psychological trick. He knows people are afraid, he knows people are greedy, so these are the two things that he goes on manipulating: fear and greed. And this is done by all the priests of all the religions in all the traditions all over the world.

Upanishads are rebellions against the priesthood. Upanishads are not at all commentaries on the Vedas — Vedas are very mundane, ordinary. Yes, once in a while you can find a sutra in the Vedas which is beautiful, but that is only one percent at the most. Ninety-nine percent is just rubbish, while the Upanishads are hundred percent pure gold — they are statements of those who have known.

The Vedas are full of prayers asking for worldly things: better crops, better cows, more money, better health, fame, power, prestige. Not only that, the Vedas are continuously praying "Destroy the enemies", "Destroy those who oppose us." They are full of jealousy, anger, violence. They have nothing to do with the Upanishads.

Upanishads are not commentaries and they are not the culmination of the Vedas either. Upanishads are a totally new beginning. The very word Upanishad is of immense importance. The word Upanishad is derived from the Sanskrit root Shad. Shad has many meanings and all are significant. The first meaning is "to sit".

The Zen people say:

Sitting silently, doing nothing,
The spring comes and the grass grows by itself.

That is the meaning of Shad: just sitting silently in deep meditation; not only sitting physically but sitting deep down psychologically too. You can sit physically in a yoga posture, but the mind goes on running, chasing; then it is not true sitting. Yes, physically you look still, but psychologically you are running in all the directions.

Shad means sitting physically and psychologically both because body and mind are not two things, not two separate entities. Body and mind is one reality. We should not use the phrase "body and mind"; we should make one word, "bodymind". The body is the outer shell of the mind and the mind is the inner part of the body. Unless both are in a sitting posture, not running anywhere — into the past, into the future — not running anywhere, just being in the present, now and here... that is the meaning of shad; it is the very meaning of meditation.

It also means "to settle". You are always in a chaos, in a state of turmoil, unsettled, always hesitating, confused, not knowing what to do, what not to do. There is no clarity inside — so many clouds, so much smoke surrounds you. When all these clouds have disappeared, when all this chaos has disappeared, when there is no confusion at all, it is called settling.

When one is settled absolutely, clarity arises, a new perspective. One starts seeing what is the case. Eyes are no more covered by any smoke; for the first time you have eyes to see that which is.

The third meaning of shad is "to approach". You are confused, you are living in darkness, you don't know who you are, you don't know the meaning of your life, of your existence. You have to approach somebody who has arrived home, who has found the way. You have to approach a Buddha, an enlightened Master — a Lao Tzu, a Zarathustra, a Jesus, a Mohammed. You have to approach somebody who is afire with God, aflame, who is radiating godliness, in whose presence you feel bathed, refreshed, in whose presence something starts falling from your heart — the whole burden, anguish, anxiety — and something starts welling up within you: a new joy, a new insight. Hence the meaning "to approach".

Upanishad is made of three words. Shad is to sit, to settle, to approach — to approach a Master, to sit by his side in a settled, silent state. And from the prefix Upa which means near, close, in tune with, in harmony, in communion... When you are settled, sitting silently by the side of the Master, doing nothing, running nowhere, then a harmony arises between you and the Master, a closeness, an intimacy, a nearness, a possibility of communion, the meeting of the heart with the heart, the meeting of the being with the being, a merging, a communion. And Ni meaning down, surrendered, in a state of prayer, in a state of egolessness.

This is the whole meaning of the word Upanishad: sitting in a settled state, unconfused, clear, approaching the Master in egolessness, surrendered, in deep prayerfulness, openness, vulnerability, so that a communion becomes possible.

This is Upanishad — what is happening right now between you and me. This sitting silently, in a deep, loving, prayerful mood, listening to me not through the intellect but through the heart, drinking, not only listening — this communion is upanishad! We are living upanishad, and that is the only way to understand what Upanishads are. It has to become an alive experience for you.

The Vedas consist of all kinds of knowledge of those days. They are a kind of Encyclopedia Britannica, of course very primitive, at least ten thousand years old — at least — it is possible they are far more older. Scholars are not decided; there is great controversy about the time when Vedas were composed. The possibility is they were not composed at one period, they were composed at different periods. There are people who say they are at least ninety thousand years old; so from ninety thousand years to ten thousand years, a long stretch of time.

The Vedas are called Samhitas; Samhita means a compilation, encyclopedia. They contain all kinds of things, all kinds of information of those days. Upanishads are pure religiousness, nothing else. Each single word is a finger pointing to the moon. They are not compilations of all kinds of knowledge; their whole insistence is for immediate experience of that which is. The emphasis is on direct experience, not borrowed — not from scriptures, not from others. It has to be your own truth; only then it liberates.

Jesus says: Truth liberates. Certainly truth liberates, but it has to be your own. If it is somebody else's, then rather than liberating it imprisons. Christians are imprisoned. Jesus is liberated. Hindus are imprisoned, Krishna is liberated. Buddhists are imprisoned Buddha is liberated. Liberation comes by experiencing the truth on your own; it has not to be just an accumulation of information, it has to be an inner transformation.

The emphasis of the Upanishads is for immediate and direct experience of godliness. And why borrow when it is possible to drink directly from the source? But information seems to be cheap. transformation seems to be arduous. Transformation means you will have to go through a great inner revolution; information requires no revolution in you, no radical change in you. Information simply is an addition: whatsoever you are you remain the same, but you become more and more knowledgeable.

Knowledgeability is not wisdom; knowledgeability is, on the contrary, a hindrance to wisdom. The more knowledgeable you become, the less is the possibility of attaining your own experience, because knowledge deceives — it deceives others, it deceives you. It goes on giving you the sense as if you know, but that "as if" has not to be forgotten. That "as if" can easily be forgotten and one can be deceived.

Remember one very significant saying in the Upanishads: Those who are ignorant, they are bound to be lost in darkness; and those who are knowledgeable, they are bound to be lost in a far more and far bigger darkness than the ignorant ones.

The ignorant person is at least sincere: he knows that he does not know; at least this much truth is there. But the knowledgeable covers up his wounds, his ignorance, his black holes. He covers them by scriptures and he starts pretending that he knows. He is harming others, but that is secondary, far more significant is that he is harming himself He will be lost in a far deeper darkness.

That's why it is very difficult for pundits, scholars, the so-called learned people, to become enlightened; it is a miracle if it happens at all. Sinners are more easily ready to go through the transformation because they have nothing to lose — except their chains, except their ignorance. But the knowledgeable person is afraid to lose his knowledge; that is his treasure. He clings to it, he protects it in every possible way. He finds rationalizations, excuses why the knowledge has to be protected. But, in fact, by protecting his knowledge he is simply protecting his ignorance. Hidden behind knowledge is his ignorance. The knowledge is just a mask which covers his original face. You cannot see his original face, he himself cannot see it. He is wearing a mask, and looking in the mirror he thinks, "This is my original face."

It is very difficult for the knowledgeable to drop his knowledge and to become ignorant again. Unless he gathers that much courage of becoming ignorant again, of becoming like a child again — innocent, not knowing anything, what Dionysius calls Agnosia, moving into a state of not knowing...

It is certainly very arduous for the knowledgeable person — his whole Life he has been accumulating knowledge. He has wasted his whole life, he has invested his whole life in knowledge. How can he drop it? So he protects it, he fights for it.

And this is the most amazing thing in the world: the prisoner is fighting so that you cannot take him out of the prison! And of course he is very clever and very cunning, so he can play with words and he can quote scriptures, but all his quotations are parrotlike; he has no understanding.

The Upanishads emphasize direct experiencing. The Vedas belong to the priests, to the scholars, to the brahmins, who are the oldest priests in the world. And of course, because they are the oldest they are the most cunning in the whole world. No other religion can defeat the Hindu priest, obviously: he has lived for so long, he has become very clever in exploiting, he has become very cunning in rationalizing, in protecting.

Upanishads are a totally different dimension. Of course they don't speak the language of rebellion — they are very soft — but the rebellion is there. Because Upanishads could not create the revolution Buddha had to speak in a harsher tone.

Buddha speaks the same truth as the Upanishads, but his way has changed. Seeing that Upanishads have failed to have any impact — because the priests started managing : Upanishads also and they started saying that Upanishads are nothing but commentaries on the Vedas — Buddha had to be more alert. He was not so soft as the Upanishads. Of course his message is the same, but two, three thousand years have passed since the Upanishads were composed and one thing Buddha had become absolutely clear: that you have to be very harsh, very hard. He has sharpened his sword.

Twenty-five centuries have again passed, the same period. Upanishads and Buddha are divided by twenty-five centuries; between me and Buddha again twenty-five centuries have passed. I have to sharpen my sword even more, because Buddha has also failed.

The ignorance of man is so deep and the priests are so cunning that one has to be really hard. If one has compassion one has to be cruel, only then this whole stupidity that exists in the name of religion can be destroyed and man can be freed. Man needs freedom from all cages, from all fetters.

Question 3

OSHO,

Would you please say something about sincerity?

— *Yoga Punya*

Man can live in two ways: either he can live according to the dictates of others — the puritans, the moralists — or he can live according to his own light. It is easy to follow others, it is convenient and comfortable, because when you follow others they feel very good and happy with you.

Your parents will be happy if you follow their ideas, although their ideas are absolutely worthless because their ideas have not made their lives illumined, and it is so apparent. They have lived in misery, still they want to impose their ideas on the children. They cannot see a simple fact: that their life has been a failure. that their life has not been creative, that their life has never tasted of bliss, that they have not been able to discover truth. They have not known the splendor of existence, they have no idea what it is all about. Still their egos insist that the children should be obedient, they should follow their dictates.

The Hindu parents will force the child to become a Hindu, and they will not even think for a single moment what has happened to them. They have followed those same ideas their whole life and their life is empty; nothing has flowered. But they enjoy the idea that their children are obedient and they are following them. They have lived in misery, in hell, and their children will live in misery and hell, but they think they love their children. With all good intentions they destroy the future of their children.

The politicians try in every possible way that the society should live according to their ideas, and of course they pretend to others and to themselves that they are doing public service. All that they are doing is destroying freedom of people. They are trying to enforce certain superstitions which were enforced on them by their parents, by their leaders, by their priests.

The politicians, the priests, the pedagogues, they are all trying to create a false humanity; they are creating insincere human beings. They may not have intended to do so, but that's what has happened. And a tree is to be judged by the fruits; it does not matter what was the intention of the gardener. If he was sowing seeds of weeds and hoping, intending, desiring that roses will come out just because of his good intentions, roses are not going to come out of the weeds. He has destroyed the whole field. To impose a certain structure of character on anybody is to make him insincere, is to make him a hypocrite.

Sincerity, Yoga Punya, means to live according to your own light. Hence the first requirement of being sincere is to be meditative. The first thing is not to be moral, is not to be good, is not to be virtuous: the most important thing is to be meditative — so that you can find a little light within yourself and then start living according to that light And as you live it grows and it gives you a deep integrity. Because it comes from your own innermost being there is no division.

When somebody says to you, "Do it, it Should be done," naturally it creates a division in you. You don't want to do it, you wanted to do something else, but somebody — the parents, the politicians, the priests, those who are in power — they want you to follow a certain route. You never wanted to follow it so you will follow it unwillingly. Your heart will not be in it, you will not be committed to it, you will not have any involvement with it. You will go through it like a slave. It is not your choice, it is not out of your freedom.

The first disciples of Jesus had chosen him; it was Their choice and they had chosen a very risky path — to be with Jesus was dangerous. It has always been so: to be with anybody who gives you freedom is dangerous because he will make you so independent that you will continuously be in a fight with the society, with the establishment, with the vested interests. You will be in a constant struggle your whole life. Of course, that struggle is worth and it is not a curse, it is a blessing, because only through that struggle you grow, you expand. Your consciousness becomes more and more clear; it becomes a peak. You have to pay for it; it is not cheap. Hence the risk.

The few people who followed Jesus were taking a dangerous path: they could have been crucified, and they were tortured in many ways. But today to be a Christian has no risk, hence it is bogus.

The people who followed Buddha were living dangerously, and to live dangerously is the only way to live. But they were sincere people: they followed their own inner voice against the whole society, against the whole tradition, convention. They followed a rebel and became rebels in their own right. Buddhists were burned alive just as early Christians were burned alive, thrown to the lions and to the wild animals, tortured in every possible way. But still they attained to the ultimate experience of godliness — they paid for it. But to be a Buddhist now is very convenient there is no problem about it, anybody can be a Buddhist. And the same is true about all religions.

Right now to be with me is dangerous. You will be continuously in trouble; wherever you will go you will be opposed. You will be opposed by the Christians, by the Hindus, by the Mohammedans, by the Jains, by the Buddhists. You will be tortured, you will be condemned, you will not be accepted anywhere. But you will become sincere, you will have some authenticity. And you will suffer all these tortures joyfully because you have chosen them.

Even to choose hell is beautiful, rather than to be forced to live in heaven. If you are forced to live in heaven it is hell, and if you choose hell it is heaven — because it is your own choice. It brings your life to its highest peak.

Sincerity means not living a double life — and almost everybody is living a double life. He says one thing, he thinks something else. He never says that which he thinks, he says that which is convenient and comfortable, he says that which will be approved, accepted, he says that which is expected by others. Now what he says and what he thinks become two different worlds. He says one thing, he goes on doing something else, and then naturally he has to hide it. He cannot expose himself because then the contradiction will be found, then he will be in trouble. He talks about beautiful things and lives an ugly life.

This is what, up to now, humanity has done to itself. It has been a very nightmarish past.

The new man is an absolute necessity now because the old is utterly rotten. The old is continuously in conflict within himself; he is fighting with himself. Whatsoever he does he feels miserable. If he follows his own inner voice he feels he is going against the society, against the powerful people, against the establishment. And that establishment has created a conscience in you; that conscience is a very tricky procedure, a strategy. It is the policeman inside you, implanted by the society, who goes on condemning you that: "This is wrong, this is not right. You should not do it, you should feel guilty for it — you are being immoral."

If you follow your voice your conscience is at daggers with you; it will not give you any rest, it will torture you, it will make you miserable. And you will become afraid — afraid that somebody may find it out. And it is very difficult to hide because life means relationship — somebody is bound to know, somebody is bound to discover. You are not alone.

That's why the cowards escaped to the monasteries, to the Himalayan caves, just for a single reason: that there they will not be found out at all. But what kind of life you can live in a cave? You have already committed suicide. To be in a cave is to be in a grave — and alive! If you are dead and in a grave, that seems right — where else you can be? But alive and in a grave — it is real hell!

In the monasteries people are living a miserable life; that's why they have such long faces — not that they are religious. Those long faces are a simple outcome of a cowardly life. If you are in the world living with people you cannot hide for long; you can deceive a few people for a time being, but not forever. And how can you deceive yourself? Even if you are not found out by others you know that you are living a double life — and the guilt...

And everybody is guilty, and the priests want you to be guilty because the more guilty you are, the more you are in the hands of the priests. You have to go to them to get rid of your guilt. You have to go to the Ganges to take a bath, you have to go to Mecca, to Kaaba, so that you can get rid of your guilt. You have to go to the Catholic priest to confess so that you can get rid of the guilt. You have to do fasting and other kinds of penances and other kinds of austerities so that you can punish yourself These are all punishments! But how can you be happy? How you can be cheerful and blissful? How can you rejoice in a life where you are constantly feeling guilty and punishing yourself, condemning yourself?

And if you choose not to follow your inner voice and follow the dictates of others — they call morality, etiquette, civilization, culture — then too that inner voice will start nagging you, it will continuously nag you. It will say you are being untrue to your nature. And if you feel that you are being untrue to your nature then your morality cannot be a rejoicing; it will be only an empty gesture.

This is what has happened to man: man has become schizophrenic.

My effort here is to help you to become one. That's why I don't teach any morality, any character. All that I teach is meditation so that you can hear your inner voice more clearly and follow it, whatsoever the cost. Because if you follow your inner voice without feeling guilty, immense is going to be your reward, and looking backwards you will find that the cost was nothing. It looked very big in the beginning, but when you have arrived at the point where sincerity becomes natural, spontaneous, when there is no more any division, no more any split in you, then you will see a celebration is happening and the cost that you have paid is nothing compared to it.

You ask me, Yoga Punya: Would You Please Say Something About Sincerity?

Sincerity is the fragrance of meditation.

Question 4

OSHO,

At this moment the Christian Broadcasting Company, NCRV, In Holland, has started a series of eight programs on spiritual movements entitled: Not To Be Believed. The producer-minister, Sipke Van Der Land, who has been here with his crew To Film You And Life At The Ashram, called the first program: Bhagwan, Sex Guru from Poona. At the end of the film he comments: "Bhagwan never looks at you, he looks over us. What kind of Mastership is this, in which someone pulls people towards him without paying any attention to them? Jesus humiliated himself to be equal with us as a servant, but not Bhagwan. Bhagwan raises himself above humanity —

haughty, a strange ruler"

Could You Please Comment On This?

— Prem Pushpa

The Christian, the Hindu, the Mohammedan, they cannot understand me — they are determined not to understand me. It is against their vested interests. They are afraid of me and they will try in every possible way to confuse people.

Because it is a Christian broadcasting company they must have come with prejudiced ideas, they must have come with a closed mind. They had come already with conclusions, hence whatsoever they say only shows something about them, nothing about me. And remember, their title is right: Not To Be Believed!

They have received many letters — I have received many letters too — and there have been many comments in the newspapers in Holland. And almost all the newspapers have asked one question: that their whole program about me does not give any indication about the title, Bhagwan, Sex Guru From Poona. Their whole program has nothing to do with the title. People are meditating, people are sitting silently listening to me, people are working... It has no relationship at all with the program. What they have filmed and what they have tried to project is totally irrelevant! But they were not even aware, it seems, that the title has no relevance with the program — it has nothing to do with sex!

And what this director has replied? — because the newspapers asked the director, "Why you have given such a title, which has no reference with the program at all? It shows a prejudiced mind!" So he has answered that, "That was our very purpose, that's our very purpose of a Christian broadcasting company: to expose everything that is not Christian." They are not concerned with truth — as if truth is Christian! Truth is neither Hindu nor Christian nor Mohammedan.

And he should be reminded that Jesus was not a Christian himself! Christianity never existed in those days. Jesus was born a Jew, lived a Jew, died a jew! I may be a little bit of Christian — in fact, more Christian than Jesus! — but Jesus cannot be Christian at all. First they should condemn Jesus — why he was not Christian; that will serve their purpose more accurately.

And they should make a film on Jesus. Jesus was moving with a prostitute, Mary Magdalene — must have been a sex guru! He was always in the company which this director would not approve of — gamblers, drunkards, prostitutes. He himself was a drunkard! He should make a film on Jesus.

And there are rumors that he was a homosexual! I don't know how far they are true, but there is a possibility... because he was constantly moving with those twelve boys! And religious people are known, very well-known, to be homosexuals. Homosexuality is a religious phenomenon! When you keep men separate from women and women separate from men, homosexuality is a natural by-product.

He has also said in one interview to a newspaper, that "Bhagwan's sannyasins say that, 'We feel immense energy, that we feel the presence of Bhagwan transforming us.' " And he says, "I lived there for a few days — I didn't feel anything!"

When Jesus was crucified there were at least one hundred thousand people present. Did they feel anything? If they had felt anything Jesus would have been saved. Those one hundred thousand people could have easily saved him, because there were only a few policemen; they could have been destroyed, killed by the masses. But nobody could feel any energy, nobody could see any godliness in Jesus. In fact, people were mocking and laughing at him.

They were waiting for him to show some miracle and they were shouting that, "You have been showing miracles, we have heard. We have heard that you used to walk on water, we have heard that you have given eyes to the blind people, we have heard that you have cured incurable diseases, we have even heard that you raised Lazarus from death, you revived him again — now show us the miracle!"

And these people came back home very frustrated because no miracle happened. Jesus died like any ordinary man. And remember, these were simple people — not journalists!

This director of NCRV, if he was present there, would have become very frustrated because he would have gone there with the whole crew to film some miracle, and it was not happening!

Do you think Hindus felt the energy of Buddha? Do you think Jains felt the energy of Buddha or Buddhists felt the energy of Mahavira? Mahavira and Buddha were both contemporaries, lived in the same part of the country, Bihar, moved in the same villages and towns continuously for forty years, many times stayed in the same village and once at least stayed in one house — half was occupied by Buddha and half by Mahavira — and still their disciples were not able to feel the energy of the other. What was happening?

Could not the Jews feel the energy of Jesus?

It is a simple phenomenon to be understood: to feel the energy you have to be in a certain state. It is like — he will understand this better — it is like carrying a radio set with you, but if you don't put it on no music will flow through it. Even if you put it on, and you don't fix the needle at a certain point it will not receive. One needs openness, and the needle has to be at a certain point; a deep harmony is needed. Whether it is with Jesus or Buddha or Mahavira, it does not matter: whomsoever you are attuned with you will feel the energy.

But he is like a man who stands before the sunrise with closed eyes and he says, "There is no sun, because I cannot see. And the people who are saying it is are all false — not to be believed! — because I cannot see, and I have been standing here for hours."

You have to open the eyes to see the sun. And the sun is a gross phenomenon: the energy of a Master is a very subtle phenomenon — unless you are in deep love you will not feel it.

And he says: Bhagwan never looks at you.

In a way he is true! I never look at you because you are two: the false and the real. I am not concerned with the false. I don't look at your mask. I don't look at the accidental in you I look to the essential, I look to the very core of your being. I am not concerned with your masks and the personality; my whole concern is with the center of your being.

And why should I look at you? He must have felt it, because I perfectly remember I never looked at him! — because there was nothing to look at, just an empty man, a container without any content. Why should I waste my time looking at such people? It is only out of compassion that they are allowed, and this too is not going to happen very long any more. In the new commune I am going to prevent all these people coming in.

I certainly look, but my ways of looking are my ways I look behind the mask, because that is where my work is.

He says:... He Looks Over Us.

That is true, because I look at the transcendental self in you and that is something over you, above you, surpassing you. You are far more than your body, far more than your mind, and I look to that "far more". And that is the real thing and that has to be brought into your focus. I am not a psychoanalyst — I am not concerned with the superficial but with that which Surpasses You. I Am concerned with your beyond.

And he says: What kind of mastership is this in which someone pulls people towards him without paying any attention to them?

Ego needs attention, ego feeds on attention, ego wants that attention should be paid to it; it is constantly hankering for attention. While he was here he must have been hankering for attention.

It has been one of the problems here: whenever people come here — journalists of all kinds — their whole effort is that the commune should pay great attention to them. They want a private interview with me, they want to ask me questions directly. I am not a politician! Of course, if they go to the president or the prime minister of any country they will give them great attention. I am not interested at all in what they write, in what they show on the television. I am not concerned at all with whether they write negatively or positively, whether they make a film supporting me or condemning me. It is all the same to me.

I exist here for my sannyasins, my whole energy is for them; it is not to be wasted on stupid people. So he must have felt that no attention is being paid to him — and I deliberately never pay any attention to such people. They come with closed minds, they come with great egos — and we are not here to nourish their egos. In the new commune they will be debarred; that will be the only attention we will pay to them!

And he says: Jesus Humiliated Himself To Be Equal With Us.

What I am going to say has nothing to do with Jesus; it has something to do with what this man, the director of NCRV, is saying. So remember it.

He says: Jesus Humiliated Himself To Be Equal With Us...

That simply means he knew that he is not equal with you! "He humiliated himself to be equal with us." He was NOT — I am, so why should I humiliate myself? For what? I am simply equal, there is no need to humiliate!

He Humiliated To Be Equal With Us As A Servant!...

I am neither a master nor a servant. I don't possess you, I don't own you. If Jesus tried to be a servant to you, that means somewhere deep down he must have been self-conscious that he possesses you, that he owns you — otherwise why? Neither are you a servant to me, why I should be a servant to you? We are all friends here! There is no need to be a servant or to be humiliating oneself.

And do you think this is true? Jesus called himself the only-begotten son of God — the only. How he can be equal to you? You are born out of sin, he was born out of a virgin mother. I am not born out of a virgin mother! My mother is here, you can ask her. And I am not the only-begotten son of God, because there is no God at all, so there is no question of my being the only-begotten son of God. This is all sheer bullshit!

The Christian God must be homosexual because the whole trinity consists of three men — no women at all! On the earth Jesus is born out of a virgin mother. That is nonsense, absurdity — illogical, unscientific! Secondly, he is the only-begotten son of God; God must have carried him in his womb. Because he is not a woman, and there is no woman in Christian trinity — unless the Holy Ghost functions in double ways!

This is not right about Jesus. He dragged the money-changers out of the temple violently; that is not the way of a humble man. With a whip in his hand he chased them out of the temple. I have not done anything like that! I never enter a temple — I never think any temple is worth entering in. And this whip — is this a way of a humble man? And driving the money-changers out of the temple!

He cursed a fig tree because they were hungry... Jesus and his disciples were hungry and the fig tree was without figs. He became very angry; he cursed the fig tree. The fig tree died immediately! This is how a humble man behaves? Then why he was crucified if he was so humble?

And doing all those so-called miracles — walking on the water, raising the dead — is this the way of a humble man? Those are all strategies to prove superiority, all those miracles.

This man, the director of NCRV, is talking sheer nonsense. He knows nothing about Jesus, he knows nothing about me.

And he says:... But not Bhagwan. Bhagwan raises himself above humanity — haughty! A strange ruler.

I have never ruled anybody. I never come out of my room to rule anybody! What kind of ruling he has seen here? I never order anybody, I don't give any commandments to anybody. And I have never said that I am above humanity. What I am saying is that everybody is above humanity! Humanity is only a bridge, not a place to live but something to be surpassed.

And "Bhagwan", the word "Bhagwan", creates misunderstanding in Christian minds, because they immediately translate it as "God". Bhagwan simply means "the Blessed One", and I am certainly a Blessed One — I cannot deny it! Just to be humble have I to falsify, start lying about myself? I am blissful, I am the Blessed One — and you can be blissful and you can also be the Blessed One. What has happened to me can happen to you, because this is your birthright too.

But he had come with a particular idea. In a way it is good that people are becoming so much afraid of me. It is good: it shows that the impact is making them tremble. Holland is becoming one of my most important orange countries. Christians are becoming afraid — it is good. Make them as much afraid as possible! Make everybody afraid of you! Let them all tremble — before they collapse! It is good...

3

By Following Nobody Knows

> Question 1
>
> OSHO,
>
> Is this a new phase of your work — two complete discourses without a single joke?
>
> — Premananda

Thank you for reminding me! I had just forgotten all about jokes! Here are two jokes for the two discourses:

A young man was driving home from work one night in the pouring rain when he noticed an attractive woman standing on the footpath, soaking wet. He stopped and offered her a ride home. When they arrived at her apartment, she invited him in for a drink.

After a few drinks, one thing led to another and very soon they were in her bedroom making love. Suddenly he realized that it was quite late and his wife would be furious with him.

Before leaving he asked the young woman for a piece of chalk. He placed it behind his ear and then proceeded to drive home.

At home his wife screamed at him "Where have you been?"

"You will never believe this, darling," the man replied. "I was driving home from work this evening in the pouring rain and I stopped to pick up a woman who was standing on the footpath. I drove her home, she invited me, we had a drink, and I have spent the last two hours making love!"

"Don't bullshit me!" the wife snarled. "You have been down at the pool hall again with the boys! I can see the chalk behind your ear!"

And the second:

A jealous husband hired the very best detective in town to spy on his wife. The detective reported back after a few days, his arm in a plaster cast.

"What happened?" the husband asked eagerly.

The detective began: "At two o'clock, Saturday afternoon, I saw your wife walking hand-in-hand with another man."

"Where did they go?" the husband demanded.

"They checked into a hotel and were given a room on the second floor."

"And then?" the husband urged.

"Then I climbed up a tree and sat on a branch watching them through the open window. They sat on the edge of the bed, kissing and hugging. Then he took off his clothes..."

"And then, what happened then?" the enraged husband blasted.

"Well, then she took off her clothes..." the detective continued warily.

"Tell me, tell me what happened next!" yelled the husband in a rage.

"Well, sir, you see, at that moment the branch I was sitting on broke. I fell to the ground and could see no more!"

You get...? You missed it! Think over it later on!

Question 2

OSHO,

Could you please tell me your opinion about J. Krishnamurti, who is saying that you won't be free and therefore not happy as long as you follow any tradition, religion or master?

— *Wolfgang*

Gautam The Buddha has divided the enlightened persons into two categories. The first category he calls the arhatas and the second bodhisattvas. The arhata and the bodhisattva are both enlightened; there is no difference between their experience, but the arhata is not a Master and the bodhisattva is a Master. The arhata has attained to the same truth but he is incapable of teaching it, because teaching is a totally different art.

For example, you can see a beautiful sunset, you can experience the beauty of it as deeply, as profoundly as any Vincent van Gogh, but that does not mean you will be able to paint it. To paint it is a totally different art. Experiencing is one thing, helping others to experience it is not the same.

There have been many arhatas but very few bodhisattvas. The bodhisattva is both enlightened and skillful to teach what has happened to him. It is the greatest art in the world; no other art can be compared with it, because to say the unsayable, to help people come out of their sleep, to find and invent devices to bring what has happened to him to those who are thirsty for it and help them to get it... it is a rare gift.

Krishnamurti is an arhata, he is not a bodhisattva. His enlightenment is as great as anybody else's enlightenment; he is a Buddha, a Jesus, a Lao Tzu. In enlightenment there are no degrees; either one is enlightened or one is not. Once a person is enlightened he has the same flavor, the same fragrance as anyone who has ever become enlightened or will ever become enlightened. But to relate the experience, to communicate the experience is not possible for all.

Once Buddha was asked, "How many people have become enlightened amongst your disciples?"

He said, "Many." He showed..."Look!" Manjushri was sitting by his side and Sariputra and Modgalyayan and Mahakashyap. He said, "These four people are right now present here — they have become enlightened."

The inquirer asked, "If they have become enlightened why they are not so famous as you are? Why nobody knows about them? Why they don't have thousands of followers?"

Buddha said, "They have become enlightened but they are not Masters. They are arhatas, they are not bodhisattvas."

The arhata knows it but cannot make it known to the others; the bodhisattva knows it and can make it known to the others. Krishnamurti is an arhata. Because of this he cannot understand the beautiful world of a Master and his disciples.

You ask me, Wolfgang: Could you please tell me your opinion about J. Krishnamurti, who is saying that you won't be free and therefore not happy as long as you follow any tradition, religion or master?

He is right. If you follow a tradition, religion or Master — remember the word "follow" — you will not be free and you will not be blissful, you will not know the ultimate truth of life: by following nobody knows it. What can you do by following a tradition? You will become an imitator. A tradition means something of the past, and enlightenment has to happen right now! A tradition may be very ancient — the more ancient it is, the more dead.

A tradition is nothing but footprints on the sands of time of the enlightened people, but those footprints are not enlightened. You can follow those footprints very religiously and they will not lead you anywhere, because each person is unique. If you remember the uniqueness of the person then no following is going to help you, because there cannot be a fixed routine.

That's the difference between science and religion: science depends on tradition. Without a Newton, without an Edison, there is no possibility for Albert Einstein to have existed at all. He needs a certain tradition; only on that tradition, on the shoulders of the past giants in the world of science, he can stand. Of course when you stand on the shoulders of somebody you can look a little farther than the person on whose shoulders you are standing, but that person is needed there.

Science is a tradition, but religion is not a tradition: it is an individual experience, utterly individual. Once something is known in the world of science it need not be discovered again, it will be foolish to discover it again. You need not discover the theory of gravitation — Newton has done it. You need not go and sit in a garden and watch an apple fall and then conclude that there must be some force in the earth that pulls it downwards; it will be simply foolish. Newton has done it; now it is part of human tradition. It can be taught to any person who has a little bit of intelligence; even schoolchildren know about it.

But in religion you have to discover again and again. No discovery becomes a heritage in religion. *Buddha* discovered, but that does not mean you can simply follow the *Buddha*. Buddha was unique, you are unique in your own right, so how *Buddha* has entered into truth is not going to help you. You are a different kind of house; the doors may be in different directions. If you simply follow Buddha blindly, that very following will be misleading.

Traditions cannot be followed. You can understand them and understanding can be of immense help, but following and understanding are totally different things.

So Krishnamurti is right when he is against following, but when he starts saying that you need not even understand, then he is wrong. Then he is speaking the language of an arhata and he is unaware of the world of the bodhisattva. Understanding is possible — you can understand Buddha.

What he is doing for forty years? What efforts has he been making for forty years? How Wolfgang came to know Krishnamurti's ideas? He is trying to explain, he is trying with great effort to make you understand. You cannot follow Krishnamurti, but you can certainly understand his vision, his perspective, and that will be an enrichment. It will not bring you enlightenment, but it can be used as a stepping-stone.

Krishnamurti says he is fortunate that he has not read any religious scriptures. That is not right. In the first place it is not factual — he has been taught when he was young all the ancient scriptures, not only of one tradition but of all the traditions, because he was brought up by theologists, Theosophists — great synthesizers of all the paths and all the religions and all the traditions. Theosophy was one of the greatest efforts ever made to bring all the traditions closer to each other: Hinduism, Mohammedanism, Christianity, Judaism, Jainism, Buddhism, Taoism. Theosophy was trying to find out the essential core of them all, and Krishnamurti was taught in every possible way all that is great. He may have forgotten about it, and I know that he must have forgotten because he will not lie, he will not say anything deliberately untrue. But he lived in a kind of hypnosis for twenty-five years.

He was taken possession by the Theosophists when he was only nine years of age, and then he had been brought up in a very special way. Many secret methods have been tried upon him: he has been taught while he was sleeping, he has been taught while he was in deep hypnosis, so he does not remember it at all.

Only recently Russian psychologists are trying to find ways how to teach children while they are asleep, because if we can teach children while they are asleep much time can be saved. And one thing more: when a child is asleep he can be taught more easily because there is no distraction. His unconscious can be taught directly, which is easier. When we teach a child through his consciousness it is difficult, because ultimately the teaching has to reach to the unconscious, only then it becomes yours. And to reach to the unconscious through the conscious it takes long time, long repetition. You have to go on repeating again and again and again, then only slowly slowly it settles to the bottom of the conscious, and from that bottom slowly it penetrates into the unconscious.

But in deep sleep, or more precisely in hypnosis — hypnosis means sleep, deliberately created sleep — you can reach directly to the unconscious; the conscious can be bypassed, and a thing can be put into the unconscious. The conscious will not know anything about it.

Krishnamurti was taught all the great scriptures in a deep

hypnosis; he has completely forgotten. Not only that: he has been even manipulated to write while he was in hypnosis. His first book, at the feet of the master, was written under hypnosis, hence he simply shrugs his shoulders when you ask about that first book — which is really a rare document of immense value. But he simply says, "I don't know anything about it, how it happened. I can't say that I have written it."

Krishnamurti has been experimented upon by Theosophists in many subtle ways, so he is not aware that he has been acquainted with all the great scriptures and all the great documents, and what he goes on saying has reflections of all those teachings They are there, but in a very subtle form. He cannot quote the scriptures, but what he says is the very essence of the scriptures.

A tradition has to be understood, and if you can understand many traditions, of course it will enrich you. It will not make you enlightened, but it will help you towards the goal, it will push you towards the goal. Don't be a follower of any tradition — don't be a Christian or a Hindu or a Mohammedan. But it will be unfortunate if you remain unaware of the beautiful words of Jesus, it will be a sheer misfortune if you don't know the great poetry of the Upanishads.

It will be as if a person has not heard any great music — Beethoven, Bach, Mozart, Wagner. If one has not heard, something will be missing in him. It will be a misfortune if you have not read Shakespeare, Milton, Dostoevsky, Kalidas, Bharbhuti, Rabindranath, Kahlil Gibran. If you have not been acquainted with Tolstoy, Chekhov, Maxim Gorky, something in you will remain missing. The same is true if you have not read Lao Tzu, Chuang Tzu, Lieh Tzu, Gautam Buddha, Bodhidharma, Baso, Lin Chi, Socrates, Pythagoras, Heraclitus. These are very different, unique perspectives, but they will all help you to become wider.

So I will not say that traditions are useless; I will say they become dangerous if you follow them blindly. Try to understand, imbibe the spirit. Forget the letter, just drink of the spirit. It is certainly dangerous to belong to a religion because that means you are encaged, imprisoned into a certain creed, dogma. You lose your freedom, you lose your inquiry, your exploration.

It is dangerous to live surrounded by a small philosophy. You will be a frog in the well; you will not know about the ocean. But to understand is a totally different phenomenon. The very effort to understand all the religions of the world will make you free of creeds and dogmas.

That's what's happening here. I am talking about all the religions for the simple reason so that you don't become addicted with one standpoint. Life is multidimensional. Certainly Moses has contributed something to it which nobody else has done. Unless you understand Moses you will miss that perspective, that dimension; that much you will be poorer.

And the people who listen to Krishnamurti, they start following him! There are Krishnamurtiites who have been listening him for forty years or even fifty years. I have come across old people of the same age as Krishnamurti w ho have listened to him for fifty years, since 1930, and they have reached nowhere. All that they have learned is a kind of negativeness: "This is wrong, that is wrong." But what is right? About that there seems to be not even a glimpse in their being.

Don't become part of a religion, but visit, be a guest to all the religions. In the temple there is a beauty, in the mosque also, a different kind of beauty, in the church again a different experience. And this is our whole heritage; the whole humanity's past belongs to you. Why choose?

The follower chooses. He insists to be a Christian; he will avoid Upanishads, he will avoid Dhammapada, he will not bother about Koran. He is unnecessarily crippling himself, paralyzing himself.

I also say don't follow, but I will not agree with the statement that: don't try to understand. Trying to understand is not following; your understanding becomes more clear, more sharpened.

Krishnamurti goes on reading detective novels. Is he following those detective novels? Is he trying to become a detective? If he can read *detective novels*, what is wrong in reading the Upanishads? And detective novels are just ordinary, juvenile, childish. Upanishads are the Himalayan peaks of human consciousness. Don't follow them — there is no need to follow anybody.

My sannyasins are not my followers, they are just my companions. The word satsang, the word upanishad, means the company of a Master. The disciple is a companion a fellow-traveler, and of course if you are traveling with somebody who knows the territory, who has explored the territory, your journey will become easier, your journey will become richer, your journey will have less unnecessary hazards; you will be able to reach the goal sooner than alone.

Traditions become dangerous only when you cling to them; then certainly there is danger. Traditions are group efforts to keep the unexpected from happening. If you become a part, then it is dangerous, because then the tradition becomes a hindrance to you for exploring. The tradition insists for belief — believe in it and believe without inquiry. That's what people are doing, what Christians and Hindus and Mohammedans are doing — believing in something they have never inquired. And to believe in something without inquiring is very disrespectful towards truth and towards your own self.

No, belief is not going to help — only knowing can free you.

And he says the same about a Master. It is true about ninety-nine so-called Masters, but it is not true about the one, the real one He is ninety-nine percent right, because wherever there are real coins there are bound to be false coins too. A tradition is dead; a religion is a philosophy, a belief, a dogma. If you believe in it, it appears significant; its arguments appear to be very great. The moment you stand by the side and look with a detached view, you can see the foolishness, the stupidity. You can see that there are assumptions which have not been proved, not been established.

One morning a great philosopher was seen walking down the street touching every pole that he passed. Someone asked him, "Hey, professor, why are you touching all those poles?"

The philosopher grinned and said, "And why are you not touching all those poles?"

It is difficult to answer why you are not touching!

The philosophers have their own arguments; you may not be able to argue against them. They may silence you; they may bring great proofs, logical arguments, rationalizations. They may silence you, but that is not going to help.

After giving a speech at Columbia University, the noted philosopher, Bertrand Russell, was answering questions from the audience. One student's critical question brought him to a full stop. For a whole minute he said nothing, his hand over his chin. Then he peered at the student and rephrased the question, making it more precise. He asked the student, "Would you say that this is still your question?"

The student answered delightfully, "Yes."

Again Lord Russell thought, this time even longer, and twice seemed about to speak. Then he said, "That's a very good question, young man. I don't believe I can answer it!"

But there are very few philosophers like Bertrand Russell who will accept that they can't answer. They will invent answers, they will go on and on creating proofs, inventing proofs. For every kind of nonsense you can find proofs, you can argue.

Religions are all based on theologies, and the very word "theology" is a contradiction in terms. "Theo" means God, "logy" means logic — logic about God. In fact, there is no logic about God; there is love but no logic. You can approach the phenomenon God or godliness through the heart, through love, but not through logic.

By following a tradition or religion, what are you doing? Your approach is bound to be through the head. Following is always from the head: you are convinced logically, hence you follow, but it is not a love affair.

Love attain is possible only when you find a loving Master. You cannot fall in love with Jesus now, you cannot fall in love with Buddha now; they are no more there. Those dew-drops have disappeared into the ocean. You can fall in love only with a living Master. Buddha must have been very beautiful, but love can happen only between two living hearts.

Krishnamurti is right about ninety-nine percent so-called gurus, but one has to take the risk. If you become too cautious you will never be able to find the true one. To find the true one you will have to pass through many untrue ones.

An American seeker reached to the Everest after a long, arduous journey around the world in search of a Master. And finally he found a great, ancient old man sitting silently on top of the Everest.

The American seeker said, "Ah, great guru, I have devoted my entire life to the quest for truth, honesty, love and justice. I have traveled to the four corners of the earth to experience every agony and every passion. Now I come to you to ask: where do I go from here?"

The guru said, "Go back and do it all over again, my son."

"Thank you, thank you! What can I ever do to repay you?"

And the guru said, "Got any American cigarettes on you?"

He is right about ninety-nine percent gurus, but he is wrong about one percent, and that one percent is really what matters. He is wrong about Buddha, he is wrong about Lao Tzu, he is wrong about Jesus.

But to find a living Master one has to search, and in fact, all those false gurus help you in a way because experiencing them you become aware of that which is false. And to know the false as false is the beginning of knowing the true as the true, the real as the real. If you are absolutely clear about the false, suddenly you become clear about what is real, what is authentic. So even the false gurus are serving, in indirect way, to the real seekers.

Wolfgang, a Master is one who will not tell you to follow him.

but he will certainly tell you to be silently with him. It has nothing to do with following. A real, authentic Master does not want to create pseudo replicas, carbon copies; he helps you to discover your original face. He will not impose any structure on you; on the contrary, he will help you to get rid of all imposed structures. He will not condition you; he will only uncondition you and then leave you to yourself He will not recondition you.

When you move from one false guru, then it happens: the new false guru will uncondition you and then recondition you. If you become a Hindu from being a Christian you will be unconditioned first so that you can get rid of your Christianity, and then Hinduism will be imposed on you.

That is what is happening to Hare Krishna people: now they are being conditioned as Hindus. They have lived in one kind of prison called Christianity, now they will be living in another kind of prison called Hinduism. It is the same, it makes no difference; only the prison is different. You get out of one prison and immediately you enter into another.

The real Master will take you out of one prison and will prevent you from entering into another prison. Certainly it is difficult to find a real Master, but that does not mean that one should not try to find; that does not mean that it is impossible — difficult of course, but not impossible. And when you have come to a Master who simply imparts his love, his being, his presence, who shares his joy, his laughter with you, and there is no desire to condition you, to force you into a certain pattern, then his presence can be of immense catalytic significance; he can be a catalytic agent. In his presence something can start happening in you which may not happen alone for centuries, maybe for lives.

J. Krishnamurti is a beautiful man but one-dimensional, very linear, one line; he follows one track. Hence you will not find any contradictions in him. For fifty years he has been repeating simply the same thing again and again. unknowingly he has conditioned people; just by repeating the same thing again and again for fifty years he has hypnotized people. He has created a great difficulty for those people: he is not a Master himself, he cannot impart his experience — he is an arhata, not a bodhisattva — and he has prevented those people from going into search for some other living Master. He has created a real mess in many people: they would have been in search of a Master but he has prevented them. His logic is clear, appealing, very appealing to the egoist, particularly to the so-called intelligentsia, very appealing, because the so-called intellegentsia is always afraid of surrender, of dropping the ego — they are egoist people. And when he says, "There is no need to follow, there is no need to go to any Master, there is no need of any initiation," they feel very happy. Their ego is saved but their ego is there.

Now the ego even has the support of Krishnamurti, and all his arguments will be used by the ego. And that's what has happened to thousands of people who have listened to him. He has not been a blessing, because of his linear logic.

In the ancient days people like Krishnamurti used to remain silent. That was the way of the arhata — because he knows that he cannot impart, he has no skill, he remains silent. He does not go around the world telling people, that "I cannot impart and nobody else can do it either."

This is for the first time an arhata has been trying to teach people, and of course it is a contradiction. The arhata is not supposed to teach, and when an arhata starts teaching he will teach against teaching, and the people who will become interested in him will be egoists.

You can find the very cultured egos around Krishnamurti, and they are there because he has become their rationalization: there is no need to surrender. And the irony is, is that Krishnamurti himself passed through many initiations, he had many Masters.

In fact, I had no Master and he had many Masters, but maybe that's why he is against Masters and I am not against! — because I had had no experience of the false. I have never been with any Master, I have worked on my own. It took long, many lives, but I have never been initiated by anybody. Maybe that's why I have a soft corner for the Masters!

And he has been forced and regimented in every possible way by the Theosophists. And they had many secrets available to them and he was initiated into all kinds of ceremonies and into all kinds of secret mysteries, esoteric, which are not available to the public. He must have become tired.

And one fact has to be remembered always: he was not willingly there — he had been chosen and adopted. He belonged to a very poor brahmin, the son of a very poor brahmin, so poor that he was not able even to educate his children. And when Annie Besant and Leadbeater found these two brothers, Krishnamurti and Nityananda, swimming in a river by the side of Adyar where is the head-quarters of the Theosophical Movement, world headquarters near Madras... Leadbeater had a certain sensibility to find out talents; he discovered many talented people. He had a certain sense to see immediately the possibility, the potential. He immediately told Annie Besant... they had gone for a morning walk and he saw these two children; Nityananda must have been eleven and Krishnamurti was nine. And he said, "These two children are of immense value — they can become world teachers!"

So they searched. They found out they belonged to a very poor man; the mother is dead, the father is just a very poor clerk in an office. It is difficult to educate, to feed the children rightly. When he heard that Annie Besant wants to adopt them he was very happy; he willingly gave the children to Annie Besant.

And of course, Nityananda and Krishnamurti both were taught like princes or even better than that. They had the most learned tutors; they went through private education in India, in France, in England, in America, all around the world. They were kept away from the public so they don't become polluted, they don't become contaminated. They were prevented from meeting ordinary people. They were brought up as special people, chosen ones — chosen to be world teachers. And great discipline was imposed on them. Of course it was all unwilling; they had not chosen the path themselves. There must have been a resistance — naturally obviously deep down they must have resisted.

Nityananda died, and my feeling is he died because of too much rigorous discipline — fasting, getting up early, three o'clock in the morning. And he became ill; still the discipline continued. They were hard taskmasters, they wanted to make supermen, and of course when you want to make somebody a superman the discipline has to be hard, arduous.

Nityananda died. That too has been a wound in Krishnamurti's mind, in his heart: that his brother was almost killed by the discipline. And twenty-five years of rigorous training must have created an antagonism, a resistance.

So when the time came for them to be declared — the Theosophists gathered from all over the world and Krishnamurti was to declare himself the new incarnation of Gautam the Buddha, the World Teacher — when he stood on the platform to declare, everybody was shocked, people could not believe because he simply denied. He said, "I am nobody's Master I don't accept any disciples, I don't teach any discipline, and I dissolve this whole organization that has been created around me."

A certain organization was created around him — six thousand members all over the world. The organization was called "The Star of the East". He dissolved the organization, he distributed the money back to the donors. because it had great money. He shocked everybody: they had worked so long on him and he simply escaped at the last moment.

And that wound has remained in him, and he cannot forgive all those Masters, their disciplines, their teachings — he cannot forgive, hence he is against. And he himself is an Arhata, he cannot be a Master. And his whole past of his life is full of resistance.

My experience is totally different, just the opposite: I had nobody to impose anything on me; whatsoever I have done I have done on my own. Hence I don't see any antagonisms in me against Masters, against disciplehood.

But certainly about ninety-nine percent I will agree with him: Muktananda, Reverend Moon, Prabhupad, all kinds of stupid people, exploiting — exploiting the great search that has arisen in humanity's heart.

Man is on a new borderline, he is going to enter into a new territory. A new step has to be taken. Hence the great inquiry all around the world about truth, about meditation, about the inward. The outer has failed: the science has proved illusory, all its promises have gone down the drain; and man knows now absolutely that "What we have been doing up to now was basically wrong — the journey has to be inward."

Now there are charlatans, people who can exploit this opportunity, but this is understandable; nothing can be done about it. The seeker has to pass through all these exploiters, deceivers, hypocrites, and has to be aware so that he can find one day the true man — the man who can uncondition you and will not recondition you again, who will leave you in absolute freedom to be yourself.

Beware of the false Masters — and there are many and of many kinds. They come in all sizes and in all shapes and they can be very attractive, because they fulfill your expectations.

The real Master will never fulfill your expectations; he has no desire to manipulate you. Fulfilling your expectations means a deep desire to manipulate you. You have to be alert, watchful. If somebody is trying to fulfill your expectations, know perfectly well he himself is not free — he cannot impart freedom to you.

In India, as in other countries and other traditions too, people have expectations, certain expectations. For example, a Christian expects that the enlightened person should be similar to Jesus; now that is absolutely impossible. Jesus cannot be repeated, need not be repeated. To repeat Jesus you will need the whole context and that context is no more possible. Jesus existed in a Jewish world, with all the expectations, desires, hopes and promises. Now that world has disappeared; two thousand years have passed. So much water has gone down the Ganges, nothing is the same any more. How can Jesus be repeated?

But the Christian expects from a true Master to be just like Jesus. No true Master can be just like Jesus. Jesus was not like Moses himself — that was the trouble. That's why Jews were so much antagonistic: they were expecting him to be just like Moses. Moses lived in a totally different world; he belonged to the Egyptian context, he grew out of that context, he makes sense only in that reference. Jesus cannot be a Moses, it is impossible. And Jews were expecting him to be just a Moses, and because he was not they killed him.

Now Christians are doing the same: they expect the true Master to be a replica of Jesus, an imitation of Jesus. No true Master can be a replica; only some fool can imitate, only some mediocre person can be a carbon copy. This is such a deep insult of one's own being — to copy somebody else — that no man of intelligence can ever do it. But the same is true about other traditions.

The Buddhists are waiting for Buddha to come, and he has to be exactly like Buddha. And the Jains have their expectations and the Hindus have their expectations. The Hindus cannot accept Mahavira as an enlightened Master because he is not like Krishna, and the Jains cannot accept Krishna as an enlightened Master because he is not like Mahavira. Jains cannot accept Buddha as an enlightened person because he is not like Mahavira, and Buddhists in their own turn cannot accept Mahavira because he is not like Buddha. No tradition can accept the enlightened persons of other traditions because the expectations differ.

For example, Jains think that the enlightened Master should be naked. Now Jesus does not fulfill that, Mohammed is not naked, Zarathustra is not naked, Krishna is not naked. On the contrary, Krishna loved beautiful clothes, he loved ornaments.

In those days in India men used to wear ornaments, and that seems to be really logical and natural. If you watch nature you will see it: look at the peacock. The female peacock is unornamental; it is the male peacock which is ornamental. Don't be misguided, when you see the beautiful peacock with its rainbow-colored feathers, remember it is the male, not the female. The female is beautiful just by being female; it needs no ornamentation. It is enough to be famale! The poor male needs some other gadgets.

When you listen to the beautiful sound of the cuckoo, remember it is the male, not the female. The female need not have such a beautiful singing voice; just to be female is enough. The female simply sits hidden in a mango grove, and the male goes on pouring his heart, writing love letters!

The whole nature is proof that the female looks ordinary and the male looks very beautiful. It is strange that why man has started behaving in a reverse way, why women try to be beautiful, use ornaments and lipstick and false eyelashes and whatnot! It is crazy! Let the man use all these things! He is poor, he needs something. The woman is perfectly beautiful as she is. Just to be feminine has a grace, a beauty; there is no need for any other addition.

In Krishna's time things were perfectly natural: men used to wear ornaments. If you have seen Krishna's statues, pictures, you will see: he is wearing silk robes, colorful robes, with a crown with a peacock feather on it, and with a flute, trying to do what the male cuckoo goes on doing, and he is standing in a dancing pose.

Now Jains cannot accept him as an enlightened person; this is not the way of being enlightened. He looks like an actor! According to Jain mythology he has gone into seventh hell — seventh is the last. Only the very dangerous people are thrown into the seventh. Even Adolf Hitler will not reach the seventh; he will be somewhere, at the most third, not more than that. Krishna is in the seventh and Krishna will not be freed in this phase of creation.

Jains have cycles: one cycle means one creation; then the whole creation becomes dissolved, disappears into nothingness, and then another creation begins, another cycle. Krishna will be released only when the second cycle begins, not in this cycle. When all these suns and moons and stars and this whole universe dissolves through the black holes when all is gone and left — nothing is left — then the second cycle starts. Krishna will come back only after the first creation is gone, not before that; it will take eternity. They are very angry at Krishna — what kind of enlightened person he is.

These expectations! Jains cannot believe that Jesus is enlightened, because according to them an enlightened person cannot be crucified — impossible. In fact, they have this myth that when Mahavira walks on the road... and he is a naked man without shoes, and you know the Indian roads. And Mahavira walked twenty-five centuries before; just try to imagine what kind of roads — he must not have been walking — roadless roads!

The story is: when he walks on the road, even if a thorn is there it immediately turns upside-down because the enlightened person is finished with all his karmas, he cannot suffer any pain any more. Pain is suffered because of your past karmas; you must have committed some sin in the past. He is finished with all the sins, he is completely free from all karmas, so no pain is possible. What to think, what to say about crucifixion?

Jains cannot believe Jesus to be enlightened. For them according to them, it is not the Jews who are crucifying him, it is not the Roman governor who is crucifying him; it is his past bad deeds, past karmas which are creating this pain for him, this agony for him.

If you just watch all these expectations you will be able to understand that no enlightened person can ever go according to your expectations; he has to live his life authentically. And if he wants to exploit you he will fulfill your expectations. If he wants to exploit the Jains he will go naked, he will fast, and they will be happy — he is a great man. If he wants to fulfill the expectations of Christians he will become a Mother Teresa of Calcutta: serve the poor the crippled, the ill. If he wants to fulfill the expectations of the Mohammedans he will become an Ayatollah Khomaniac — take the sword — because that's what Mohammed did. And remember, Mohammedans believe that it was out of compassion, because if somebody is going into hell, even if he can be prevented by a sword he should be prevented. And anybody who is not a Mohammedan is going to hell, so convert everybody into a Mohammedan, by whatsoever means it has to be done but it has to be done. So Ayatollah Khomaniac is the most perfect Mohammedan Master right now!

These fools can pretend because they have to look at the crowd, what are their expectations; they can fulfill their expectations. But a true living Master is bound to be totally free from your expectations. He cannot adjust with you; if you have to be with him you have to adjust with him.

And that's why egoists find it difficult to be with a Master, and they enjoy the company of Krishnamurti — for the simple reason because he is not asking you to dissolve your ego or surrender or to adjust in any way. He is not asking anything to you. He is not giving you any insight, he is simply making clear the standpoint of an Arhata. But the arhata has never been helpful to anybody, and he cannot be helpful.

And now there have arisen many new kinds of gurus; they are mushrooming all over the world. Religious gurus are there and then there are psychoanalysts and therapists. They are taking the place; they are becoming very important. And of course they understand something about the mechanism of the mind and they can help you a little bit, but they themselves are in a deep mess.

Conversation between two psychiatrists:

"Most of my patients are disturbed. Let me ask you some questions — to give you an example. Which has smooth curves and sometimes is uncontrollable?"

"A baseball pitcher, of course."

"Next, what wears a skirt and has lips that bring you pleasure?"

"Obviously, a Scotsman playing a bagpipe."

"You know the answers, but it's amazing what strange replies I get from my patients!"

These psychoanalysts, now they are the New Age gurus. They

know certain tricks about the mind, but they have no idea of the innermost core of your being. You have to be very careful and cautious because there has never been such a tremendous desire for transformation, hence there are bound to be many people who will not miss this opportunity to exploit you.

In that sense Krishnamurti is right, but only about ninety-nine percent. And to me that is nothing to be compared with the remaining one percent. Those ninety-nine percent can be ignored, that one percent should not be forgotten because that is the only hope: a Master who can make you free, who does not make you a slave; a Master who can make you unconditioned and does not recondition you; a Master who does not give you any doctrine, dogma, a creed to believe in, but shares his joy, his celebration with you.

Question 3

OSHO,

Please tell a joke which I can laugh at for the rest of my life.
— *Prem Raquibo*

There is no joke like that; it is impossible. It cannot happen in the very nature of things, because a joke can be laughed at only when you hear it for the first time. You cannot laugh at it for the rest of your life, unless you are so stupid, so utterly stupid, that each time you hear it you have completely forgotten that you have heard it before. And you will be telling it to yourself because who is going to tell you your whole life? I can tell you only once, then you will have to tell it to yourself. Either you have to be utterly stupid or mad!

I have heard about a man who was sitting in a waiting room on a railway station, and the train was late — as Indian trains always are. In India they say the timetable exists so that you can know how much the train is late. Otherwise how you will know how much it is late? Late it is going to be! And in India they say a ticket is valid for twenty-four hours. It is valid for twenty-four hours because nobody knows when the train will come. If it comes in twenty-four hours, that too is a miracle!

So he was waiting, sitting in his chair, and the other people in the waiting room were a little bit getting puzzled. Finally one person became so curious he could not contain his curiosity. He said, "Sir, I should not interfere, but what is going on?" — because the man was sitting there with closed eyes; his lips were moving. Sometimes he will giggle and sometimes he will frown; sometimes he will laugh loudly and sometimes he will make a gesture of his hands as if he is throwing something away. What was going on?

The man asked, "What you are doing? It is none of our business and we should not interfere, and it is absolutely private what you are doing, but excuse me... if you can enlighten me a little bit?"

The man said, "There is nothing private about it — I am telling jokes to myself!"

The man said, "That's... that I can understand. Sometimes you giggle and you laugh loudly — you must be having fun. But sometimes you frown and you make such ugly face and you throw something, push away something by your hands."

He said, "Yes, when I hear a joke which I have heard before!"

He is telling jokes to himself!

Now, Raquibo, one joke for your whole life...? It has never happened! You can laugh only at the first time, because the whole art, the secret of a joke is the unexpected ending. That is the whole secret — the unexpected turn. The joke first moves in a certain line, and then takes such an unexpected turn that logically you are shocked for a moment. You were moving along the joke expecting certain things to happen, and then what happens is not the logical thing. Something illogical happens — and it is that illogical makes the joke beautiful, that makes you burst into a laughter.

Logic is not fun, it is a serious thing. And when you start hearing a joke, of course your mind starts functioning logically. You start expecting logically that this is going to happen, this is going to happen, and then something comes at the end which you could not have imagined. It is so illogical, so ridiculous. it is so absurd! The shock... and the whole energy was getting into one direction, mounting up to a climax, and then suddenly everything goes berserk. The whole energy explodes into laughter. It is a certain tension that is released. The logic creates tension and the joke releases it. That is the punchline which does the trick.

But this can happen only once. If you know the punchline, then it is very difficult for you to enjoy it because you will be expecting it. You already know it; now it has become part of your logic. So there cannot be any mounting energy, there cannot be any tension; you will sit relaxedly.

A man entering middle age had been bothered for some time by his prick. It had grown very crooked and had sprouted warts and hairs in the most inappropriate places. His condition had worsened over the years and he decided to seek medical advice.

The local doctor examined his tool thoroughly and stated that amputation was the only possibility for a specimen such as his.

The poor fellow went to another doctor for a second opinion. He also gave the thing a very thorough examination, then stated that it had to come off.

Now in a state of panic, the man went to a specialist for a final opinion. He examined the prick at length, leaned back in his armchair for a while in contemplation, then said, "No, sir, I think that amputation is unnecessary." The patient sighed with relief "Yes," continued the doctor, "in no time at all it will fall off by itself!"

4

Surrender Is Of The Heart

Question 1

OSHO,

My friend, who has a Ph.D. in Computing, and whose thesis was on "Artificial Intelligence", says that man is a Biochemical Computer and nothing more. The Buddha has said that all things are composite and there is no self, no soul, no spirit, no "I", which seems to agree with my friend's viewpoint. Could you please help me, because I feel that there is something missing from these views but I can't see it myself.

— *Prem Hamid,*

Man certainly is a biocomputer, but something more too. About ninety-nine point nine percent of people it can be said that they are only biocomputers and nothing more. Ordinarily one is only the body and the mind, and both are composites. Unless one moves into meditation one cannot find that which is something more, something transcendental to body and mind.

The psychologists, particularly the behaviorists, have been studying man for half a century, but they study the ordinary man, and of course their thesis is proved by all their studies. The ordinary man, the unconscious man, has nothing more in him than the bodymind composite. The body is the outer side of the mind and the mind the inner side of the body. Both are born and both will die one day.

But there is something more. That something more makes a man awakened, enlightened, a Buddha, a Christ. But a Buddha or a Christ is not available to be studied by Pavlov, Skinner, Delgado and others. Their study is about the unconscious man, and of course when you study the unconscious man you will not find anything transcendental in him. The transcendental exists in the unconscious man only as a potential, as a possibility; it is not yet realized, it is not yet a reality. Hence you cannot study it.

You can study it only in a Buddha, but even then studying is obviously very difficult, just very close to the impossible, because what you will study in a Buddha will again be his behavior. And if you are determined that there is nothing more, if you have already concluded, then even in his behavior you will see only mechanical reactions, you will not see his spontaneity. To see that spontaneity you have also to become a participant in meditation.

Psychology can become only a real psychology when meditation becomes its foundation. The word "psychology" means the science of the soul. Modern psychology is not yet a science of the soul.

Buddha certainly has denied the self, the ego, the "I", but he has not denied the soul and the self and the soul are not synonymous. He denies the self because the self exists only in the unconscious man. The unconscious man needs a certain idea of "I", otherwise he will be without a center. He does not know his real center. He has to invent a false center so that he can at least function in the world, otherwise his functioning will become impossible. He needs a certain idea of "I".

You must have heard about Descartes' famous statement: "Cogito ergo sum — I think, therefore I am."

A professor, teaching the philosophy of Descartes, was asked by a student, "Sir, I think, but how do I know that I am?"

The professor pretended to peer around the classroom. "Who is asking the question?" he said.

"I am," replied the student.

One needs a certain idea of "I", otherwise functioning will become impossible. So because we don't know the real "I" we substitute it by a false "I" — something invented, composite.

Buddha denies the self because to him "self" simply is another name for the ego, with a little color of spirituality, otherwise there is no difference. His word is anatta. Atta means "self", anatta means "no-self". But he is not denying the soul. In fact he says when the self is completely dropped, then only you will come to know the soul. But he does not say anything about it because nothing can be said about it.

His approach is via negativa. He says: You are not the body, you are not the mind, you are not the self He goes on denying, eliminating. He eliminates everything that you can conceive of, and then he does not say anything what is left. That which is left is your reality: that utterly pure sky without clouds, no thought, no identity, no emotion, no desire, no ego — nothing is left. All clouds have disappeared... just the pure sky.

It is inexpressible, unnameable, indefinable. That's why he keeps absolutely silent about it. He knows it that if anything is said about it you will immediately jump back to your old idea of the self If he says, "There is a soul in you," what you are going to understand? You will think that, "He calls it soul and we call it self — it is the same. The supreme self maybe, the spiritual self; it is not ordinary ego. "But spiritual or unspiritual, the idea of my being a separate entity is the point.

Buddha denies that you are a separate entity from the whole. You are one with the organic unity of existence, so there is no need to say anything about your separateness. Even the word "soul" will give you a certain idea of separateness; you are bound to understand it in your own unconscious way.

Hamid, your friend says that: Man is a biochemical computer and nothing more.

Can a biochemical computer say that? Can a biochemical computer deny the self, the soul? No biocomputer or any other kind of computer has any idea of self or no-self. Your friend is doing it — certainly he is not a biochemical computer. No biochemical computer can write a thesis on artificial intelligence! Do you think artificial intelligence can write a thesis about artificial intelligence? Something more is needed.

And he is absolutely wrong in thinking that Buddha says also the same thing:

... That all things are composite and there is no self no soul, no spirit, no "I".

He is wrong to think that Buddha agrees with his viewpoint — not at all. Buddha's experience is of meditation. Without meditation nobody can have any idea what Buddha is saying about. Your friend's observation is from the standpoint of a scientific onlooker. It is not his experience, it is his observation. He is studying biochemical computers, artificial intelligence, from the outside. Who is studying outside?

Can you conceive two computers studying each other? The computer can have only that which has been fed into it; it cannot have more than that. The information has to be given to it, then it keeps it in its memory — it is a memory system. It can do miracles as far as mathematics is concerned. A computer can be far more efficient than any Albert Einstein as far as mathematics is concerned, but a computer cannot be a meditator. Can you imagine a computer just sitting silently doing nothing, the spring comes and the grass grows by itself...?

There are many qualities which are impossible for the computer. A computer cannot be in love. You can keep many computers together — they will not fall in love! A computer cannot have any experience of beauty. A computer cannot know any bliss. A computer cannot have any awareness. A computer is incapable of feeling silence. And these are the qualities which prove that man has something more than artificial intelligence.

Artificial intelligence can do scientific work, mathematical work, calculation — great calculation and very quick and very efficiently, because it is a machine. But a machine cannot be aware of what it is doing. A computer cannot feel boredom, a computer cannot feel meaninglessness, a computer cannot experience anguish. A computer cannot start an enquiry about truth, it cannot renounce the world and become a sannyasin, it cannot go to the mountains or to the monasteries. It cannot conceive of anything beyond the mechanical — and all that is significant is beyond the mechanical.

A policeman starts chasing a car after noticing that the driver is a computer, a robot — wearing a hat, smoking a cigar and driving with one hand hanging out of the window.

He finally succeeds in stopping the car. He approaches it and sees to his surprise that there is a man sitting next to the computer.

"Are you mad?" exclaims the officer, "letting your computer drive?"

"Excuse me, officer," replies the man, "I asked him for a lift!"

Yes, in stories it is possible, but not in reality.

Mr. Polanski enjoys playing with cuckoo clocks. One rainy Sunday morning he takes his cuckoo clock apart and puts it back together again.

At twelve o'clock the family gathers, waiting for the pretty little bird to sing its song... nothing happens. They wait till one o'clock — no cuckoo. At two o'clock they are still waiting for the bird to appear. Finally, at three o'clock, the little door opens and the cuckoo comes out.

"Dammit!" it squeaks. "Do any of you guys know the time?"

Question 2
OSHO

You spoke yesterday about Krishnamurti and Masters, and that we can understand, we can know, we can surrender and we can fall in love with the master, but we should not follow and believe in the master. Is it possible to surrender without believing? My heart says to me that to surrender and to believe is the same. I cannot feel the difference. what is surrender and belief? I want to believe. I need to believe! if you say that meditation is the source and I do meditation, I believe you, I trust you.

— Dhyan Anna

Surrender is not possible at all if you believe, because belief is of the head and surrender is of the heart. Belief means you are convinced logically, intellectually, that what is being said is right. The argument appeals to you. Belief has nothing to do with the heart; it is absolutely of the mind, a mind phenomenon. Belief is not a love affair.

Belief means intellectually you are convinced because you cannot see any argument which can destroy it; all the arguments that you can manage prove it. But deep down there is bound to be an undercurrent of doubt. Belief cannot destroy doubt, it can only cover it up. It can cover so perfectly that you may forget about the doubt, but it is always there. Just scratch a little bit any believer and you will find the doubt there. That's why believers have always been afraid of listening to anything that goes against their belief.

The Catholic Church goes on prohibiting the Catholics: not to read this, not to read that. They go on putting books on their black list which are banned for the Catholics. The Vatican library has thousands of tremendously beautiful documents with it — for thousands of years they have been gathering — of all those scriptures that they have burned, banned, prohibited. But they have kept a few copies in the Vatican library just as a historical past, and what has been done in the past and what has been destroyed in the past — some proofs of that. Anything that went against Christianity was destroyed.

The same has been done by Mohammedans, by the Hindus, by almost all the believers of the world. Why this fear? — because they are all aware of the fact that the believer is not free of doubt; the doubt is there and anybody can raise the dust again. Somehow they have managed it to settle, somehow they have covered the wound, but the wound has not healed; it is there, and underneath the cover it goes on spreading.

People believe in God, but does that mean their doubt has dropped? If the doubt is no more there, what is the need of belief? Belief is an antidote, it is a medicine. If you are healthy no medicine is needed: if there is no doubt in you no belief is needed.

Belief is very superficial; it divides you. The believer is only the superficial part of you and the remaining part, the major part, the nine-tenths of your being, remains full of doubts. There is turmoil within every believer and he is afraid, really afraid to come across something which may disturb his belief — and anything can disturb his belief.

Communists are not allowed to read anything against communism. In Russia, government does not allow anything that goes against communism. Why this fear? The fear is because they know that if things against communism come into their country, people will start thinking again; their doubts will arise.

Anna, the first thing you have to understand is: believing is of the head and surrender is of the heart. Surrender is not a belief, it is not an intellectual conviction — it is just the ultimate in love. You cannot give any proofs for your surrender; you can give thousand and one logical proof for your belief, but for your surrender you cannot supply a single proof. And whatsoever you say will look absurd to yourself; it will fall short. Surrender has a transcendental beauty, and belief is so ordinary and the proof is so mundane.

That is the trouble why people feel a little embarrassed if you ask about their love. If you ask a man why he has fallen in love with a certain woman he will feel a little embarrassed. You are asking something which cannot be answered, hence the embarrassment. Why...? He can manage to say something, but neither he will be convincing you nor he himself will feel that it is worth saying. He can say the woman is beautiful, that's why... but these are all rationalizations, not reasons for his surrender.

Surrender has no reasons, no motives at all. Surrender simply means a happening, not a doing. Belief is a doing — you do it, you make every effort — but surrender happens from the beyond. You are simply possessed by it.

Lovers know it, how they become possessed. If you say, "Because the woman is beautiful," the other person can say, "But nobody else has fallen in love with her. And she has been beautiful even before you had met her, and she is beautiful, but I have not fallen in love with her. How come you have fallen in love with her?"

Surrender Is Of The Heart

In fact, that is a rationalization, it is not true. Somehow he is trying to save his face. He does not want to say that he does not know why it has happened — it has simply happened. He does not want to accept that he is living something irrational, that he has allowed something illogical to happen to him.

The reality is: the woman looks beautiful because you have fallen in love with her, not vice versa. It is not because of her beauty that you have fallen in love, otherwise the whole world would have fallen in love before you. Just the opposite is the case: she looks beautiful to you because you are in love. Love beautifies.

And falling in love with a man or a woman is the lowest kind of love. When you fall in love with a Buddha or a Christ or a Krishna it is the highest kind of love, the crescendo. It is just far out! It is outlandish! You cannot even give any reasons for your ordinary love — what reasons you can give when you fall in love with a Master? There are no reasons at all.

Just the other day Vivek was telling me a joke. She said, "Osho, do you know why the Jews have short necks?"

And I said...(Osho shrugs his shoulders)

And she said, "Yes, that's why!"

When you love, what you can say except shrug your shoulders? And if you go on shrugging your shoulders the whole day you will have a short neck!

Anna, you ask me: Is it possible to surrender without believing?

Not only it is possible without believing, it is only possible if there is no believing. With belief there is no possibility — belief is a false substitute. Surrender happens out of trust, and trust and belief are not synonymous.

That is where Anna is confused: she thinks trust and belief are the same — they are not. Belief is of the head, trust is of the heart. Belief has arguments about it, trust has no arguments. Belief is intellectual, trust is supra-intellectual. You cannot say a single word in favor of your trust, and if you say you can be immediately refuted very easily. Any fool can destroy your argument for trust, because in fact there is no argument possible.

You say, Anna: My heart says to me that to surrender and to believe is the same.

It is not the heart, Anna, it is the head. You are confused. You don't know what is the heart and what is the head — and this is the case with almost everybody. People live through their heads. Even if they love, they love via the head. They say, "I think I am in love." I think — that comes first and then comes love. It is not a question of thinking at all; whether you think or not does not matter. If you are in love, you are in love. Love does not come via the head.

You say: My heart says to me that to surrender and to believe is the same.

No, it is your head which is telling you that both are the same: to believe is to surrender. This is the language of the head — belief is the language of the head. Surrender belongs to a totally different dimension; it has nothing to do with belief. That's why belief can be disturbed, but surrender cannot be disturbed.

And this has been my experience of working with thousands of sannyasins: almost always it happens that whenever a man comes to me his approach is intellectual. There are a few exceptions, it is not an absolute rule; but it can be said that almost ninety-nine percent men are head-oriented, and when a man comes to me he comes through logical conviction. Listening to me, trying to understand me, if he feels convinced he becomes a sannyasin.

But his sannyas has not much value. Any day he can drop the sannyas. Anybody can destroy his belief because it is based on logic, and logic is just a game. If you come across a person who is more logical than you he will destroy your proofs.

I have never come across a single proof which cannot be destroyed. In fact, to prove anything is difficult to disprove is very easy. If you say, "The sunset is beautiful." it can be argued it is not, and more easily. Anybody can object, anybody can say, "Give me the proof! What do you mean by beauty? What is beauty? And how can you prove that this sunset is beautiful?" And you will be at a loss. You know it is beautiful, but that knowing is not of the head, that knowing is of the heart — and heart Cannot argue, it simply knows.

The problem is: the head has all the questions and the heart has all the answers. The head has all the doubts and the beliefs and the heart has only the trust. That is the flavor of the heart.

There is a beautiful story of Chekhov, a parable:

In a village there was one man who was thought to be an utter idiot, and of course he felt very offended. He tried in every way to convince people, but the more he tried the more it became known that he is a fool.

A mystic was passing through the village, and the idiot went to the mystic and said, "Somehow save me — my life has become impossible! The people of this place think I am an idiot. How can I get rid of this? — because it is torturing me day and night. It has become a nightmare! I am afraid even to face anybody in the town, because wherever I go people start laughing. I have become a laughingstock! Only you can show me the way. What should I do?"

The mystic said, "This is very simple. From tomorrow morning you start asking people such questions which cannot be answered."

He said, "For example, what?"

The mystic said, "If somebody says, 'Look, how beautiful is the rose!' you immediately raise the question: 'Who says? What is the proof? What is beauty?' If somebody talks about time, immediately ask, 'What is time?' If somebody asks about God, ask him, 'Give me the proof!' Somebody talks about love, don't miss the opportunity — just go on asking! Don't make any statement from your side. You simply ask the questions and make people feel embarrassed, because these are the questions nobody can answer!"

And within seven days the man was thought by the villagers as one of the greatest geniuses, because now he was not making any statement so he was not available for you to refute. He was simply denying others.

That is the whole art of atheism: just go on saying no, and nobody can convince you. Yes comes from the heart, and the head is very efficient in saying no. And nobody can prove... nothing can be proved by the head. And higher the value, the more difficult it is to prove.

When men come to me they come through the intellect; their sannyas is not very reliable. But when women come to me... and of course, again there are exceptions, but very few, the same proportion. Ninety-nine percent women are going to remain sannyasins.

That's why I have given my commune totally to be disciplined, to be controlled by the women sannyasins — for the simple reason because their approach to me is through the heart; they are more reliable. One percent men are reliable, one percent women are not reliable — they can drop sannyas. But ninety-nine percent women are reliable: they come through the heart. Nobody can refute their hearts. Their approach is through trust and love.

Anna, you have to understand the difference between the head and the heart. It will take a little because the society has made everybody confused. Everybody is in a mess — nobody knows where is the heart and where is the head.

Just be here — she is new — soon you will be able to feel the difference clearly.

You say: I cannot feel the difference.

Yes, right now it will be difficult, but become a little more silent. In silence the distinction will come very loud.

You say: I want to believe. I need to believe!

That's why it is difficult for you to make the difference. You are desperately in need to believe, you are afraid not to believe, because you don't know anything about trust. Once you know of

Surrender Is Of The Heart

trust, who bothers about belief? Who cares? Belief is nobody's need. It is the strategy of the priests imposed on you that belief is a need — it is not a need. Trust certainly is a need, is a nourishment, but belief is just artificial food, maybe very colorful, but not nourishing.

> You Say: If You Say That Meditation Is The Source And I Do Meditation, I Believe You, I Trust You.

Please, trust but don't believe. And of course, meditation is the way, the source — that's why I have given you the name Dhyan Anna. Dhyan Anna means meditation, prayer. Through meditation you will come to prayer Prayer is the highest form of love, of trust. Through meditation one finds the heart, and prayer arises. And through meditation ultimately one finds the being. And the moment you have found the being there is nothing more to be found... you have come home.

Question 3

OSHO,

You can read in the bible that Jesus warned about other Masters coming in the future. Do you think his warnings were also including you? Your message is very different from important parts of the teachings of Jesus. How is it possible that enlightened Masters can say so many contrary things?

— Dieter

One thing of great importance has to be understood first. Jesus became enlightened only at the last moment on the cross. Hence the statements that he has made before that experience are not of an enlightened person — close, very close, approximate, but as far as truth is concerned there is nothing like approximate truth.

This thing has not been told to Christians at all, that Jesus became enlightened at the very last moment. On the cross he became enlightened, on the cross he became a Christ.

To me the cross is important not for the same reasons as it is for Christians. To them the cross is important because Jesus was crucified, and the cross has become the symbol of crucifixion. To me that is absolutely wrong — that is a kind of life-negation, that is worshipping death, that is making too much fuss about crucifixion.

I call Christianity "Crossianity" because it is not concerned with Christ, it is more concerned with the cross. I also love the symbol of cross, but for a totally different reason: not because of crucifixion but because Jesus became enlightened on the cross, he became aware of the immortality of his ultimate being. To me it is not crucifixion, not death, but the beginning of eternal life.

At the last moment Jesus says to God, "Have you forsaken me?" And that shows that he was still living in the mind, expecting, desiring, hoping — even from God. There were a few expectations that at the last moment some miracle would happen. Not only the people who had gathered there were expecting a miracle looking at the sky — that a divine hand will appear and Jesus will be raised to ultimate glory; he will be saved at the last moment — but Jesus himself was also waiting.

He says, "Have you forsaken me?" What does it mean? It is a complaint, it is not a prayer. It is frustration, it is disappointment. And disappointment is possible only if there was some deep desire, some longing to be fulfilled. God has failed him — he has not come to his rescue. He was hoping.

And these are the signs of an unenlightened person. These are symbolic of the ego, of the head, of the mind, of the very process of the mind.

But he was a man of great intelligence too: immediately he recognized that what he is saying is wrong, the very desire is wrong. One should not expect anything from the universe, one should not feel disappointed. one should not feel frustrated. This is not trust! This is not a love affair! This is not an absolute yes, it is a conditional yes: "You fulfill these conditions, then of course I will be grateful. But because conditions have not been fulfilled I am angry." There is anger in his voice; there is anxiety, disappointment.

But he understood the point, and immediately he corrected it. A single moment... and he is no more Jesus, he becomes Christ. Suddenly he looked at the sky and said, "Forgive me! Let thy kingdom come, let thy will be done — not mine. Let thy will be done!"

This is surrender. He has dropped the mind, he has dropped the ego and all the expectationS. "Let thy will be done." In this egoless state he became enlightened. But unfortunately it happened at the very last moment, and he had no time left.

Buddha lived for forty years after his enlightenment, hence whatsoever he says has a totally different significance than what Jesus says in the New Testament. It is poetry, beautiful, but still he is groping in the dark, making every effort to reach to the light, but he reached to the light at the very last moment. He could not say a single word. He died enlightened, but he could not live enlightened. He died too early — he was only thirty-three. If you understand this, then your question will be very simple.

You Ask Me, Dieter: You can read in the Bible that Jesus warned about other Masters coming in the future.

That is the fear of an unenlightened person, the fear that somebody may replace him, that somebody may come and may convince people of other things. That fear is perfectly understandable in an unenlightened person, because he is jealous. There is fear that once he is gone his teaching may be destroyed. He is too much concerned about the future.

The unenlightened person lives in the past or in the future, and Jesus did both the things in the New Testament. He is talking continuously about the past; he is trying to prove that "I am the Messiah you have been waiting for. I am the man who has been predicted by the prophets of old. The Old Testament has simply prepared the way for me!" He is too much concerned about the past. He is too much concerned in convincing the Jews that he is the expected Messiah. Who cares?

People have asked me, "Buddha, we have heard, is going to come back after twenty-five centuries. Twenty-five centuries have passed. Are you the Buddha?" Why should I be? I am just myself! Why I should be the Buddha? He did his thing, I am going to do my thing. I am not anybody's carbon copy! Why should I be a Buddha? If he wants to come, that is up to him, but I am nobody's incarnation.

Hindus have asked me that "Krishna says, 'Whenever there is need I will come.' Are you that one?" I am not, absolutely not! I am just myself. If Krishna has to fulfill his promise he will come!

Jesus is too much concerned about the past. In fact, that concern brought him the whole trouble. If he had not bothered about being the Messiah Jews may not have crucified him, because then they started asking about the signs that the Messiah has to give, and then they started asking that "You have to fulfill this and you have to fulfill that — only then we can accept you, that you are the Messiah." And then he went into unnecessary argumentation, but his whole effort was to prove that "I am the expected Messiah." This is concern for the past, and only an unenlightened person is concerned about the past.

And he is very much concerned about the future also. He warns about other Masters coming in the future. "And beware of them," he says, "because they will distract you; they will distract you from the path" — the path that he has shown. He is making sure that no follower is taken away from the fold even when he is gone. This is too much businesslike!

And the reason is that he became enlightened at the very last moment and he had no time to correct to change his statements. His statements were made in an unenlightened state.

That's why you find his approach towards God very childish. He calls God abba — papa, daddy! There is no daddy — daddy is dead! It is childish. It is the need of a child, because the child cannot be without the father hence God becomes the father.

And a strange thing has happened: now Christian priests are called fathers. A monastery is defined by someone: a place where unwed fathers live. They don't have any wife, they don't have any children, and they are fathers. What kind of fathers are these? But if God can be a father without a wife, then of course they can also be fathers without wife. Catholic priests being called fathers. Catholic nuns being called mothers, sisters, Mother Superiors! People who have renounced life, renounced families, are still clinging to some ideas of the family. Now God becomes the father, but the father is needed.

Jesus remained a little childish in his approach towards God. Buddha has a maturity, tremendous maturity. He is so mature that he can say there is no God. Existence is enough, more is not needed. There is no creator, creation is enough. Creation itself is divine creativity; it is the process of creativity.

This fear of Jesus simply shows the fear of a Jew businessman! He is afraid his customers may go to somebody else. He is making sure that even in the future the customers never leave the shop! He will be gone, that much is certain, sooner or later he will be gone, but he is making sure that his priests will go on dominating the world; his representatives, his popes, will go on and on always dominating the world.

The very idea to dominate the world, to change the whole world into Christianity, is in some subtle sense an ego trip, an ego number. But it is understandable from an unenlightened person; you cannot expect more than that.

And you ask me: Do you think his warnings were also including you?

The future is absolutely unknown. Nobody knows the future; not even the enlightened person knows about the future. That is the beauty of the future: it is unpredictable. Yes, few inferences can be made, but they are only inferences.

But all the religions have tried to prove that their founders are all-knowing, omniscient. Jains say Mahavira is omniscient: he knows whole past, whole present, whole future. And that is sheer stupidity, because it is a well-known fact — Buddha has mentioned it, they were contemporaries — that Mahavira is known to have begged from a house where nobody had lived for years: and he was standing in front of the house with his begging bowl!

And he was told by the neighbors that, "That house is empty and has been empty for years! And you are an omniscient person — can't you see that there is nobody in the house?" And he knows all about the future — he does not know about this house in front of him! In fact, if people have not lived in that house for many years, even an unenlightened person will be able to infer, looking at the situation of the house — the dust that has collected, the doors that are closed for years — that nobody lives here. You can see easily whether people live in this house or not. Where people live the house has a different quality, aliveness; where nobody lives the house is dead.

Buddha also mentions, just jokingly, about Mahavira, that once he was walking on the road early in the morning. It was a winter morning, too much mist was there, and he stepped on the tail of a dog! And when the dog barked, then he became aware that there is a dog. And he knows all about the past and all about the future!

Nobody knows about the future or about the past. The enlightened person knows only himself, and that's enough. Knowing himself, essentially he knows everybody — essentially, remember, not in details. Essentially he understands everybody because he knows himself. Knowing himself he knows your potential, your possibility. Knowing himself he knows that you are in darkness. Knowing himself he knows how he has reached to his light, and he can help you to reach to the same light.

But the enlightened person knows only himself and nothing more. He knows himself totally absolutely, his whole being is full of light, but that does not mean that he knows everything about the whole existence and past and future, all. That is sheer nonsense! Because of this nonsense so many problems have arisen for religion.

The Bible talks about the earth as if it is flat. That was the problem: that in the Middle Ages the scientists who discovered for the first time that the earth is a globe, circular, round, got into trouble because they were going against the Bible, and the Bible is omniscient. How can you dare to say something against Moses, against Jesus and all the prophets? — because they talk about the earth as flat.

The Bible thinks that the sun goes around the earth, and one can understand why, because we all see the sun moving, in the morning rising and in the evening setting. We see the arc of the sun going around: it is a common inference.

When for the first time Galileo discovered that this is wrong, this is only apparently so, it is a visual illusion, the truth is just the opposite — the earth goes around the sun, not the sun around the earth — he got into trouble. He was very old when he discovered it, seventy or more, and very ill. When his book was published he was called by the Pope. He went there, and he must have been a man of great understanding... I love that man. Many have condemned him for this same thing, but I don't condemn him. I respect him for the same thing for which he has been condemned for three hundred years or more.

The Pope asked him that, "Have you written this?"

He said, "Yes, I have written."

The Pope said, "This goes against the Bible. Are you ready to change it? Otherwise you will be killed or burned alive!"

He said, "I am perfectly ready to change it. You need not take so much trouble of burning me — forgive me. I declare that it is the sun who goes around the earth, not the earth. But remember, my declaration will not make any change — the earth still will go around the sun! Who bothers about Galileo?" He said, "Neither the sun will listen nor the earth will listen. But if it is offensive to you, I am perfectly ready to change it!"

People have thought that he was cowardly; I don't think so. He had a sense of humor! He was not a coward, but he was not stupid — that much is certain. It would have been stupidity to insist for such a small thing. Why bother about it? He was not suicidal — that much is certain. If he had been suicidal, if he had carried some idea of suicide in him, then this was a good chance to become a martyr. Then suicide takes spiritual color: one becomes a martyr, a revolutionary.

But he laughed at the whole thing like a joke and he said, "I will change it immediately — I declare!" But he reminded the Pope that, "My declaration won't make any difference at all — nobody listens to me."

There is the point which he made clear at the end and he corrected with a footnote. And in the footnote he wrote that. "Although I am correcting it because it goes against the Bible — and I am the last person to disturb anybody's religion — but the truth is the earth goes around the sun."

These people... if you try to look into the Vedas, into Gita, into the Bible, into the Koran, you will find thousand and one things which are absolutely wrong, but I can understand why they are wrong. They were writing thousands of years before, and at that time that was the general notion; they were simply talking in that way.

Even today although we know that the earth goes around the sun, our language still carries the old idea — sunrise, sunset — and I think it is going to remain forever; we will not change the language. What does it mean now? It means nothing! There is no sunrise and no sunset, because the sun never goes around the earth, so what do you mean by rising and setting? But the language carries the old idea because the language was created in those days.

Neither Jesus knows nor Mahavira nor Buddha nor anybody else about the future, but the followers try in every possible way to make their Master omniscient, omnipresent, omnipotent! And these are all ego trips. And if the Master himself is yet unenlightened he will pretend himself.

Jesus certainly says that, "Be alert, cautious because there will be many who will come and who will speak in such a way, in such a convincing way that you can be distracted from the right path." He

Surrender Is Of The Heart

is simply afraid. Otherwise, the right path should not be afraid at all.

The truth is going to win. It is not Jesus or Krishna or Buddha or Mahavira who are going to win: it is always the truth which wins. So why be worried? But to keep people imprisoned these warnings help; these warnings make people afraid.

He knew nothing about me, he cannot know. I don't know anything about the coming Masters in the world, and I will not make you beware of the coming Masters. I would like you to enjoy all the Masters you will find in the future. Don't miss a single opportunity. Enjoy the truth from whatsoever source it comes. The question is of being with truth, not with me. If you are with truth you are with me. Truth is nobody's possession; it is neither mine nor Christ's nor Buddha's.

In Buddha's time Buddha was the most clearcut expression of truth, that's why people were with him. In Jesus' time few people were with Jesus because they could see something beautiful in him. And this has been always so. It you are with me you are not with me — you are with truth. Because you feel truth being imparted, communicated, showered on you, that's why you are with me. So wherever you find truth in the future when I am not here, nourish yourself from it. Don't cling to persons. Persons are insignificant, truth is significant.

And You Ask, Dieter: Your message is very different from important parts of the teachings of Jesus.

It is bound to be so, because two thousand years have passed. How I can be exactly the same as Jesus and why should I be? There is no need. In two thousand years much has changed: the language, the people's understanding, the people's approach. Man has become more mature. Jesus speaks in a very childish way.

Of course, the people, the Masters who will come after me will be speaking in a far more better way than I am speaking, obviously, because they would have learned more. As time passes better and better expressions will be available. But we start clinging and that creates trouble.

Jesus spoke in his context, I am speaking in my context. He could not speak in the way twentieth century will understand. I cannot speak in the way that Jesus had chosen because those people are no more here for whom he was speaking. A different humanity is here; a far more mature, far more ripe humanity is here.

Man has come of age. Now to talk about God as the father is foolish; after Sigmund Freud it is foolish. Jesus had no idea of Sigmund Freud; I have to take care of Sigmund Freud too, because Sigmund Freud will say that talk about God as father is simply a projection, and he is right. It is your longing to belong to a father figure, it is your childish desire to be dependent on somebody — you don't want to be independent. Now after Sigmund Freud I cannot speak in the same way as Jesus spoke. But the ultimate experience is the same, the expression will be different.

What Jesus experienced at the last moment on the cross I have experienced, but that experience is of absolute silence. To bring it into language, to create methods to help others to experience it, certainly I am in a far better position than Jesus or Buddha or Mahavira. Naturally, the Masters who will follow me will be in a far better position than me. They will have a far more accurate approach towards truth, because the man is continuously growing. Man is not deteriorating, man is growing, man is reaching to higher peaks.

And You Ask: How it is possible that enlightened masters can say so many contrary things?

They only appear contrary — because the language changes, expressions change, ways and methods change; otherwise they are not contrary. And a man like me is bound to be not only contrary to Jesus and Buddha and Mahavira: I am going to be many times contradictory to myself for the simple reason that I am trying to bring all the religions in a higher synthesis; different approaches have to be joined together. I am creating an orchestra.

Surrender Is Of The Heart

Buddha is a solo flute-player. Of course when you are playing flute solo it has a consistency, but it is not that much rich as when the flute becomes part of an orchestra. Then it has a totally different kind of richness, multidimensionality. But then you have to be in tune with others; you have to be continuously alert not to fall out of step. Somebody is playing a tabla and somebody is playing the sitar and you are playing the flute; all the three have to be in harmony. And of course they are three different instruments, very different from each other, but to bring them into harmony can create a higher kind of music.

Jesus is a solo player, Buddha too, Mahavira too. In the past it was bound to be so because they all lived in small worlds. Buddha never went out of Bihar, just a small province of this country; Jesus was confined, Krishna was confined. Now the whole world has become a small village, a global village. You can see it — the whole world has gathered here! Buddha was not so fortunate; he was surrounded by Biharis. Jesus was surrounded by Jews. Krishna was surrounded by Hindus. They could only be solo players; they were bound because their listeners, the people they were working with were of a certain tradition.

Now I am working with all the traditions together. Jews are here and Hindus and Mohammedans and Christians and Parsis and Sikhs and Jains and Buddhists. All traditions have gathered here. It is a unique experiment in the whole history of humanity; it has never happened in this way.

Even people who are moving into different countries are still carrying their solo instruments. For example, Maharishi Mahesh Yogi, although he works in the West. But the method that he calls Transcendental Meditation is a very old Hindu method of chanting a mantra; it is neither transcendental nor meditation; it is just an old rubbish of chanting a mantra! Any word will do; you go on repeating it continuously. It creates a state of autohypnosis and nothing more. Although he is working in the West, but he is using only an autohypnotic method invented thousands of years before by the Hindus.

Now there are Zen monks working in America, there are Zen centers in America, but what they are doing there is the old method of Buddha. There are Sufis working in the West, but they are using the method invented by Jalaluddin Rumi, one thousand years old.

I am using all the possible methods, and when all these methods meet of course there is going to be great contradiction. If you don't understand you will see only contradictions and contradictions. If you understand then you will understand the harmony of all these instruments together.

People are doing Vipassana and doing the Sufi dancing and doing Yoga and doing Tantra and using Zen methods, zazen and other methods. And not only the old methods — they are doing all that is happened into this century after Sigmund Freud, all the psychological methods, all the psychotherapy groups.

This is a meeting of the whole world. It is a universal religiousness that I am creating here. It is bound to be multi-dimensional if you understand. If you don't understand, if you still cling to a certain tradition, then it will look contradictory to you.

Question 4

OSHO,
What is the difference between experiencing and indulging?
— Deva Tapodhana

The difference between experiencing and indulging is that of awareness; there is no other difference no other distinction. If you are not aware, it is indulgence; if you are aware, it is experiencing — the Same thing. It may be eating food, it may be making love, listening to music. enjoying the night sky full of stars — whatsoever it is. If you are not consciously there, if you are not a witness to it, if you remain unconscious, mechanical, robotlike, then it is indulgence. If you are aware, then it is experiencing. And experiencing is beautiful, indulgence is ugly. But remember the distinction that I am making.

Surrender Is Of The Heart

In the past all the religions have labeled things; I am not labeling things. They have labeled things: "This is indulgence and this is experiencing." I am not labeling things — things cannot be labeled. Things are the same.

Buddha eating his food and you eating your food: as far as the outer, objective viewpoint is concerned both are doing the same. You are eating, Buddha is eating. What it is? Buddha is experiencing, you are indulging. The difference is not in the act, it is in your awareness. Buddha eating is eating as a witness, and he will eat only that much which is needed because he is totally aware. He will enjoy food, he will enjoy more than you can enjoy, because he is more aware. You will not enjoy the food: you simply go on stuffing it, you don't enjoy. And you are not there at all to enjoy, in fact; you are somewhere else, always somewhere else. You are never where you are — somewhere else. You may be in the shop, you may be in the field, you may be in the factory, you may be talking to a friend: physically you are eating, but psychologically you are not there.

Buddha is there totally: physically, psychologically, spiritually. When he is eating he is simply eating.

A Zen Master, Rinzai, was asked, "What is your sadhana? What is your spiritual practice?"

He said, "Nothing much, nothing much to brag about; it is very simple: when I feel hungry I eat and when I feel sleepy I go to sleep."

The man said, "But that's what we all do!"

Rinzai said, "There you are wrong — take your words back — because I have lived like you, I have both the experiences. I have lived like a robot — the way you are I have been — so I know the difference. You eat when you are not hungry, you eat because it is time to eat, you eat because the food is delicious, you eat because you are invited to eat. You don't care what is the need. You sleep because it is a habit; whether you need it or not is not the point. And while you are eating you are not only eating, you are doing thousand and one other things — maybe making love in your fantasy. And when you are asleep certainly you are not doing only one thing, sleeping — you are dreaming. The whole night your mind goes on and on creating dreams upon dreams."

So I don't label, Tapodhana, anything as experiencing and indulging. The question is of awareness.

Two drunks in a tavern see a bug fall down on the bar. The first drunk says, "A bug."

The other nods and says, "A bug."

The first peers again and says, "Ladybug."

The other drunk says, "Damn good eyesight!"

A talkative drunkard at a circus looked mystified at a contortionist as the performer went through his act. Unable to control himself, he cried, "What is the matter? You look like I am drunk!"

There is a story about a small youngster who was abandoned by his parents in Yellowstone National Park. He was raised by a pack of wild dogs. Years later he was found walking on all fours, eating raw meat and living in the open. He was put in school where in one year he breezed through grammar school, high school and college. The day after he got his Ph.D. he was killed — chasing a car.

Even if you get your Ph.D. you are going to chase the car — unconscious habit! Knowledgeable you can become, but that is not going to transform you; you will continue to indulge. You can escape from the world, but that will not make any difference: you will still indulge.

Learn how to be aware.

A train is speeding through the countryside when, from a distance, the driver notices what looks like a couple involved in passionate lovemaking, lying right on the tracks.

The engine driver pulls the whistle... once, twice, then again and again, but there is no response from the couple. The engine driver starts to panic and, as a last resort, slams on the emergency brake. The lovers continue in their play, oblivious.

Finally the train screeches to a halt just a few feet away from the couple. The engine driver is furious. He gets out of his cabin and storms over to them.

"What the fuck are you doing?" he screams at them. "Did not you see the train coming? Did not you hear the whistle? You should be at home, behind bedroom doors!"

The man on the tracks looks up at the driver very coolly and says, "Listen, mate, she was coming. I was coming, and you were coming... but you had the brakes!"

5

Bound In Deep Togetherness

OSHO,
    The One Self Never Moves,
    Yet Is Too Swift For The Mind.
    The Senses Cannot Reach It,
    Yet Is Ever Beyond Their Grasp.
    Remaining Still, It Outstrips All Activity,
    Yet In It Rests The Breath Of All That Moves.

    It Moves, Yet Moves Not.
    It Is Far, Yet It Is Near.
    It Is Within All This,
    And Yet Without All This.

    He Who Sees Everything As Nothing But The Self,
    And The Self In Everything He Sees,
    Such A Seer Withdraws From Nothing.
    For The Enlightened, All That Exists
    Is Nothing But The Self,
    So How Could Any Suffering Or Delusion
    Continue For Those Who Know This Oneness?

    He Who Pervades All, Is Radiant,
    Unbounded And Untainted,
    Invulnerable And Pure.
    He Is The Knower, The One Mind,
    Omnipresent And Self-Sufficient.
    He Has Harmonized Diversity
    Throughout Eternal Time.

Aum

Purnamadah
Purnamidam
Purnat Purnamudachyate
Purnasya Purnamadaya
Purnameva Vashishyate.

Aum

That Is The Whole.
This Is The Whole.
From Wholeness Emerges Wholeness.
Wholeness Coming From Wholeness,
Wholeness Still Remains

Aum represents the music of existence, the soundless sound, the sound of silence, when your whole being hums with joy. Aum represents the ultimate harmony, what Heraclitus calls "the hidden harmony". To become one with this music of existence is to attain flowering, fulfillment.

The moment you lose your discord with the whole, the moment you are in tune with the whole — attunement simply means "at-onement" — when you are one with the whole, every fiber of your being, every cell of your being dances, for no reason at all. It is the dance for dance's sake, joy which is uncaused, hence it is eternal — joy which is unmotivated. joy which is not dependent on anything. It is your intrinsic, natural music, your spontaneity.

All the Upanishads begin with this remembrance:

Aum

That Is The Whole.
This Is The Whole.

That represents the innermost core of this. It is called that because it is not known to you yet. Those who know, for them there is only this and no that, or only that and no this. The duality disappears, but for the blind the duality is there. Everything is dual, if you are not fully aware — divided.

This means that which you can see and that means which is invisible. This is the wheel and that is the axle. The wheel moves on the axle but the axle moves not. All movement depends on something unmoving: all change depends on something eternal Time depends on timelessness. Birth and death happen into something which is never born and never dies.

This represents all that is known to the unenlightened and that which is known when you become enlightened. When you are full of light you have clarity, perception, transparency; you can see through and through. In that vision, this starts melting into that; the circumference disappears into the center. The center is naturally hidden, it is bound to be hidden; only the circumference is available to the senses. You can see only the surface, you cannot see the depths. If you go to the ocean you can see only the surface and the surfacial turmoil; you cannot see the depth. To see the depth you will have to dive deep, and as far as the ultimate that is concerned, only diving deep won't do: you will have to dive so deep that you disappear totally, become one with it. In that oneness God is realized.

The people who go on arguing about God know nothing about God. Those who know, they cannot argue about God. Yes, their very presence is a proof, their very existence radiates the ultimate, their "thisness" is overflowing with "thatness", but they cannot prove logically, intellectually the existence of God. God is not an object, hence it cannot be put before you. It cannot be made a collective experience.

That's why science goes on denying God, and science will go on denying God because science depends on collective observation; it believes only in that which can be observed by everybody. It believes in the rock because the rock can be watched by everybody; everybody can agree that it exists.

The word "object" is significant; "object" means that which hinders. If you try to pass through a wall you will be hit hard by the wall. The wall is an object: it objects your passing through it.

Bound In Deep Togetherness

You cannot pass through a rock — it objects, it prevents, it hinders.

God is not an object — you can pass through God, you are passing through God every moment. You are breathing God; your very heartbeat is God's heartbeat. But God is so close... even the word "close" is not right because the word "close" or "closeness" shows distance.

This fan is close to me, but it is separate. This microphone is even more closer, but still it is separate. The body is even more closer, but it is still separate. God is inseparable with you; hence even the word "closeness" is not right. God is your very being, your very consciousness. It cannot be an object, it cannot prevent you; it helps you, it nourishes you. It is your subjectivity. Because it is your innermost core it remains hidden even from yourself — unless you take a one-hundred-eighty-degree turn, unless you recoil upon yourself.

You must have seen the symbol — a very ancient symbol and very significant too — of a snake eating its own tail. Many ancient mystery schools used that symbol; it is certainly very indicative. The snake eating its own tail means one-hundred-eighty-degree turn. The snake is turned upon itself, the consciousness has recoiled upon itself

And the snake has represented in almost all the cultures of the world wisdom Jesus says: Be ye as wise as a snake. And in the East snake, the serpent, has symbolized the inner energy of man, kundalini; hence it is called serpent power. The energy is coiled at the lowest center of your being; when it uncoils, the snake starts rising upwards. It simply represents that there is something in the snake which can be used as a metaphor.

The snake can catch hold of its own tail; the dog cannot do it. Dogs try — you must have seen dogs trying — and the more they try, the more crazy they go, because the tail goes on jumping with them. They think it is something separate. They try to catch hold of it, and when they cannot catch hold of it... of course they try desperately, but the more they try the more they are at a loss. Only the snake can do it, no other animal.

The same happens in enlightenment: your energy starts moving upon itself, it becomes a circle.

God is your subjectivity; you cannot find God anywhere else. But once you have found God within you you will find him everywhere else too. All the arguments are stupid, and these arguments are really childish. Whatever proofs have been given of God are so childish that one wonders what these theologians were doing. They prove by their arguments only one thing: that they were fools!

God is an experience, unprovable, because your senses cannot reach him. If God was an object, your senses will be able to reach. God is not a thought either, hence your mind cannot grasp it. But we have made God an object; statues have been created. Those statues are objects; they are made of stone or wood or some other material. And to make God an object is the greatest blasphemy because God is subjectivity. You are changing the whole idea of God; you are reducing it into a thing. God is not a thing.

That's why Gautam the Buddha calls God "nothingness". Remember, when he uses the word "nothingness" he means "no-thingness" — he does not negate. He is not saying there is no God; the word "nothing" simply means it is not a thing.

And the temples and the churches, they have all made God a thing, even though there may not be any statue — in the mosques there are no statues. But people are praying to God as if he is there, not deep in your own consciousness but somewhere else. It is the same! — whether you are bowing down to a statue or to a God somewhere above the clouds, still it is an object. Whom you are praying? Your prayer means that you have accepted the idea of God's separateness from you — he has to be prayed. You are the prayer and he is the prayed. You are the praiser and he is the praised. The separation is accepted, and that is irreligiousness.

But people go on fighting on each and everything. In fact, they want to fight; fight seems to be their joy. Then God is one of the most beautiful excuses to fight because it can never be conclusively decided.

In a one-horse town in front of the general store two men were fighting. A ten year-old boy was among the spectators who were enjoying the battle. A stranger came along and asked the youngster what was going on.

"My father and a man are having a real fight," explained the boy.

"Which one is your father?" the stranger asked.

"That," said the boy, "is what they are fighting about!"

And this is what religious people have been doing for centuries. They think they are creating great philosophical ideas. Professors of philosophy and professors of theology don't know anything about themselves, but they are trying to prove that their idea of God is true. They themselves live in absolute unconsciousness. If they were not unconscious they would not argue about God; they will live God, they will radiate God. God would be their fragrance, their presence.

An absent-minded professor of philosophy was going out to dinner one evening with his wife.

"I don't like that tie you have on, "she said. "I wish you would go upstairs and put on another."

The professor quietly obeyed. Minute after minute passed until finally the impatient wife went upstairs to see what had happened. In his room she found her husband undressed and getting into bed.

Old habit! The moment he took out his tie he thought the time has come to go to bed.

And these are the people who go on proposing great systems of thought. Immanuel Kant has created one of the greatest philosophical systems in the world, and he himself was such an unaware man that it seems almost impossible how a man can be so unaware. There are thousands of anecdotes about his life.

One day he came home after his evening walk... He was a very regular person in his habits, in his routines. He never got married for the simple reason that the woman may disturb his pattern. He never allowed any friendship because then you have to be polite to the friends. And if you want to go to bed and your friend is sitting, just out of etiquette, mannerism, you have to go on talking. And he was such a mechanical man that at exactly nine — and nine meant nine, not a minute before, not a minute after — he will go to bed. He never married for the simple reason because women are illogical and they won't understand, and there will be unnecessary quarrels.

He kept a servant, and the servant used to declare only time. There was no need to say anything, he will simply come and say, "Sir, it is nine," and he will jump into the bed.

The servant was puzzled that it was almost ten in the night and his light was still on, so he went to have a look what has happened. He looked from the window and he could not believe his eyes: he was standing in a corner of the room with closed eyes, and his walking stick was Lying on the bed! When he came after the walk he forgot who is who — just a little confusion! And it was nine o'clock so there was no time even to think about the matter, to figure it out, who is who. He was in such a hurry!

The servant came in, shook him and asked, "What is the matter? What are you doing?"

And he said, "I was also thinking what is the matter — because I am feeling very tired! Now I know what is the matter." When he saw the walking stick on the bed resting, then he realized.

And these people have created great systems of thought, and they talk about God and they talk about truth and they talk about love and they talk about beauty and they define what is virtue and what is sin. So unconscious!

In the East we have a totally different approach. You cannot think such a phenomenon with a Gautam Buddha or with an Upanishadic seer, because the whole approach is of being more and more conscious. One has to be a flame of consciousness, one has to be alert and aware. On one hand is Immanuel Kant, on other hand is Gautam Buddha.

His chief disciple Ananda, who lived with him for forty years and served him with great love... He used to watch him in every possible way, because he was continuously following him like a shadow, and each of his movements was beautiful, it was a grace. He was also watching him when he was asleep because he used to sleep in the same room in case the Master needs him in the night, he used to watch him while he was asleep. Awake or asleep, his grace was the same, his beauty was the same, his silence was the same.

One day he asked Buddha that, "I should not ask such questions — it looks so stupid — but I cannot contain my curiosity. You sleep, but I have watched you for hours. Sometimes in the middle of the night I wake up and watch you, sometimes just before you get up early in the morning I watch you, but my experience has been such that it seems to me that you are still awake even while asleep. You look so alive, so fresh! And one thing more — you never change your posture. You go to sleep and you wake up in the same posture. What is the secret of it?"

Buddha said, "There is no secret in it. The Body goes to sleep; once you are awake you are awake! — whether it is day or night makes no difference, the inner flame goes on burning. The body goes to sleep because the body gets tired, and now there is no mind any more so no question of the mind arises at all."

There are only two things. In the unenlightened person there are three things: the body, the mind, the soul. And because of the mind he cannot see the soul. The mind is a turmoil, a chaos; it is all smoke, it is all clouds. The enlightened has no mind; there is only silence. So he has the body and he has the soul. The body tires, needs rest, but the soul is never tired, needs no rest; it is always awake. The body is always asleep and the soul is always awake. The nature of body is to be unconscious and the nature of the soul is to be conscious. These are intrinsic qualities. Once the mind is no more there, then even in your sleep only the body sleeps, not you.

In the East we have called these people religious: those who have known such awakening which cannot be clouded by any sleep any more. The West has been thinking about Kant and Hegel and Fichte and Bertrand Russell and Nietzsche and Wittgenstein — these people, as if they are great explorers of truth. They are thinkers.

And remember always, only a blind man thinks about light The man who has eyes knows it: he need not think about it. These are blind people — howsoever clever they are in argumentation but they are blind.

The Upanishad belongs to the seers. It expresses that which is experienced in the ultimate accord where you are no more a separate entity from the whole, when the dewdrop slips from the lotus leaf and becomes the ocean.

The first sutra:

The One Self Never Moves, Yet Is Too Swift For The Mind.

You will come across many self-contradictory statements, for the simple reason because truth is paradoxical. It has to be paradoxical for the simple reason because it contains the whole, and the whole means the contradictory also is contained in it. It contains both the poles, the negative and the positive. It contains the day and night, life and death, summer and winter. It contains all opposites; in it those opposites are no more opposites, they are complementaries. So don't think them as contradictions.

To the seer, to the one who has come to the ultimate peak of meditation, one who has attained samadhi, all the polarities are joined together into one existence. They are not separate — nothing is separate. The existence is one organic unity, hence to say anything about it will have to be paradoxical if it has to cover the whole truth. So you will come again and again from different sides. The contradictions have to be dissolved, they have to be talked about, so that you become aware of their complementariness.

The first is:

The One Self Never Moves, Yet Is Too Swift For The Mind.

It never moves and yet it is too swift, unmoving and yet moving. But remember, these are not separate, these two phenomenon: movement and non-movement. Again let me remind you of the metaphor of the wheel and the axle: the axle remains unmoving; it is because of the unmoving axle that the wheel moves. They support each other. If the axle also moves then the wheel will not be able to move. By remaining unmoving it is supporting the wheel to move.

The world is the wheel. The Sanskrit word for the world is samsara; samsara simply means the wheel — literally it means the wheel. That's why Sanskrit is a language belonging to a totally different category: it is a transformed language, transformed by the seers. Each word has been coined in such a way that it can be used in two ways: it can be used in a mundane sense, it can also be used in a sacred sense. It is the most expressive language about the ultimate, about the inexpressible.

The Sanskrit word for the world is samsara; samsara means the wheel. It goes on moving. But don't forget the axle, the very center upon which the whole movement depends, and it has to be unmoving. The wheel and axle are not enemies; they are in partnership, a deep friendship. They are together; they are bound in a deep togetherness.

The One Self Never Moves, Yet Is Too Swift For The Mind.

One more thing has to be understood: whenever the Upanishads say "the one Self", remember, it is exactly what Buddha says when he calls the ultimate reality "no-self". Their expression is opposite to each other. Upanishads speak the language of affirmation, Buddha speaks the language of negation. Upanishads are via affirmativa, and the approach of Buddha — or at least the expression of Buddha — is via negativa. Both are valid approaches; it depends with whom you are speaking.

The Upanishads were spoken in a different context; they were spoken twenty-five centuries before Buddha arrived — from today, five thousand years before today. It was a totally different world. The Upanishadic seers were not moving from one place to another place; they were not talking to the crowds, they were not arguing with the skeptical minds. They were talking only to their disciples, chosen few; it was a totally different context. To talk to your own disciples is certainly different than to talk to those who are skeptical, doubtful, antagonistic.

The days when the Isha Upanishad was born were the days of very innocence, deep innocence. People were simple, non-philosophical. They were not much concerned about logic; they were trusting people, honest, sincere, authentic. And then the Upanishadic seers lived in their small ashrams.

The ashram, the commune of the Master and the disciples, is an Upanishadic discovery. It is not a monastery; that is a totally different phenomenon. In English, ordinarily the ashram is translated as a monastery — it is not a monastery. A monastery is something against the world; a monastery means you have escaped from the world; a monastery simply shows a condemnation of the world.

The ashram is not a condemnation of the world. Rather it is a learning place — where you learn the art of how to live in the world. People used to go to Upanishadic Masters to learn how to live in the world.

In those days this was the process of life. Assuming that a person was going to live hundred years, life was divided in four parts. First twenty-five years everybody has to be with some awakened Master so that he can have a taste of the beyond, so he can have some experience of the sacred. This first stage was called brahmacharya. Remember, to translate brahmacharya as "celibacy" is not right. The word brahmacharya simply means living like a god, living with the experience of the Brahma, the absolute, living meditatively. If I am to translate brahmacharya I will translate it as "the life of meditation".

Those twenty-five years, the beginning part of life... it will look strange. Why God has to be experienced in the beginning? — for many reasons. First: the first part of life is the most innocent part, most courageous, adventurous, alive, intelligent. Once you become burdened with life's experiences you start becoming cunning. To live in a world and not to be cunning is very difficult. To face the world you will have to be cunning, to face the world you will have to be on guard, cautious; otherwise you will be cheated, you will be exploited. To be in the world you have to be continuously fighting and competing; you have to be ambitious and violent and aggressive. And if all these experiences become part of your consciousness — and they are bound to become part — then trust will be more difficult, doubt will be more easy.

I have heard:

Johnson was a compulsive gambler, but always willing to give and share. So when he lost all his money in a poker game, Brown, one of his cronies, gave him a twenty-dollar bill to tide him over till the next day. On his way home, a shabbily dressed woman approached him with a hard-luck story.

"I can't go on," she pleaded. "I haven't eaten all day. If you don't help me, I'm going to drown myself"

Generous Johnson handed her the twenty-dollar bill.

"I'll never forget your kindness, "she said gratefully. "You have restored my faith in mankind."

The next morning Johnson noticed a newspaper item about the body of an unknown woman that had been fished out of the river. The description of her clothes fitted the woman he had befriended. He was puzzled.

He met Brown at lunch.

"What did you do after you left us yesterday?" asked Brown.

"I walked home," said Johnson.

"Did you spend any money?"

"No. Why?"

"That's good," said Brown with a smile. "We were wondering what would happen when you tried to spend that phony twenty-dollar bill I gave you."

In this world you are bound to be corrupted — this world is so corrupted. It is because of this fact that in the days of the Upanishads, the knowers, the seers have decided that before you have any experience of the world it is better to have some taste of God, because that taste will save you from the corrupting influences of the world. If you have known something higher, then the lower cannot disturb you; if you have known something deeper, then the superficial does not matter. It is very scientific and very psychological

The first part of life, twenty-five years, had to be devoted to meditation, living with a Master, serving the Master, being with the Master, enjoying his presence, rejoicing his presence. It was not a monastery; it was a school, an academy, a real university to learn the art of life.

And when after twenty-five years the second stage used to begin... it was the stage called the stage of the householder, grihastha. Then one gets married, goes to work in the world, earns money, lives a worldly life, but now he has an inner center, a grounding. The world cannot disturb him, and he knows that that experience has to be again achieved, that light has to be again achieved. Whatsoever glimpses he has got in those twenty-five years will haunt him, will remind him again and again that this world is only momentary. He will not become mad after money or power or prestige. He will do all the actions of the world but remain deep down unmoved. He will become a wheel as far as the outside is concerned, but inside he will remain an axle, unaffected, cool. Whether success comes or failure it will be all the same. Whether he becomes rich or poor it will be all the same. Whether he becomes very famous or remains a nobody it is all the same, because he has experienced a joy within himself; now he cannot be deceived by anything from the outside.

And this experience is also needed to enforce, to reinforce the first experience of twenty-five years. This is an examination, this is a criterion whether what you have achieved you have really achieved it, or it was only in the light of the Master, in his presence, something borrowed. You have to go into the world — that is the

Bound In Deep Togetherness

test — so that you can see that it is something that has become part of your own being and nothing can take it away. Even coming away from the Master is not going to affect it; it is your own, authentically your own. This is a beautiful, scientific procedure.

And after twenty-five years when the person will be reaching the age fifty, his children will be ready to come from the ashrams, from those extraordinary devices for learning. His children will be now ready. They must be getting twenty-five years old and they will be on the way back to home. Now they will be getting married and they will take the place of the father.

And try to see the eastern insight into human psyche: when the son comes back and he gets married, and if the father still goes on reproducing children, it is ugly. It is like when your small son is born and he plays with toy boats and you are also playing with toy boats. It will be stupid; you will simply show that you are retarded. If you go on carrying a teddy bear... it is perfectly okay for a child, but a man of fifty years carrying a teddy bear and cannot go to sleep without a teddy bear will be ugly; it will show immaturity; the man has not grown.

Fifty is the time — enough! Twenty-five years you have lived in the world; it is enough to see that it is only a drama. It is enough to give you an experience of its falseness, of its illusoriness. It is made of the same stuff dreams are made. It is enough to see. And now your children will be playing the same game, and you are also playing the same game; it does not look right.

The moment your son comes back, in the days of Upanishads, the father will start removing himself away from the jobs, the work, the money, the power game — all the games. Now the son has to be given the place, not reluctantly — rejoicingly, happily. Now let him play the games. Otherwise fathers are also in the same game, their children are in the same game, even their grandchildren are in the same game. The grandchildren are chasing girls and the grandfathers are chasing girls! It looks so ugly, as if nobody seems to have grown up. Maybe physically they are old, but not psychologically mature.

To grow old is not to grow up, remember it. To grow up is a psychological process. So when a man was fifty he would start giving place to his children, and there was no competition. Now there is competition in every field.

Somebody like Morarji Desai, at the age of eighty-five still trying again to be the prime minister of the country... Then what about the children? If you are interested in the teddy bears, then what about the children? What about the young people who really need space and opportunity? These old fools go on and on; they don't stop. There is no retiring age for the politicians, no retiring age for the wealthy. They never retire, they only die. Only then reluctantly they have to retire, otherwise they won't retire.

There is a college in London, a medical college; the man who founded the college, who gave the money, he presided his whole life on the board of the directors, and when he died his will was opened and all were puzzled and shocked. His will was that "My whole money is for the college, provided I still continue to preside." After death... and he is still presiding! After two hundred years he is still presiding in that medical college. His body has been preserved. His body sits in the place of the chairman... and the board meeting and he presides. Of course somebody else does the whole work as acting president, but the real president is there in the chair! Even people don't want to retire after death — he has not retired.

Now just think of that meeting, how the other directors who are alive will be feeling, sitting with a dead man, a corpse! And he is the president, and they must be addressing him, "Sir, president sir..."

But this is the situation all over the world! In Sri Lanka a man of ninety years age is now the prime minister! Now these dead people are bound to create bad feelings in younger generation, and they say it is the younger generation which is wrong. It is not so.

When people used to live not that long, when people used to live not more than seventy years, it was okay; the younger generation could tolerate them, hoping that they are going to die sooner or later — don't get into a hurry, don't kill them. But medical science has now made it possible for people to live indefinitely.

In Russia there are thousands of people who have crossed the age one hundred fifty, and they are still working. Now what do you want? Younger generation is bound to be angry. Sooner or later younger people will start killing these old people — they have to be killed! How long you can tolerate? They will destroy your whole life! By the time you are hundred they may die, but then other younger people are there who will push you into the grave!

It was very psychological that when your children are back from the gurukul... the ashrams were called gurukuls. Gurukul means the place where the Master lives and his family — his disciples are his family — where the Master lives with his disciples — the family of the Master, the commune of the Master.

When the children started coming, the father, the mother, the elders have to vacate and joyously, because now they are being relieved. Twenty-five years they will still remain in the home so that they can help their children to be in the world, so they can hand over everything to the children. By the time their grandchildren start coming home they will go back to the ashrams.

This is the full circle of life, four stages. It begins in the ashram, it ends in the ashram. It begins in the ashram as a disciple and it ends in the ashram as a Master. The circle is complete. A man after seventy-five years of age — twenty-five years' experience with a Master, then twenty-five years' testing time in the world, then twenty-five years of slow withdrawal, not a hasty renunciation, a very meditative withdrawal, slowly... and then back into the forest, into the ashram. Now he comes as a Master in his own right; a fully lived life, experienced in all possible ways, sacred and mundane, he becomes a Master himself... and children will be coming again.

The Master in the Upanishads was talking to innocent people, unpolluted by the world, unskeptical, uncorrupted trusting, loving.

Buddha after twenty-five centuries was speaking to a totally different audience. Ashrams had disappeared, died; the whole beautiful institution died. It died because of the Jains — they are the culprits, because Jains insisted that the Masters should not live in one place. Jains have a very life-negative attitude and they are as old as the Upanishads. They insisted on asceticism, they insisted on renouncing the world, and they insisted that one should not live in one place because if you live in one place long enough you may get attached to the place. Their fear of attachment was so much, they were so much obsessed with the fear they were living in a kind of phobia, in a panic.

The Jain muni, the Jain monk, is allowed to stay only three days in a town, then he should leave, because if he stays longer than that there is a possibility he may start growing friendship, he may become loving to people, he may become attached to the place, to people, he may not like to move.

Jains are against ashrams. Ashram means the Master lives there permanently with his disciples. Jains insisted that the Jain monk should be a wanderer; he should not stay anywhere. They destroyed the beautiful institution of the Upanishads, they destroyed it completely. And they appealed more to people because people are so foolish, they become attracted to any kind of unnatural thing. They became attracted to the Jain munis; they thought these are the real renouncers of the world — because the Upanishadic seers lived very ordinarily, just as everybody else lives. The only difference was they used to live in forests. Of course, to live in the forests was far more beautiful than to life in the marketplace. They were not against the marketplace, but they knew the beauty of the forest, the nature and all its joys and all its climates. They were not there against the world; they loved the beauty of nature. They were not for any negative reason, they were there for a positive reason. They loved the trees, the wild animals, the flowers, the silence of the forests. They were in immense love with the forest. They were poets. Their going to the forest was not renunciation, it was rejoicing in nature. Remember the difference.

Jains started a totally different kind of tradition in India — the

Bound In Deep Togetherness

tradition of the wanderer — and they destroyed the whole institution of the ashram. And the wanderers cannot be Masters, because what can you teach in three days living in a place? And they go on moving. They are afraid, very much afraid of relating to people. What can they teach? They are themselves afraid, living out of fear; their whole orientation is fear of the world. They destroyed the beautiful universities that existed around Masters.

My effort here is to create again a real ashram, a real commune. That's why I want to move to the forests. I am not against the world, against the marketplace, but I know the beauty of the hills, of the lakes, of the oceans, and I would like you to experience it and to experience it with me so you can share my vision, so you can dance with the trees and sing with the birds, so that you can start feeling the humming sound that comes when you meet with the universe... aum... so that you can feel that music, the eternal music, the celestial music.

Buddha came after the Jains have destroyed completely the institution of the ashrams. He had to talk to the skeptical, he had to talk to the crowd, he had to talk to people who had never known any meditation. Hence he had chosen the expression of the negative. He will say, "The ultimate is a no-self." But Upanishads say, "The ultimate is the supreme Self," but they both mean the same thing.

The Senses Cannot Reach It.
It Is Ever Beyond Their Grasp.

Obviously — the senses are to grasp the objective world. You can see with your eyes the whole world, except your eyes themselves. If you want to see your eyes you will have to have a mirror, and then too you are not seeing your eyes, you are only seeing the reflection in the mirror. And those are not your eyes, just a reflection, and the reflection may not be correct; it all depends on the mirror and the quality of the mirror. The mirror may be made in India! — and you may be seeing somebody else's eyes which have nothing to do with you. And you must have seen, there are many kinds of mirrors. In some mirrors you look very small. In some mirrors very tall, in some mirrors very fat, in some mirrors very thin. It all depends on the mirror how you look. In fact, I don't think there is any mirror which exactly represents you, hundred percent; there cannot be.

See the point: your eyes are capable of seeing everything except themselves; your hand can grasp everything except itself. Your senses are made for the external reality; they are your reaches towards the external. But to the internal they are impotent; they cannot grasp your interiority, and that is where your reality is. They can catch hold of the wheel, but the axle remains beyond them.

> Remaining Still, It Outstrips All Activity,
> Yet In It Rests The Breath Of All That Moves.

It is the axle.

> ... In It Rests The Breath Of All That Moves.

And once you have experienced your absolute, unmoving center, then you know all activity depends on it — although it is not active.

This is the meaning of the Upanishadic emphasis of "action in inaction", or the Zen emphasis of "effortless effort", or Bohidharma's statement that if you can just sit silently doing nothing, everything will happen. You are not to do anything, just sit silently so you can have an experience of your axle. Sitting silently you become more aware of the axle than of the wheel. If you are active you remain on the wheel, the merry-go-round... or the sorry-go-round, it all depends on you — more or less it is sorry-go-round! You cling to the wheel and the wheel goes on moving.

Sitting silently simply means settling at the very center where all activity ceases, but it is also the source of all activity. The inactive is the source of activity, the nothing is the source of all things.

> It Moves, Yet Moves Not.

You walk, you go for a morning walk: in a way you are moving, in a way you are not moving. Your body is moving, your mind is moving, but your consciousness is the same. You were a

Bound In Deep Togetherness

child, then you became young, then old. Everything has moved and yet nothing has moved; your consciousness is still the same.

That's why it is very difficult... if you don't keep a record, if you don't have a birth certificate, if you don't have a calendar, it is very difficult to judge your age. If you close your eyes and you try to figure out how old you are, you will not be able to figure it out at all.

That's why if you go to the primitive tribes where no clocks exist, no calendars, and nobody knows when he was born because people cannot count beyond their ten fingers... Even the person who can count the ten fingers is thought to be very literate, educated, cultured. He becomes the priest or the chief! If you ask people, "How old you are?" they will not be able to answer you; there is no way.

You cannot judge by your own inner being; some outer measurement is needed. Why? — because when you close your eyes and you look within it is always the same, it never changes — and in a way, everything has changed. You will not be able to recognize your photograph when you were one day old — or do you think you will be able to recognize? And in the mother's womb, in nine months' time, you passed through all the stages that life has passed through — millions of years. First you were like a fish and finally you were like a monkey — and very few people grow out of that stage!

Darwin may be right about a few people — a Buddha, a Christ, a Zarathustra, a Lao Tzu... in fact, I cannot count even Darwin! He may be right about a few people, that they have evolved beyond the monkeys, but as far as others are concerned they have only descended from the trees — that is true — but they have not evolved. They have not become better than the monkeys.

Just watch your mind and you will see: the monkey goes on jumping. Your mind is a monkey and it takes longer jumps — quantum leaps — than any monkey can ever do. The monkey can jump from one branch to another branch, from one tree to another tree, but not much, but you can jump from the earth to the moon. Your mind has become a greater monkey.

Every child comes to that stage in the mother's womb. If you are shown a picture or a series of pictures you will not be able to believe that "This is me!" The first day in the mother's womb, do you think you will be able to recognize? It will be just a dot, almost invisible to the naked eyes; you will need a microscope to see it. And then... but all those changes are peripheral; at the center you are still the same. Nothing has changed, nothing ever changes.

Watch when you are going for a morning walk tomorrow: the body moves, but something in you remains unmoving.

It Moves, Yet Moves Not.
It Is Far, Yet It Is Near.

It is far if you go through the mind, it is very far. In fact, it is so far you will never reach it. But if you go through meditation it is very near, nearer than your own ego; it is the nearest. It is your very being, but it depends. If you go through the mind, then you have taken the longest route possible; if you go through no-mind, then you have taken the shortest route possible.

It Is Within All This, And Yet Without All This.

It is within and without both. But first you have to experience it within because that is the nearest point, the nearest door you can enter into the temple of God. And then once you have experienced it as your very self you will know it is everybody's self. Then you will see it in the tree and in the rock, in the animals, in the people — you will see it everywhere. Once you have recognized it within yourself you cannot miss recognizing it anywhere.

He Who Sees Everything As Nothing But The Self And The Self In Everything He Sees, Such A Seer Withdraws From Nothing.

The whole idea of renunciation is non-Aryan, but Indians think that that is their culture. That is just absolute unawareness of what they are talking about. Renunciation is a non-Aryan phenomenon; it has nothing to do with the Indian culture or Indian religion. It has

Bound In Deep Togetherness

come from the Jains, and Jains are not part of Indian culture.

When Aryans came to India, nearabout ten thousand years before, India was a very civilized country. When the Aryans came India was flourishing; it was not unpopulated. Now explorers have discovered Harappa and Mohenjodaro. These two cities, they must have gone into tremendous calamities because both the cities show indications that seven times they were destroyed. Because they have gone digging and they have found seven layers; the oldest is the seventh at the bottom. One is unable even to comprehend how old the oldest is, but somehow it was destroyed — maybe a great earthquake, some upheaval in the earth — and it is covered with earth. Then the second time again the city was populated and the third time...: seven times it has been populated and destroyed. Naturally it has been destroyed by some natural calamity and the possibility is that the Himalaya was rising up very close by, and when such a great mountain rises, then all around it there are great upheavals, bound to be so. Such a great, huge... the greatest mountain coming up means for thousands of miles around everything will change. And Himalaya is still growing. It is the youngest mountain in the world — still growing, still becoming higher. But when the first time it must have arisen out of the earth you can think what calamity must not have surrounded the whole of North India; Harappa and Mohenjodaro were destroyed seven times.

In Harappa and Mohenjodaro statues have been found which can only be related to the religion of the Jains — naked statues, sitting like Mahavira in a lotus posture or standing like Mahavira, meditating. Only Jains are known to meditate standing: no other religion has prescribed meditation has to be done in a standing posture. And they are all naked — only the Jain religion has believed in naked Masters. Harappa and Mohenjodaro must have survived a little bit. Jain religion seems to be far older than Hindu religion; it must have come from Harappa and Mohenjodaro. Harappa and Mohenjodaro must have been Jain cultures; remnants of it remained and they infiltrated the Aryan mind.

Otherwise the Aryans have never been in favor of withdrawing from life; they have always rejoiced in life. But Jains have contaminated the whole mind; they have succeeded in corrupting the whole idea.

Such A Seer, Says The Isha Upanishad, Withdraws From Nothing.

There is no need to withdraw because all is God! To withdraw from the world means to withdraw from God's manifestation. It is an unholy act to withdraw, to renounce. The Upanishads believe in rejoicing, not in renouncing, and that's my approach too.

Hence I would like to say to the so-called defenders of Indian culture that they are not really defenders of Indian culture. I am, because whatsoever I am saying is rooted in the Upanishadic vision: Rejoice in everything, because all is God! From the lowest to the highest, everything is divine. I am certainly against the Jain attitude of withdrawal, renouncing, but I am not against the Upanishadic attitude — I am all for it.

For The Enlightened, All That Exists Is Nothing But The Self...
The supreme Self, God himself.
So How Could Any Suffering Or Delusion Continue For Those Who Know This Oneness?

There is no question of suffering or delusion. The moment you drop your ego and you become one with the whole, all suffering disappears. Suffering is only illusory; it is a dream, a nightmare. When you wake up, all dreams disappear. Just like that: when you become awake. aware, all suffering disappears. Life becomes a sheer joy, a dance, a celebration!

He Who Pervades All, Is Radiant...

God means that which pervades all, and he is very radiant. All that you need is to open your eyes. But first you have to see his radiance within yourself; then only you will be able to recognize it on the outside. He is unbounded, because the universe is vast and there are no boundaries. He is untainted, because there is no other thing that can taint it.

These are immense declarations: you are untainted, you are radiant, you are unbounded. Just drop the ego and you become one with this infinity, with this eternity that existence is.

He Is Invulnerable And Pure.

So are you.

He Is The Knower, The One Mind...

What Buddha calls no-mind, Upanishads call the one mind", but they mean the same thing.

He Is The Knower...

God is the knower. When you become a knower you are a god. To Know is to be a god, because he is the knower:

Omnipresent...

He is present everywhere, because there is nothing else that can be present.

Remember, Upanishads don't believe in any devil, any Satan, they don't believe in any hell, because all is divine — how can there be a hell? Hell is your creation, the shadow of the ego. It is just a delusion — it exists not.

He Has Harmonized Diversity Throughout Eternal Time.

God is the harmony of all that is, and you can watch — everything is harmonious. The trees are swaying with the wind; there is harmony. They are not fighting the wind, they are dancing with the wind. The stars are moving in tremendous harmony. This vast existence is a great orchestra: all is tuned with everything else. There is no conflict, no division, no disharmony.

Only man can believe that he is separate because he has onsciousness, and consciousness gives you the alternative. Either you can think yourself separate — then you fall in misery and hell — or you can try to understand the oneness and suddenly there is bliss. To be one with the whole is bliss: to be separate with the whole is misery.

Aum

Purnamadah
Purnamidam
Purnat Purnamudachyate
Purnasya Purnamadaya
Purnameva Vashisyate.

Aum

That Is The Whole.
This Is The Whole.
From Wholeness Emerges Wholeness.
Wholeness Coming From Wholeness,
Wholeness Still Remains.

6

Absolute Lobe, Absolute Freedom

Question 1

OSHO,

Sitting fretfully, squirming endlessly, does the spring still come and the grass Grow by itself?

— *Anand Daniel*

The spring still comes. It does not depend whether you are sitting silently or fretfully, whether you are sitting or not sitting at all. It does not depend on you; it comes on its own accord. And the grass goes on growing, but if you are not sitting silently you will miss it. It will come, but you will not be able to feel it. It will come, but you will not be able to experience it. The grass will grow, but you will not grow.

The sun rises, the night disappears, but the light is only for those who have eyes and only for those who open their eyes: otherwise you will remain in darkness. The sun will be there, the light will be there, but you will not be bathed in its light; you will remain the same.

The whole question is whether you are closed or open. Silence opens you; the inner noise keeps you closed to existence, within and without both. The outside is a beautiful world: the whole sky with the stars, the flowers, the birds singing, the clouds floating, the rivers, the mountains. And the inside world is even far more beautiful, because the outside is the manifest part of the inside and the inside is vaster than the outside. The unmanifest is unlimited, the manifest is bound to be limited. The unmanifest contains all the future possibilities; the manifest contains only that which has become actual in the past. The unmanifest contains all the universes that will ever happen in the coming eternity. Of course, it is far bigger than the outer.

Between the two is the mind. Between the within and the without there is a wall — a China Wall — of thoughts, desires, memories, expectations, frustrations. And because of the thick wall and the constant noise that is bound to be there... each memory hankering to be listened to, each desire nagging you to be fulfilled, each imagination forcing you to be realized, each expectation torturing you, goading you so that you can succeed in fulfilling it. The noise is great; there is great conflict. The desires are antagonistic to each other.

If you want to be powerful, of course you will have to choose a few desires and you will have to leave a few desires. There are desires to be famous, desires to be wealthy, desires to be powerful, and desires to be healthy, and desires to be loved, and desires to be creative; they all cannot be fulfilled simultaneously. And whenever you choose, the unchosen desires will nag you; they will try to drag you towards themselves.

This chaos cannot allow you to see either the beauty that surrounds you or the beauty that resides in you it cannot allow you to see the rainbows on the circumference and it cannot allow you to see the source of all joy, of all truth, of all beauty within you — the kingdom of God within you.

You ask me, Daniel: Sitting fretfully, squirming endlessly, does the spring still come...?

Certainly... the spring comes, but not for you. You are not available, you are not there. You are so much occupied, so much engaged, you can't see out, you can't see in. Your eyes are covered with layers of desires and thoughts.

The grass certainly goes on growing, because the grass is sitting silently doing nothing — but you are not sitting silently, doing nothing. If you can sit silently doing nothing like the grass you will also grow.

That's the way how the ignorant becomes enlightened: becoming silent... just now... just a moment of silence, a pause... and you can hear the songs of the birds and you can suddenly feel the silence. Then there are no more five thousand sannyasins here: the Buddha Hall is empty, and that emptiness is a great experience. It is ecstatic!

The spring is felt suddenly — it can be felt right now! Then nothing distracts you. This noise of the plane is not a distraction; it will even deepen your silence, it will become a contrast to the silence, it will help define the silence.

The outer noise is not a distraction; but the mind inside remaining continuously in an insane state is the only distraction.

And there are foolish people who renounce the world in search of silence. The world does not disturb you; what disturbs is your mind — and they don't renounce the mind. When a Hindu becomes a monk he still remains a Hindu. Do you see the absurdity? He has renounced the Hindu society, but he still carries the idea of being a Hindu! If you have renounced the Hindu society... then this idea of being a Hindu was given by the same society, how can you carry it?

Somebody becomes a Christian monk, but he still remains a Christian — a Catholic, a Protestant... The mind is so stupid; if you look at its stupidities you will be surprised, amazed! How can you be a Catholic if you have renounced the world? But people renounce the world, they don't renounce the mind — and the mind is a byproduct of the world! The child is raised by the Hindus, then he becomes a Hindu, because the parents are cultivating Hindu ideology — or Christian, or Mohammedan, or Jain.

Just the other day I was talking about how Jainism destroyed the beautiful concept of the Upanishadic ashrams. When I passed around the Buddha Hall going back, I looked particularly at my Jain sannyasins — they were not looking happy! Even my sannyasins! But whenever I criticize Hinduism and I have seen the same sannyasins — so joyous. Of course Hindus feel offended.

Even my sannyasins somehow deep down go on carrying their mind.

I don't teach you to renounce the world, I teach you to renounce the mind. And that's what is meant by this immensely beautiful Zen saying:

Sitting silently, doing nothing,
The spring comes and the grass grows by itself.

All that is needed on your part is just to be absolutely silent And that's exactly the meaning of the word upanishad: sitting silently, doing nothing, by the side of a Master — that means by the side of spring — allowing the spring to possess you, to take you along with it like a tidal wave.

Your inner being is not something that has to be developed; it is already perfect. No spiritual development is needed, only it has to be discovered. And once silence falls over you, you start discovering it. It is the noise and the dust that the mind creates that goes on hindering the discovery.

Question 1

OSHO,

My parents are so disappointed in me, they worry all the time. They have made my being here possible, so how can I turn from them? What do I owe to my parents?

— *Prem Shunya*

The trouble with the family is that children grow out of childhood, but parents never grow out of their parenthood! Man has not even yet learned that parenthood is not something that you have to cling to it forever. When the child is a grown-up person your parenthood is finished. The child needed it — he was helpless. He needed the mother, the father, their protection; but when the child can stand on his own, the parents have to learn how to withdraw from the life of the child. And because parents never withdraw from the life of the child they remain a constant anxiety to themselves and to the children. They destroy, they create guilt; they don't help beyond a certain limit.

To be a parent is a great art. To give birth to children is nothing — any animal can do it; it is a natural, biological, instinctive process. To give birth to a child is nothing great, it is nothing special; it is very ordinary. But to be a parent is something extraordinary; very few people are really capable of being parents.

And the criterion is that the real parents will give freedom. They will not impose themselves upon the child, they will not encroach upon his space. From the very beginning their effort will be to help the child to be himself or to be herself. They are to support, they are to strengthen, they are to nourish, but not to impose their ideas, not to give the shoulds and should-nots. They are not to create slaves.

But that's what parents all over the world go on doing: their whole effort is to fulfill their ambitions through the child. Of course nobody has been ever able to fulfill his ambitions, so every parent is in a turmoil. He knows the death is coming close by every day, he can feel the death is growing bigger and bigger and life is shrinking, and his ambitions are still unfulfilled, his desires are still not realized. He knows that he has been a failure. He is perfectly aware that he will die with empty hands -- just the way he had come, with empty hands, he will go.

Now his whole effort is how to implant his ambitions into the child. He will be gone, but the child will live according to him. What he has not been able to do, the child will be able to do. At least through the child he will fulfill certain dreams.

It is not going to happen. All that is going to happen is the child will remain unfulfilled as the parent and the child will go on doing the same to his children. This goes on and on from one generation to another generation. We go on giving our diseases; we go on infecting children with our ideas which have not proved valid in our own lives.

Somebody has lived as a Christian, and his life can show that no bliss has happened through it. Somebody had lived like a Hindu and you can see that his life is a hell but he wants his children to be Hindus or Christians or Mohammedans. How unconscious man is!

I have heard:

A very sad, mournful man visited a doctor in London. Seating himself in a chair in the waiting room and glumly ignoring the other patients he awaited his turn. Finally the doctor motioned him into the inner office where after a careful examination the man appeared even more serious, sad and miserable than ever.

"There's nothing really the matter with you," explained the doctor, "you are merely depressed. What you need is to forget your work and your worries. Go out and see a Charlie Chaplin movie and have a good laugh!"

A sad look spread over the little man's face. "But I am Charlie Chaplin!" he said.

It is a very strange world! You don"t know people's real lives; all that you know is their masks. You see them in the churches, you see them in the clubs, in the hotels, in the dancing halls, and it seems everybody is rejoicing, everybody is living a heavenly life, except you — of course, because you know how miserable you are within. And the same is the case with everybody else! They are all wearing masks, deceiving everybody, but how can you deceive yourself? You know that the mask is not your original face.

But the parents go on pretending before their children, go on deceiving their own children. They are not even authentic with their own children! They will not confess that their life has been a failure; on the contrary, they will pretend that they have been very successful. And they would like the children also to live in the same way as they have lived.

Prem Shunya, you ask: My parents are so disappointed in me...

Don't be worried at all — all parents are disappointed in their children! And I say all, without any exception. Even the parents of Gautam the Buddha were very much disappointed in him, the parents of Jesus Christ were very much disappointed in him, obviously. They had lived a certain kind of life — they were orthodox Jews — and this son, this Jesus, was going against many traditional ideas, conventions. Jesus' father, Joseph, must have hoped that now he is growing old the son will help him in his carpentry, in his work, in his shop — and the stupid son started talking about kingdom of God! Do you think he was very much happy in his old age?

Gautam Buddha's father was very old and he had only one son, and that too was born to him when he was very old His whole life he has waited and prayed and worshipped and did all kinds of religious rituals so that he can have a son, because who is going to look after his great kingdom? And then one day the son disappeared from the palace. Do you think he was very happy? He was so angry, violently angry, he would have killed Gautam Buddha if he had found him! His police, his detectives were searching all over the kingdom. "Where he is hiding? Bring him to me!"

And Buddha knew it, that he will be caught by his father's agents, so the first thing he did was he left the boundary of his father's kingdom; escaped into another kingdom, and for twelve years nothing was heard about him.

When he became enlightened he came back home to share his joy, to say to the father that, "I have arrived home," that "I have realized," that "I have known the truth — and this is the way."

But the father was so angry, he was trembling and shaking — he was old, very old. He shouted at Buddha and he said, "You are a disgrace to me!" He saw Buddha — he was standing there in a beggar's robe with a begging bowl — and he said, "How you dare to stand before me like a beggar? You are the son of an emperor, and in our family there has never been a beggar! My father was an emperor, his father was too, and for centuries we have been emperors! You have disgraced the whole heritage!"

Buddha listened for half an hour, he didn't say a single word. When the father ran out of gas, cooled down a little... tears were coming out of his eyes, tears of anger, frustration. Then Buddha said, "I ask for only one favor. Please wipe your tears and look at me — I am not the same person who had left the home, I am totally transformed. But your eyes are so full of tears you cannot see. And you are still talking to somebody who is no more! He has died."

And this triggered another anger, and the father said, "You are trying to teach me? Do you think I am a fool? Can't I recognize my own son? My blood is running in your veins — and I cannot recognize you?"

Buddha said, "Please don't misunderstand me. The body certainly belongs to you, but not my consciousness. And my consciousness is my reality, not my body. And you are right that your father was an emperor and his father too, but as far as I know about myself I was a beggar in my past life and I was a beggar in a previous life too, because I have been searching for truth. My body has come through you, but you have been just like a passage. You have not created me, you have been a medium, and my consciousness has nothing to do with your consciousness. And what I am saying is that now I have come home with a new consciousness, I have gone through a rebirth. Just look at me, look at my joy!"

And the father looked at the son, not believing what he is saying. But one thing was certainly there: that he was so angry but the son has not reacted at all. That was absolutely new — he knew his son. If he was just the old person he would have become as angry as the father or even more, because he was young and his blood was hotter than the father's. But he is not angry at all, there is absolute peace on his face, a great silence. He is undisturbed, undistracted by the father's anger. The father has abused him, but it seems not to have affected him at all.

He wiped his tears from the old eyes, looked again, saw the new grace...

Shunya, your parents will be disappointed in you because they must have been trying to fulfill some expectations through you.

Now you have become a sannyasin, all their expectations have fallen to the ground. Naturally they are disappointed but don't become guilty because of it, otherwise they will destroy your joy, your silence your growth You remain undisturbed, unworried. Don't feel any guilt. Your life is yours and you have to live according to your own light.

And when you have arrived at the source of joy, your inner bliss, go to them to share. They will be angry — wait, because anger is not anything permanent; it comes like a cloud and passes. Wait! Go there, be with them, but only when you are certain that you can still remain cool, only when you know that nothing will create any reaction in you, only when you know that you will be able to respond with love even though they are angry. And that will be the only way to help them.

You say: They worry all the time.

That is their business! And don't think that if you had followed their ideas they would not have worried. They would have still worried; that is their conditioning. Their parents must have worried and their parents' parents must have worried; that is their heritage. And you have disappointed them because you are no more worrying. You are going astray! They are miserable, their parents have been miserable, and so on, so forth... up to Adam and Eve! And you are going astray, hence the great worry.

But if you become worried you miss an opportunity, and then they have dragged you again back into the same mire. They will feel good, they will rejoice that you have come back to the old traditional, conventional way, but that is not going to help you or them.

If you remain to be independent, if you attain to the fragrance of freedom, if you become more meditative — and that's why you are here: to become more meditative, to be more silent, more loving, more blissful — then one day you can share your bliss. To share first you have to have it; you can share only that which you have already got.

Right now you can also worry, but two persons worrying simply multiply worries; they don't help each other.

You say: They worry all the time.

It must have become their conditioning. It is the conditioning of everybody in the world.

A rabbi was being hosted by a family, and the man of the house, impressed by the honor, warned his children to behave seriously at the dinner table because the great rabbi is coming. But during the course of the meal they laughed at something and he ordered them from the table.

The rabbi then arose and prepared to leave.

"Anything wrong?" asked the concerned father.

"Well," said the rabbi, "I laughed too!"

You don't be worried about their seriousness, about their worrying about you. They are trying unconsciously to make you feel guilty. Don't let them succeed, because if they succeed they will destroy you and they will also destroy an opportunity for them which would have become possible through you.

You say: They have made my being here possible.

Be thankful for that, but there is no need to feel guilty.

So how can I turn from them?

There is no need to turn from them, but there is no need either to follow them. Go on loving them. When you meditate, after each meditation pray to the existence that "Something of my meditativeness should reach to my parents."

Be prayerful for them, be loving to them, but don't follow them. That won't help you or them.

You say: What do I owe to my parents?

You owe this: that you have to be yourself. You owe this: that you have to be blissful, that you have to be ecstatic, that you have to become a celebration unto yourself, that you have to learn to laugh and rejoice. This is what you owe to them: you owe to them enlightenment.

Become enlightened like Gautam the Buddha and then go to your parents to share your joy Right now what can you do? Right now nothing is possible. Right now you can only pray.

So I am not saying turn away from them, I am saying don't follow them, and this is the only way you can be of some help to them. They have helped you physically, you have to help them spiritually. That will be the only way to repay them.

Question 2

OSHO,

Why is it I feel fully alive only when I am in love? I tell myself that I should be able to spark myself without the other, but so far no luck. Is this some stupid "waiting for godot" game I am playing with myself? When the last love affair ended I swore to myself I was not going to let the same old deadening process happen, but here I am again feeling half alive, waiting for him to come.

— *Prem Idama*

One remains in the need of the other to that point, up to that experience, when one enters into one's own innermost core. Unless one knows oneself one remains in the need of the other. But the need of the other is very paradoxical; its nature is paradoxical.

When you are alone you feel lonely, you feel the other is missed; your life seems to be only half it loses joy, it loses flow, flowering; it remains undernourished. If you are with the other, then a new problem arises because the other starts encroaching on your space. He starts making conditions upon you, he starts demanding things from you, he starts destroying your freedom — and that hurts.

So when you are with somebody, only for a few days when the honeymoon is still there... and the more intelligent you are, the smaller will be the honeymoon, remember. Only for utterly stupid people it can be a long affair; insensitive people it can be a lifelong thing. But if you are intelligent, sensitive, soon you will realize what you have done. The other is destroying your freedom, and suddenly you become aware that you need your freedom because freedom is of immense value. And you decide never to bother with the other.

Again when you are alone you are free, but something is missing — because your aloneness is not true aloneness; it is only loneliness, it is a negative state. You forget all about freedom. Free you are, but what to do with this freedom? Love is not there, and both are essential needs.

And up to now humanity has lived in such an insane way that you can fulfill only one need: either you can be free, but then you have to drop the idea of love... That's what monks and nuns of all the religions have been doing: drop the idea of love, you are free; there is nobody to hinder you, there is nobody to interfere with you, nobody to make any demands, nobody to possess you. But then their life becomes cold, almost dead.

You can go to any monastery and look at the monks and the nuns: their life is ugly. It stinks of death; it is not fragrant with life. There is no dance, no joy, no song. All songs have disappeared, all joy is dead. They are paralyzed — how they can dance? They are crippled — how they can dance? There is nothing to dance about. Their energies are stuck, they are no more flowing. For the flow the other is needed; without the other there is no flow.

And the majority of humanity has decided for love and dropped the idea of freedom. Then people are living like slaves. Man has reduced the woman into a thing, a commodity, and of course the woman has done the same in her own subtle way: she has made all the husbands henpecked.

I have heard:

In New York a few henpecked husbands joined hands together. They made a club to protest, to fight — Men's Liberation Movement, or something like that! And of course they chose one of the most henpecked husbands the president of the club.

The first meeting happened, but the president never turned up. They were all worried. They all rushed to his home and they asked him, "What is the matter? Have you forgotten?"

He said, "No, but my wife won't allow me. She says, 'You go out, and I will never allow you in!' And that much risk I cannot take."

I have heard about the doors of paradise there are two boards — there are two doors in fact. On one board is written: "Those who are henpecked should stand here." This is the door for them, and the other is for those few rare human beings who are not henpecked. St. Peter has been waiting and waiting that some day somebody will turn who will stand on the other door which is not meant for the hen-pecked ones, but nobody ever stood on that gate.

One day St. Peter was surprised: a very small, thin, weak man came and stood there. Peter was puzzled, amazed. He asked the man, "Can you read?"

He said, "Yes, I can read — I am a Ph.D., a professor of philosophy!"

Then Peter said, "This door is meant only for those who are not henpecked husbands. Why you are standing here when the whole queue is standing at the other door?"

He said, "What can I do? My wife has told me to stand here! And even if God says to me, I cannot leave this place unless my wife allows!"

Man has reduced woman into a slave and the woman has reduced man into a slave. And of course both hate the slavery, both resist it. They are constantly fighting; any small excuse and the fight starts.

But the real fight is somewhere else deep down; the real fight is that they are asking for freedom. They cannot say it so clearly, they may have forgotten completely. For thousands of years this is the way people have lived. They have seen their father and their mother have lived the same way, they have seen their grandparents have lived in the same way... this is the way people live — they have accepted it. Their freedom is destroyed.

It is as if we are trying to fly in the sky with one wing. Few people have the wing of love and a few people have the wing of freedom — both are incapable of flying. Both the wings are needed.

Idama, you say: Why is it I feel fully alive only when I am in love?

It is perfectly natural, there is nothing wrong in it. It is how it should be. Love is a natural need; it is like food. If you are hungry, of course you will feel a deep unease. Without love your soul is hungry; love is a soul nourishment. Just as body needs food, water, air, the soul needs love. But the soul also needs freedom, and it is one of the most strange things that we have not accepted this fact yet.

If you love there is no need to destroy your freedom. They both can exist together; there is no antagonism between them. It is because of our foolishness that we have created the antagonism. Hence the monks think the worldly people are fools, and the worldly people deep down know that the monks are fools — they are missing all the joys of life.

A great priest was asked, "What is love?"

The priest said, "A word made up of two vowels, two consonants and two fools!"

That is their condemnation of love. Because all the religions have condemned love; they have praised freedom very much. In India we call the ultimate experience moksha; moksha means absolute freedom.

You say: I tell myself that I should be able to spark myself without the other, but so far no luck.

It will remain so, it will not change. You should rather change your conditioning about love and freedom. Love the person, but give the person total freedom. Love the person, but from the very beginning make it clear that you are not selling your freedom.

And if you cannot make it happen in this commune, here with

me, you cannot make it happen anywhere else. This is the beginning of a new humanity. Of course it is only a seed now, but soon you will see it will grow in a vast tree. But we are experimenting upon many things. One of the dimensions of our experiment is to make love and freedom possible together, their coexistence together. Love a person but don't possess, and don't be possessed. Insist for freedom, and don't lose love! There is no need. There is no natural enmity between freedom and love; it is a created enmity. Of course for centuries it has been so, so you have become accustomed about it; it has become a conditioned thing.

An old farmer down South could barely speak above a whisper. Leaning on a fence by the side of a country road he was watching a dozen razorbacks in a patch of woodland. Every few minutes the hogs would scramble through a hole in the fence, tear across the road to another patch of woodland, and immediately afterward scurry back again.

"What's the matter with them hogs anyway?" a passing stranger asked.

"There ain't nothing the matter with them," the old farmer whispered hoarsely. "Them hogs belongs to me and before I lost my voice I used to call them to their feed. After I lost my voice I used to tap on this fence rail with my stick at feeding time."

He paused and shook his head gravely. "And now," he added, "them cussed woodpeckers up in them trees has got them poor hogs plumb crazy!"

Just a conditioning! Now those woodpeckers are driving them hogs plumb crazy — because when they do the knocking they rush, thinking that it is food time.

That's what is happening to humanity.

One of the disciples of Pavlov, the founder of the conditioned reflex — the discoverer of the theory of the conditioned reflex — was trying an experiment on the same lines. He bought a puppy and decided to condition him to stand up and bark for his food. He held the pup's food just out of reach, barked a few times, then set it on the floor before him. The idea was that the pup would associate standing up and barking with getting his food and learn to do so when hungry.

This went on for about a week, but the little dog failed to learn. After another week the man gave up the experiment and simply put the food down before the dog, but the pup refused to eat it. He was waiting for his master to stand and bark! Now he had become conditioned.

It is only a conditioning, it can be dropped. Just you need, Idama, a little meditativeness. Meditation simply means the process of unconditioning the mind. Whatsoever the society has done has to be undone. When you are unconditioned you will be able to see the beauty of love and freedom together; they are two aspects of the same coin. If you really love the person you will give him or her absolute freedom — that's a gift of love. And when there is freedom, love responds tremendously. When you give freedom to somebody you have given the greatest gift, and love comes rushing towards you.

You ask me: Is this some stupid "waiting for godot" game I am playing with myself?

No, Idama.

When the last love affair ended, I swore to myself I was not going to let the same old deadening process happen, but here I am again feeling half alive, waiting for him to come.

But just by swearing, just by deciding, you cannot change yourself. You have to understand. Love is a basic need, as basic as freedom, so both have to be fulfilled. And a man who is full of love and free is the most beautiful phenomenon in the world. And when two persons of such beauty meet, their relationship is not a relationship at all. It is a relating. It is a constant, river like flow. It is continuously growing towards greater heights.

The ultimate height of love and freedom is the experience of God. In God you will find both: tremendous love, absolute love, and absolute freedom.

Question 3

OSHO,

Why are you not getting bored while you are telling the same stories and the same jokes?

— Divakar Bharti

The first thing to be understood is that Divakar Bharti is an Indian, and Indians are absolutely unable to understand jokes! They don't have any jokes in India. I have not come across a single Indian joke. Indians are serious people — spiritual people, religious people! They talk only of great things: God, heaven, hell, the theory of karma and rebirth.

When you tell a joke to an Indian he feels offended... you see? He feels offended, insulted! You look at his face — he feels embarrassed. Talk about something esoteric — bullshit him! — and then he is perfectly happy. He never laughs, he cannot; laughter is beyond him. He has forgotten laughter.

That's why, Divakar, the question has arisen in you. Otherwise each joke, in a different context, is different. The joke in itself may be an old one — and in fact, there are no new jokes in the world. The proverb that there is nothing new under the sun may not be right about other things, but about jokes it is absolutely right. If Adam and Eve come back to the earth they will recognize only the jokes and nothing else! The same jokes, but the context goes on changing, and in a different context the same joke has a different meaning.

But because you cannot understand the jokes you must be feeling bored.

G.C. Lichtenberg has a profound statement. He says: A person reveals his character by nothing so clearly as the joke he resents.

I have heard:

It is said: The gravest fish is an oyster, the gravest bird is an owl, the gravest beast is a donkey, and the gravest man is an Indian fool.

There are fools of all kinds, they come in all shapes and sizes, but the Indian is the best! Each race reacts, responds differently about jokes...

If you tell the German a joke, he laughs once, just to be polite. If you tell the same joke to a Frenchman he also laughs once because he understands immediately. If you tell the same joke to an Englishman he laughs twice: first to be polite, and second when in the middle of the night he gets it. If you tell the same joke to an American he laughs, but not loudly, and says that "I have heard it before!" If you tell the same joke to a Jew, instead of laughing he says, "It is an old joke, and what is more, you are telling it all wrong!"

And I don't feel bored because I cannot feel bored — it is simply impossible for me. I have completely forgotten how to feel bored! You can go on telling me the same joke again and again and I will always find some new meaning, some new nuance, some new color, some new dimension to it, but I cannot feel bored because I am no more. To feel bored you need the ego; it is the ego that feels bored. When the ego is no more there it is impossible to feel bored.

A simple-minded old woman had a cow that fell sick. In her distress she called the rabbi to pray for its recovery.

To comfort the poor woman, the rabbi walked around the cow three times intoning, "If she dies, she dies, but if she lives, she lives." Happily the cow recovered.

Some time later the rabbi became ill and the woman, recalling how he had cured her cow, visited him. She walked around his bed three times, solemnly repeating, "If he dies, he dies, but if he lives, he lives." Whereupon the rabbi burst out into sidesplitting laughter which soon led to his recovery.

I cannot feel bored — I am no more there. And I don't remember what I have said to you yesterday, so how I can say the same joke again? It is never the same, it cannot be. I never remember what has been said by me, and I have been telling to people thousands of things for all these last twenty-five years.

I never read any of my books, I never listen to any of my lectures — why should I feel bored?

But Divakar, you are in a wrong place here. This is not the place for serious people like you! You should find some old Hindu monastery.

The little red man woke up, opened up his little red curtains and looked out at the little red sunrise. He showered in his little red bathroom, put on his little red clothes and left his little red house. Getting into his little red car, he drove through the little red town to his little red office block. There he went up in the little red elevator to the tenth floor, walked along the little red corridor and entered his little red office. He sat down at his little red desk and read his little red newspaper. Deciding that his life was too boring to live any more, he took out a little red knife and slashed his little red wrists.

Ten minutes later his little red secretary entered his little red office and found her little red boss covered in little red blood. She grabbed the little red telephone and phoned the little red hospital. Soon a little red ambulance arrived. The little red attendants rushed into the little red office, put the little red man on a little red stretcher and raced across the little red town to the little red hospital. Quickly they carried the little red man into the little red operating theater and placed him on a little red table.

One minute later the door to the little red operating theater opened and in walked a little green man. "Sorry!" he said. "I seem to have walked into the wrong joke!"

This is not a place for you — little red world, and you are a green man here! You have walked in a wrong joke, Divakar — walk out!

Question 4

OSHO,

How do you always find new names to give to your sannyasins?

— *Prem Pramod*

Two women were looking into new arrivals in a bookshop. One woman was very much interested in one book; the title of the book was: How to Torture Your Husband. She told to the other woman, "Look at this book! I am going to purchase it! Are you also interested in it?"

The other woman said, "No, I have my own system!"

I also have my own system, but I cannot tell you! Certainly I have given more names than anybody may have ever given in the whole history — almost two hundred thousand sannyasins are there in the world! — but my system is such that I can give names to the whole humanity.

One Red Indian boy was asking his father, "Father, what is the way how you give names to new children? Your name is Black Horse, my mother's name is Buffalo, my uncle's name is White Cloud — how you manage to find out what is the true name for the new arrival, the new child?"

The father said, "It is not difficult — we have a system. Whenever a child is born, the eldest member of the family — the grandfather, the grandmother or the father — goes out of the house, and whatsoever he sees first... For example when my grandfather went out he saw a black horse; that's how I am named Black Horse. But why you are asking Two Dogs Fucking?"

That was his name!

I have my own system, but I cannot tell you!

Just the other night I gave sannyas to a beautiful woman; her name is Diotima. I called her Dhyan Diotima. Diotima is a mythological name: in Greek mythology Diotima is the priestess of love or goddess of love. But it can be derived from another root also, diota; and diota means a jar with a neck and two handles.

So I told the woman that "This is your situation right now: a jar with a neck and two handles. That's what a woman is all about! But through meditation you can become a priestess of love; that transformation is possible. Otherwise you will remain just a jar with a neck and two handles!"

It is not very difficult, and the more names I have given the easier it has become, because I have become more proficient! I can find some way, either from the root of the word... and there are different roots; even in one language a word means many things. Sometimes a word has different roots in different languages: in one language it means one thing, in another language it means another thing. And it is very easily possible to play with words, and names are nothing but a game.

I give you a new name only to make you feel that names are not important. Your old name can simply disappear because it was only a label, it can be changed. You are not the name. To insist this fact, to emphasize this fact upon your consciousness, that the name is not your reality...

Every child comes into the world without a name, but we have to give a name; it has some utility. It is absolutely false, but in a vast world with millions of people it will be difficult to manage if nobody had any name; it will become almost impossible to manage. Some names are needed; false they are, but they work, they have a utility. They have no reality, but utility certainly they have.

But ordinarily you grow with your name; in fact, you become conscious only later on. Your name is deeper than your consciousness, hence there arises an identity with the name. You start feeling, "This is my name, this is me."

When you become a sannyasin I want to destroy that identity, because this is the beginning of destruction of all identities. First I destroy the identity with the name, then I will destroy the identity with the body, then the identity with the mind, then the identity with the heart. When all these identities have been destroyed you will be able to know who you are: the unidentified, the nameless, the formless, the indefinable. And that is only a pure witness in you; nothing can be said about it, no word is adequate to explain it.

Hence I change the name — to give you a break, to give you the idea that name is just a given thing. Your old name disappears, a new name becomes your reality, but now you will not get so much identified because you are now more mature. The first name was given when you were a small child; you were not aware. Now you are a little bit aware. And by becoming a sannyasin you are becoming committed to more and more awareness, to a life of witnessing in which all identities have to be dropped.

A man is absolutely free only when there is no identity left. You are neither a Christian nor a Hindu nor a Mohammedan; you are neither an Indian nor a Japanese nor a German; you are neither a man nor a woman. You are just a pure consciousness, and that consciousness is eternal. The Upanishads are talking about that consciousness.

The only thing to be learned in the communion with the Master is that witness, that watcher, that seer, that watcher on the hills who is beyond everything. Everything falls short of it which is transcendental. To know that transcendental reality of you I start by changing your name; that is just taking one brick out of your false edifice. And then if you allow me to take one brick, I will go on taking other bricks. I change your clothes just to give you a discontinuity with the past.

You have to become discontinuous to the past. Unless you die to the past you cannot be reborn, you cannot be here-now. The past has to be completely dropped and forgotten — it was a dream, nothing more — and out of the past arises the future. If the past is dropped, the future disappears. Then the only reality is now and here. And to be here and now, absolutely here and now, is to know all that is worth knowing, is to really live an authentic, sincere life, a life full of truth and bliss and godliness.

Each Moment — Miracles !

Question 1

OSHO,

Can an enlightened person be wrong? This refers to what you told us about J. Krishnamurti, who keeps on saying that one does not need a Master, which is actually not right please comment.

— Prem Pantha

An enlightened person can never be wrong. Neither J. Krishnamurti is wrong, but he never considers the situation in which you are. He considers only the space in which he is, and that freedom is part of enlightenment.

The enlightened person has reached the highest peak of consciousness; his abode is on Everest. Now it is his freedom to speak according to the peak, the sunlit peak where he is, or to consider the people who are still in the dark valley, who know nothing about the light, for whom the peak of the Everest is only a dream, only a perhaps. This is the freedom of the enlightened person. Krishnamurti speaks in terms where he is.

I speak in terms where you are, I consider you, because if I am speaking to you, you have to be taken in consideration. I have to lead you towards the highest peak, but the journey will begin in the dark valley, in your unconsciousness. If I talk about my experience, absolutely inconsiderate of you, I am right, but I am not useful to you.

An enlightened person is never wrong, but he can be useful or he can be useless.

J. Krishnamurti is useless! He is perfectly right; about that there is no question, because I know the peak and what he is saying is certainly true — from the vision of the peak. Those who have arrived, for them the journey becomes almost a dream phenomenon. For those who have not arrived the journey is real, the goal is just a dream. They are living in two different worlds. When you are talking to a madman you have to consider him; if you don't consider him you cannot help him.

Once a madman was brought to me. He had this crazy idea that one afternoon when he was sleeping, a fly has entered his mouth. And because he used to sleep with open mouth, nobody can deny the possibility. And since then he was very much disturbed because the fly was roaming inside him, jumping inside him, moving in his belly, going to his bladder, circulating in his bloodstream, sometimes in his head, sometimes in his feet. And of course he could not do anything because he was continuously occupied, obsessed with the fly.

He was taken to the psychoanalysts and they said, "This is just in your mind — there is no fly! And no fly can move in your bloodstream, there is no possibility. Even if a fly has entered it must have died! And now six months have passed; it cannot be alive inside you."

He listened, but he could not believe it because his experience was far more solid. He was taken to the doctors and everybody examined him and they did everything, but finally they will say, "It is just a mental thing. You are imagining." He will listen what they were saying, but he could not trust because his experience was far more certain than their words.

His family brought him to me as a last resort. The man was looking very tired because he was being taken to one person, then to another, then all kinds of physicians — allopaths and homeopaths and naturopaths — and he was really tired. In the first place the fly was tiring him, and now all these "pathies", medicines. And everybody was insulting him — that was his feeling, that they were saying that he was just imagining. Is he a fool or is he mad, that he will imagine such a thing? They were all humiliating him — that was his feeling.

I looked at the man and I said, "It is so clear that the fly is inside!"

For a moment he was puzzled. He could not believe me, because nobody has said that to him — because nobody has considered him. And they all were right and I was wrong — there was no fly, but the madman has to be considered.

And I said, "All those fools are just wasting your time; you should have come here first. It is such a simple thing to bring the fly out; there is no need to bother. Medicines won't help — you are not ill. Psycholanalysis will not help — you are not crazy."

And immediately he was a changed man! He looked at his wife and said, "Now what do you say? This is the right man," he said, "who really knows. And all those fools were trying to convince me that there is no fly. It is there!"

I said to him that, "It is simple — we will take it out. You lie down."

I covered him with a blanket and told him to keep his eyes closed and "I will do some mantra, some magic, and we will bring the fly out. You just keep quiet so that the fly sits somewhere. Otherwise the fly is continuously running — where to catch it?"

He said, "That looks logical. I will keep absolutely still!"

And I said, "Don't open your eyes. Just remain silent, breathe slowly, so the fly settles somewhere, so we can catch hold of it!"

Then I rushed into the house to find a fly. It was a little bit difficult because for the first time I was trying that, but finally I succeeded — I could get a fly in a bottle. And I came to the man, I moved my hand on his body, and I asked him, "Where the fly is?" And he said, "In the belly." And I touched the belly and I said, "Of course it is there!" And I convinced him that I perfectly believe in him and then I uncovered his blanket and showed him the fly.

And he said to the wife, "Now see! And give this bottle to me; I will go to all those fools and take all the fees that they have taken from me! I have wasted thousands of rupees, and all that they did was they told me I am mad! And now I don't feel the fly anywhere, because it is in the bottle!"

He took the bottle, he went to the doctors.

One of the doctors who knew me, he came to see me. He said, "How you managed? Six months a fly can live in the body? And that man has taken his fee back from me, because he was making such a fuss that I said, 'Better give it back to him!' And he proved that he was right!"

I said, "It is not the point who is right."

Gautam the Buddha defines truth as "that which works". This is the ancientmost pragmatic definition of truth: "that which works"! All the devices are truth in this sense: they work; they are only devices. The Buddha's work is upaya; upaya exactly means device.

Meditation is an upaya, a device. It simply helps you to get rid of that which you have not got in the first place — the fly: the ego, the misery, the anguish! It helps you to get free of it, but in fact it is not there. But it is not to be told...

And Krishnamurti has been doing that: he has been telling crazy people that the fly does not exist and you don't need any doctor. I say to you: the fly exists and you need the doctor! Because just by telling to you that the fly does not exist is not going to help you at all.

For thousands of years you have been told the ego does not exist. Has it helped you in any way? There have been people who have told, in this country particularly, that the whole world is illusory, maya, it does not exist, but has it helped India in any way? The true test is there: whether it has helped, whether it has made people more authentic, more real. It has not helped at all. It has made people more deeply cunning, split, schizophrenic; it has made them hypocrites.

All the religions have done this, because they don't consider you. And you are far more important than the ultimate truth, because the ultimate truth has nothing to do with you right now. You are living in a dreamworld; some device is needed which can help you to come out of it. The moment you are out of it, you will know it was a dream — but a person who is dreaming, to tell him that it is all dream is meaningless.

Have you not observed in your dreams that when you are dreaming it looks real? And every morning you have found that it was unreal but again in the night you forget all your understanding of the day — again the dream becomes real. It has been happening again and again: every night the dream becomes real, every morning you know it is false, but that knowing does not help. In the dream one can even dream that this is a dream.

And that's what has happened in India: people are living in maya, deeply in it, and still talking that "This is all maya." And this talk too is part of their dream; it does not destroy the dream. In fact it makes the dream more rooted in them, because now there is no need to get rid of it — because it is a dream! So why get rid of it? It does not matter.

In a subtle way all the religions have done this: they have talked from the highest peak to the people for whom that peak does not exist yet. The people are living in darkness, and you go on telling them that darkness has no existence. It is true — darkness has no existence, it is only the absence of light — but just by saying to people that darkness has no existence is not going to bring light in.

That's what Krishnamurti is doing; it has been done by many people. Nagarjuna did it — Krishnamurti is not new, not at least in the East. Nagarjuna did it: he said, "Everything is false. The world is false, the ego is false, nothing exists. Because nothing exists you are already free. There is no need for any meditation, there is no need for any Master. There is no need to find out any device, strategy, technique, because in the first place there is no problem. Why go on looking for solutions? Those solutions will create more problems; they are not going to help."

Nagarjuna did it; before Nagarjuna, Mahakashyap did it, and it has been a long tradition. Zen people have been saying the same thing for centuries. Krishnamurti never uses the word "Zen", but whatsoever he is talking is nothing but Zen — simple Zen.

Zen says no effort is needed, nothing has to be done. When nothing has to be done, what is the need of a Master? — because the Master will tell you to do something. Nothing has to be done — what is the need of the scriptures? — because the scriptures will tell you to do something, to know something. Nothing has to be done, nothing has to be known. You are already there where you are trying to reach.

And I know this is true, but to talk about this ultimate truth to people who are living in tremendous darkness is futile.

Prem Pantha, no enlightened person can ever be wrong, but only few enlightened persons have been of help. The majority of enlightened people have been of no help at all, for the simple reason because they never considered the other.

In fact, George Gurdjieff used to say, "Don't consider the other." It was one of his basic teachings: "Don't consider the other. Just say what is absolutely true." But the absolute truth is truth only when experienced; people are living in relative truth.

My approach is different from Krishnamurti's. I know that one day you will come to that point where nothing is needed — no Master, no teaching, no scripture — but right now the scripture can be of help, the methods can be of help, and certainly a living Master can be of immense help.

The function of the Master is to give you that which you already have and to take away that which you don't have at all.

Question 2

OSHO,

Jesus, Buddha, Krishna, etc., certainly were enlightened Masters. But Buddhism, Hinduism, Christianity and whatsoever has developed from them, have not much to do with the ideas of the Masters. Osho, I am sure you are an enlightened Master too, but what can we do, or what at all is possible to do, to prevent oshoism?

— *Hermann*

Each Moment – Miracles !

Nothing can be done at all, and don't waste your time. Whatsoever has happened was natural. Christianity was bound to happen, it was inevitable. When a man like Christ walks on the earth he will leave footprints on the sands of time, and people will worship those footprints. Christianity is nothing but worship of the footprints; it leads you nowhere. But it is bound to happen.

It is as inevitable as the birth of a child brings the death in; you cannot avoid the death. If the child is born, the death is going to happen. And of course we have known that so many people were born before and so many people have died, so when your child is born you may try to do something so he need not die. That is impossible — birth brings death.

When a living Master is there, sooner or later the Master will be gone and there will be a dead teaching left. That dead teaching becomes Christianity, Hinduism, Buddhism; it will become Oshoism too. Nothing can be done about it — in fact, your very concern is the beginning of it, even the fear. That means Christianity has not happened yet, but the anti-Christian has arrived.

And I am alive! Oshoism will happen, Hermann, when I am gone, but to you it has already happened and you are trying to find out ways how to prevent it. And why you should bother? Who are you to decide for others? You are not a sannyasin, you are not part of my commune, you have no communion with me, you have not tasted of the wine that is available here — and you are worried about others, that these people will worship the bottles when the wine is gone! (At this point a cuckoo bursts loudly into song.)...

Look...! It always happens exactly at the time — even birds agree with me! The bird was saying, "Hermann, you are a fool!" You drink right now! and who are you to bother about the future? And why you should prevent people from Oshoism? If they want it, then that is their business! Why you should take the responsibility? Why you should prevent people from their freedom? If they want to worship something dead they are entitled to it!

But to me you are far more foolish than those people. At least they will be worshipping a bottle — and you are missing the wine! You drink the wine and leave the bottle! If people want to play with the bottle they will play; they are collectors. There are collectors who collect bottles of wine, and sometimes it helps too.

I have heard one case:

In the First World War two brothers separated. The father divided all his property, because he was getting old and he was worried about the younger son — because he was a drunkard and he will destroy the whole thing, and even the eldest son will suffer because of the younger. So he divided them equally.

And a miracle happened. In the First World War the value of money went so low, as it always goes in wartime: things become very costly and money loses its purchasing capacity. The drunkard had one habit of collecting bottles. He finished with the whole money, he drank and he enjoyed. And the other son was so miserly that he was clinging to the money that he has got, but money was going down every day.

And the miracle was this: that a moment came when the money became almost useless, almost valueless, and the younger son sold all his bottles and he had more money than the elder brother. He enjoyed the wine and he sold the bottles! And the elder was a fool — he was just clinging to the money.

Life is very mysterious, and the ways of God are very strange. And God is always for the drunkards! He loves these crazy people.

Hermann, if you really feel that I am an enlightened person, then what are you doing here? Drink out of my enlightenment! Others are drinking. And I don't think that you think that I am enlightened, because the way you say:

Osho, I am sure you are an enlightened master too...

You are not sure. When people are not sure, only then they use the word "sure"! If you are sure, then take the jump in! Then why you are standing on the bank? And while the river is alive, do something so that you can quench your thirst. And leave it to others.

Oshoism is bound to happen — I am not worried about it. It is a natural phenomenon. Don't become obsessed with it. Christianity has happened, Buddhism has happened, Jainism has happened, Hinduism, Mohammedanism, all kinds of "isms". They are not unnatural, otherwise they would not have happened.

There are people who can connect themselves only with dead Masters — and you seem to be one of those people, you can also connect with dead Masters. Now you are much concerned about Jesus, Buddha, Krishna, because they are dead. Now a few are Christians — they are concerned with the dead. Now a few are anti-Christians — they are also concerned with the dead...

Bertrand Russell has written a book: Why I am not a Christian. Why bother about it? There are people who are writing books why they are Christians and there are people who are writing books why they are not Christians. Both are wasting their time!

Friedrich Nietzsche became so obsessed with anti-Christianity that in the last years of his life, when he became mad, he started signing his name as "Antichrist Friedrich Nietsche". Friedrich Nietzsche became secondary; that anti-Christ attitude became more primary. And he was not really anti-Christ, he was only anti-Christian, but when you start moving in a certain direction, if you are logical, you will reach to the logical end. First he started condemning Christianity, and then slowly slowly he found that Christianity is a byproduct of Christ, so naturally he started condemning Christ, and for everything! Sometimes he will go to such absurd lengths to condemn Christ and he will find such rationalizations, such excuses, that one has to say one thing: that he was really imaginative and really logical.

For example, Jesus at the last moment prays to God on the cross that, "Forgive these people, my father, because they know not what they are doing." It is one of the most beautiful utterances, but Friedrich Nietzsche became so obsessed with anti-Christianity that he cannot accept even such a beautiful statement. And if you are not interested to accept anything as beautiful, if you are bent upon to find something wrong, you can always find. He found something wrong even in this. He said, "This means Jesus thinks only he knows and everybody else is ignorant."

Look at his approach. Jesus is praying to God, "Forgive these people. They are crucifying me only because they know not what they are doing." Friedrich Nietzsche condemns it — even this beautiful statement is condemned. He finds a logical reason, that this shows only an egoistic approach, that "I know, and all these people are fools, ignorant. They know not, so forgive them." This asking, praying to God to forgive the people, is an egoistic approach; it is not love, it is ego, according to Friedrich Nietzsche.

Jesus has said, "If somebody slaps you on one cheek, give him the other too." Now this is one of the greatest statements ever made by anybody, of tremendous beauty, of deep love, of nonviolence — but Friedrich Nietzsche condemns it. He says, "This is humiliating to the other person. This is insulting the other person's integrity, his humanity. When somebody hits you on one cheek and you give him the other you are showing him, 'Look how saintly I am, holier-than-thou, and you are just an animal.' You are insulting him!" Nietzsche says it will be far better to hit him back, because that means you have accepted him on equal terms; you are not lowering him. And if you listen to his logic you can find there is something in it.

Logic is a game; it can be played from both the sides. Logic is a prostitute — it can be with anybody, whosoever is ready to pay.

Nietzsche remained his whole life concerned against Christianity and against Christ. Now this is sheer wastage! There are people who are praying to Christ and there are people who are condemning Christ, but both are concerned with the dead person. And if you are concerned, I think praying is far better than condemning, because the person who is praying may get something out of it, but the person who is condemning is not going to get anything out of it.

My approach, Hermann, is that if you happen to meet a Jesus, a Buddha, a Krishna, don't miss the opportunity. And don't become

Each Moment – Miracles !

concerned about others — respect them. They have their own life and they have to decide about it. And millions will always decide to be with a dead Master because that is convenient, comfortable. A living Master is always uncomfortable, inconvenient.

Just think of yourself, Hermann, to be with Jesus when he was alive: there were thousand and one difficulties...

One day Jesus is a guest in a house and Mary Magdalene came — and she was a prostitute! — and she started washing Christ's feet with a very costly perfume, with a very costly oil. Judas could not tolerate it — he was a socialist! He is the real founder of communism in the world; Karl Marx, et cetera, are just offshoots.

He immediately said to Jesus, "This is not right! This perfume, this perfumed oil is so costly that if we sell it we can feast all the poor of this town for at least three days. And this is sheer wastage — you should not allow such a wastage. A man like you should immediately stop.

"Secondly" — now he is far more religious than Jesus — "a prostitute should not be allowed to touch your feet; it is prohibited. A man like you, a man of God, should not allow a prostitute to touch him."

And Jesus said, "Look at her heart. Thousands of people come to me, but rarely I see such love, such surrender. How can I say to her, 'Don't touch me'? That will be ugly!"

Now to be with this man who is going against the whole tradition of religion is dangerous. To be with this man who is allowing the woman to destroy a precious thing which can feed the poor people... and what Jesus says?

Jesus says, "When I am gone the poor people will still be with you, so there is no hurry; you can feed them later on. While the bridegroom is here, celebrate!"

Now, Hermann, will you be ready to say yes to Jesus...? Immediately your rational mind will say, "This is not right! He is not concerned about the poor people at all. He is not concerned about the tradition of the sages at all. He is very unsocialistic, he does not understand anything of economics, he is not compassionate to the poor."

Do you think Mother Teresa of Calcutta would have agreed with him? Impossible! She would have said that "This can help many orphans. We can open a school for the poor children or we can purchase medicine for the ill, and what are you doing?"

Do you think Jesus can get a Nobel Prize? I don't think — impossible. You will rather agree with Judas — he is more rational, more socialistic than Jesus.

To be with Buddha would have been difficult for you, Hermann, because to be with Buddha means surrender, total surrender. The ego has to be put aside.

It is very easy to be with dead Masters because to be with dead Masters is very nourishing to the ego — that you are a follower of Jesus, follower of Buddha, follower of Krishna. But to be with Krishna would have been really impossible — he had sixteen thousand wives! Hermann, would you agree with this man? What kind of enlightened man is this Krishna? Sixteen thousand wives! And they were not all married to him — many he had stolen — they were married to other people! How can you agree with this man?

And he persuaded Arjuna to go into war, and the reasons that he gave were that, "The soul is eternal, so don't be bothered. You can kill — the soul is not killed, only the body, and the body is dead anyway. So there is no violence involved, because the soul is immortal and the body is mortal. You are only separating the immortal from the mortal, there is nothing wrong in it — just separating the essential from the non-essential.

Do you think you would have agreed?

That's why people create Christianity, Buddhism, Hinduism, Mohammedanism — it is easier, very easy, because then you can manage the dead Master according to your ideas. You can put your ideas in his mouth, you can ignore the ideas that go against you,

Each Moment – Miracles!

you can interpret, manipulate, rationalize... you can do thousand and one things because the Master is no more there.

So many people need dead Masters, that is their need. And remember one economic law: wherever there is demand there will be supply. Because people need dead Masters, that's why the Pope is needed — a representative of a dead Master. The Shankaracharya is needed — a representative of a dead Shankara. Ayatollah Khomaniac is needed — a representative of a dead Mohammed. People need, that's why these things happen, and nothing can be done about it.

My concern is not at all about the future. I accept the way things are; they cannot be otherwise. My insistence is: while I am here, if you are really interested in transforming your life, then the opportunity is available. Don't miss it.

Question 3

OSHO,

I always feel that I have to ask you a lot of things. I feel a burden inside. But every time I form a question it looks ridiculous and stupid.

— Atmananda Bharati

It is ridiculous and it is stupid — you are perfectly right in not asking. And even if you ask, do you think I answer? I never answer any question, I simply destroy the question! It is not answering it, it is destroying it. It is hitting the question from all sides. It is a kind of murder: murdering the question, and, if possible, the questioner too! So nothing is left, because if the questioner is left he will again ask.

You see here are five thousand people. Many are killed already! They don't ask; they have understood that I never answer any question. I just play around the question a little bit, and if you are acquainted with me and I know that you will not escape, then I start hitting you. If I think you will escape, then for a few days I behave very politely!

I never answer anything. I am an ancient Jew...

Once a rabbi was asked by a Christian priest, "Rabbi, will you please give me a straight answer to a plain question? Why is it that the Jews always answer a question by asking one?"

The rabbi reflected for a moment, then replied, "Do they?"

The prosecutor was questioning a Jew witness.

"Do you know the man who has just testified?"

"How should I know him?" said the Jew.

"He said you borrowed five thousand dollars from him. Did you?"

"Why should I borrow money from him?" said the Jew.

Visibly annoyed, the judge interrupted, "Why do you answer every question put to you with another question?"

"Why not?" said the Jew.

In a lawsuit for damages the Jewish lawyer for the plaintiff had long experience with juries. He gave force to his words by all kinds of body movements, waving his arms, hammering with his fists, his face expressing a raging storm of feelings. Finally he sat down, his voice drained, his body exhausted.

Defense counsel arose, who was also a Jew, and began to mimic his opponent. He swung his arms freely in front of the jury, twisting and distorting his face, pointing with fingers, tearing his passion to tatters — without ever uttering a word.

After a few minutes he smoothed his hair and straightened his tie and said quickly to the jury, "Now that I have answered every argument of my learned opponent, let me discuss with you the facts in this case."

You see my hands go on making all kinds of gestures? That is just an old Jewish tradition!

You ask, Atmananda Bharati: I always feel that I have to ask you a lot of things.

Everybody feels, because the mind is like a tree. Just as on a tree leaves grow, on the mind questions grow. And my effort here is not to prune the leaves, because pruning simply makes the foliage thicker. My effort here is to cut the roots, very roots, so the tree dies.

Everybody comes here with a lot of questions, but whether you ask them or not they are worthless. I answer them just to keep you engaged here, to keep you occupied. And side by side the real work goes on: in meditations, in therapy groups, I have put people to cut your roots. I go on answering so that you feel that your philosophical inquiry is satisfied, and you remain occupied with questions and answers. And I have put my people... meanwhile they are cutting your roots. Sooner or later your roots are gone, then leaves disappear on their own accord.

When all questions disappear, the answer is found, never before it. The answer is never found by questioning; the answer is found by dropping all questions, questioning as such, because the answer is your own experience of silence, joy, godliness. That is the answer. Unless that is found, questions will go on arising.

But it is good that you yourself have started feeling that:

Every time I form a question it looks ridiculous and stupid.

All questions are ridiculous and stupid.

Question 4

OSHO,

In the Mahabharata. Yudhishtirha was asked a question: "What is surprising?" (Kim ashcharayam) by a yaksha. If you were in his place, what would be your answer?

— *Alkhilesh Bharti*

The most surprising thing in life is that nobody seems to be surprised! People take life for granted. Otherwise everything is a mystery, everything is simply amazing! It is a miracle that a seed becomes a tree. that as the sun rises in the morning the birds start singing. It is a miracle! Each moment you come across miracles and still you don't look surprised. This is the greatest surprising thing in life

My answer would have been that people take life for granted — this is the most surprising thing. Only children don't take it for granted. That's why children have beauty a grace, an innocence. They are always living in wonder; everything brings awe. Collecting pebbles on the seashore or seashells... watch the children, with what joy they are running, with what joy they are collecting — just colored stones, as if they have found great diamonds collecting flowers, wild flowers, and look into their eyes... or running after butterflies, watch them. Their whole being, each cell of their body is mystified. And that's the most important quality that make life worth living.

The person who loses his quality to be surprised is dead. The moment your surprise is dead, you are dead. The moment your wonder is dead, you are dead. The moment you become incapable of feeling awe, you have gone impotent.

To be born with the gift of laughter and a sense that the world is mad is the quality that makes life worth living — not only worth living but worth dancing, worth celebrating.

An old farmer visited a circus for the first time. He stood before the dromedary's cage, eyes popping and mouth agape at the strange beast within. The circus proper began and the crowds left for the main show, but still the old man stood before the cage in stunned silence, appraising every detail of the misshapen legs, the cloven hoofs, the pendulous upper lip, and the curiously mounded back of the sleepy-eyed beast.

Fifteen minutes passed. Then the farmer turned away in disgust. "Hell!" he exclaimed. "There ain't no such animal!"

Rather than feeling surprised people would like to deny: "There ain't no such animal!" That makes you at ease again; otherwise a restlessness arises in you.

I have heard about a general, a great military general who was posted in Paris. He took his small son one morning to the garden, just for a morning walk. He was very happy that the child was very much fascinated by the statue of Napoleon mounted on a horse, a big marble statue. And the child said, "Daddy, Napoleon is so beautiful, so great! Can you bring me every day when you come for a morning walk just to have a look at the great Napoleon?"

The father being a general, was very much happy that the child is also becoming interested into people like Napoleon: "This is a good sign! Sooner or later he will also become a great general."

After six months he was transferred, and he took his son for the last time to the garden so that he can say goodbye to Napoleon. And the son went there, tears in his eyes, and he said to the father that, "I had always wanted to ask one question, but I become so fascinated with the great Napoleon when I come to the garden that I always forgot to ask the question. Now this is the last day and I would like to inquire. Who is this guy, always sitting on top of poor Napoleon?"

I was reminded of this story just few days before... In a press conference, Morarji Desai was asked, "If people want you to become the prime minister of India again, will you be ready?"

And he said, "Yes, if people want me to ride on a donkey, even then I will be ready."

I was reminded about this story. There will be a problem: how people will know — "Who is this guy riding on poor poor Morarji Desai?" And how they will make a distinction who is who?

That's why in India in a marriage procession when the bridegroom goes to the house of the bride he rides on a horse. A small child asked his father, "Why the bridegroom always rides on a horse? Why not on a donkey?"

The father said, "You don't understand. If he rides on the donkey, then how the bride is going to find who is the bridegroom? A donkey riding on a donkey will be very difficult to make distinctions!"

Morarji Desai riding on a donkey... it will be really a great joy to see a donkey riding on a donkey!

If you look at life you will find everywhere immense surprises.

He was fifty and had spent the best years of his life with a woman whose constant criticism had driven him mad. Now, in poor health and with his business on the verge of bankruptcy, he made up his mind. He went to the dining room, fastened his tie over the chandelier, and was about to end it all. At that moment his wife entered the room.

"John!" she cried, shocked at the scene before her. "That is your best tie!"

A young man vacationing in the upper Midwest woods decided to write to his girl, but, having no stationery with him, walked to the trading post. The attendant was a young, well-stacked girl with a sensual appeal.

"Do you keep stationery?" he asked.

"Well," she smiled, "I do until the last few seconds, and then I go wild!"

Just watch around!

A soldier disembarked in New York after two long years abroad and was met by his beautiful wife.

Alone at last in their room at the hotel, they were disturbed by the sudden clamor in the corridor and a cry of "Let me in!"

The rattled soldier jumped out of bed and panted, "It must be your husband!"

His distracted mate reassured him. "Don't be foolish!" she said. "He is thousands of miles away somewhere in Europe!"

One just needs a clear perspective, and each moment you are in for a great surprise.

She was very nearsighted and very pretty, but too vain to wear glasses on her honeymoon and unable to wear contact lenses.

Each Moment – Miracles !

When she returned from her honeymoon, her mother immediately got in touch with the occultist. "You must see my daughter at once," she pleaded. "It is an emergency!"

"There is nothing to be excited about," he reassured her. "She is nearsighted, that's all."

"That's all?" repeated the mother. "Why, this young man she has got with her is not the same one she went on her honeymoon with!"

The only thing that is most surprising is that you don't look surprised. And this is how your life becomes a life of boredom, a life of sadness.

Bring your surprising quality back as you had it in your childhood. Again look with those same innocent eyes. Dionysius calls it agnosia, a state of not-knowing, and Upanishads call it dhyana, samadhi, a state of not-knowing. It is not ignorance.

Ignorance and knowledge belong to the same dimension: ignorance means less knowledge, knowledge means less ignorance; the difference is of degrees agnosia, samadhi, is not ignorance; it is beyond ignorance and knowledge both. It is a pure state of wonder. When you are full of wonder, existence is full of God.

Question 5

OSHO,

I spent thirteen years in different nuns' convents, and was born in a family composed of one priest, two nuns, one monk and one missionary. With such a number, any jokes you tell on these people provoke a healing laughter for which I am grateful. Could you tell us some more good ones?

— Kavisho

This is really surprising — such a great family, and you still survived! Not only that, you have arrived here! That's what makes me hopeful about humanity. That's why I never lose hope.

Two men met at a bar and struck up a conversation After a while one of them said, "You think you have family problems?

Listen to my situation. A few years ago I met a young widow with a grown-up daughter and we got married. Later my father married my stepdaughter. That made my stepdaughter my stepmother, and my father became my stepson. Also my wife became the mother-in-law of her father-in-law. Then the daughter of my wife, my stepmother, had a son. This boy was my half-brother because he was my fathers son, but he was also the son of my wife's daughter which made him my wife's grandson. That made me the grandfather of my half-brother. This was nothing until my wife and I had a son. Now the sister of my son, my mother-in-law, is also the grandmother. This makes my father the brother-in-law of my child, whose stepsister is my fathers wife.

"I am my stepmother's brother-in-law, my wife is her own child's aunt, my son is my father's nephew — and I am my own grandfather. And you think you have family problems!"

Kavisho feel grateful to God: to be born in such a family is rare. It is a unique opportunity!

A Catholic nun in a small residential hotel complained to the desk clerk that the man in the adjoining room kept annoying her with indecent songs.

"You must be mistaken," replied the clerk politely "Mr. Pritchard never sings any songs."

"I know," replied the Catholic nun, "but he whistles them."

Grandma was in her eighties. She tired easily, had little appetite, and was sometimes confused mentally. Her son called the doctor, who arrived shortly and was shown up to Grandma's room. Half an hour later he came down.

"There's no need to worry" he explained. "I have given her a thorough examination and there is nothing really wrong with her except her age. She will be all right."

Son and daughter-in-law, much relieved, went upstairs to see her. "Well, mother," asked her son, "how did you like the doctor?"

"Oh, so that was the doctor?" she said. "I thought he acted

rather familiar for a clergyman!"

The young couple moved from their small town to the big city, leaving behind family and relatives, mostly elderly. Their young son still continued to include them in his nightly prayers. One night he seemed to have forgotten Uncle Joseph. Strangely enough, the next day they learned that Uncle Joseph had passed away.

Some months later he again skipped a name in his prayers — Aunt Mary. The next day they learned that Aunt Mary had passed away.

Thereafter they listened most carefully to his nightly prayers to discover if any blessings were left out. Sure enough, several weeks later, after "God bless Mommy" he omitted "God bless Daddy." This panicked his father, who did not dare go downstairs all night or even leave the bedroom, but stayed in bed worrying about his child's supernatural powers of prophecy.

The next morning they got word from their former home town that their friendly priest had died.

And the last, Kavisho:

A salesman is forced to share a room with a rabbi in a crowded hotel. He enters the room and finds the rabbi kneeling in a corner, rocking on his heels while murmuring his prayers.

"Hi!" says the salesman. "I'm your new roommate."

The rabbi nods without interrupting his prayers.

"Well then, which bed shall I take?"

The rabbi points to one bed, continuing to pray.

The salesman nervously unpacks his bag, then all of a sudden says, "Say, rabbi, do you mind if I bring up a girl?"

The rabbi, still praying, holds up two fingers.

8

Knowing Nothing About Everything

Question 1

OSHO,

Is there something wrong with me? I feel proud to be a polack!

— *Prem Kavita*

There is nothing wrong to be a Polack. Polacks are as beautiful as anybody else, or a little more, a little more juicy.

A sign outside a police station read: Man Wanted For Rape. Next day three Polacks applied for the job.

But it is certainly wrong to feel proud. Whether one feels to be proud as an Indian or as a Polack or as an Englishman, it does not matter. These are just excuses. The real thing is that the ego wants some support. The ego cannot stand on its own feet; it needs crutches. It claims that "My country is the best country in the world, my religion the most superior, my culture the most evolved," and so on, so forth.

Anything can be used as a prop for the ego, and that's certainly wrong, particularly for the sannyasin, because the whole effort of sannyas is to drop the ego in all its possible forms, subtle or gross, manifest or unmanifest, direct or indirect.

One has to be constantly aware of the tricks of the ego; its ways are subtle. If you throw it out from one door it enters from the other door — and in a new disguise. Unless you are really alert it is going to grab you from the back.

Many times you feel the misery that is created by the ego and

Knowing Nothing About Everything

many times you have dropped it, but it again creates new temptations. And because the temptations are new you think it is not the old ditch you are falling in. It is the same ditch — of course painted with fresh colors, changed a little bit here and there, renovated...

Beware of the ego! Pride is not good for a sannyasin. That's the only difference between a sannyasin and a non-sannyasin. The old idea of sannyas was to renounce the world; my idea of sannyas is to renounce the ego, because even if you renounce the world the ego will go on hidden within you wherever you go. In fact, when it starts taking on spiritual colors it becomes far more difficult to get rid of it.

Just like if your chains are made not of ordinary steel but of purest of golds, studded with diamonds — then you will not like to drop them. To you they will appear like ornaments, and if somebody says, "These are chains," you will be offended, you will be angry.

A Hindu is offended if you say to him that to be a Hindu is to be in a prison. A Mohammedan is angry if you say to him that to be a Mohammedan means to be a slave. The same is true about the Christians and the Jains and the Buddhists.

But to be proud simply means you are thinking yourself separate from existence. Secondly: you are thinking of yourself as special.

To be a sannyasin means to be just natural. You are not higher than anybody and you are not lower than anybody. You are simply part of the same existence. How can one be lower or higher? It is not only a question of being on equal terms with human beings; you are on equal terms with the trees, with the rocks, with the stars. Simply there is nobody inside you who feels separate. This is true equality, and the true equality is always rooted in equanimity, equilibrium.

To feel higher in any way is simply a proof that deep down you are suffering from an inferiority complex it is just a compensation.

The politician feels higher than others because he has power, political power. The wealthy feels higher than others because he has power, economic power. And the so-called spiritual person also feels higher than others because he has again the same kind of thing: power — spiritual power, purity, morality, virtue. But these are nothing but properties.

In my vision a sannyasin is utterly ordinary and in that very ordinariness the extraordinary explodes.

Question 2

OSHO,

The other day in darshan you were talking about women and transforming their energy. You said that in the past Masters such as Jesus Mahavira, and even Gautam the Buddha were not able to understand and transform women's energy and allow it to come to a peak. You said that this time here with you it will be possible for women as well as for men to flower and come to a peak. Somehow I was touched by this very deeply. Can you say something more about this difference between man and woman and how you work with us in different ways?

— *Anand Maria*

The difference between man and woman is not much; the difference is simple. It is like a man by your side is standing on his head: what is the difference between you who is standing on his legs and the man who is doing a headstand, a sirshasana? In fact, none. You are both the same — but in a way there is a difference. The difference is that the man who is standing on his head is upside-down. That's the only difference between man and a woman.

What is conscious in man is unconscious in women, and what is unconscious in women is conscious in men. Man is man only in his consciousness; in his unconsciousness he is woman, feminine. That's why whenever you feel a man in any way moving closer to his unconscious he becomes softer, feminine, loving, tender.

That's why the people who are condemned by the society, the

sinners, are more loving people than your so-called saints. Your so-called saints are hung up in the conscious; they don't allow their unconscious, they repress it. They disassociate themselves from their unconscious, they condemn it. They create a distance between themselves and the unconscious; they define themselves only through the conscious. That's why they look so hard.

Look at the faces of your so-called saints — the moralists, the puritans, the people who are continuously carrying the load of "holier-than-thou", just look at their faces, and you will find hard lines, stiffness, uptightness — a quality which cannot be called soft, tender, loving.

Watch the so-called sinners, the condemned people, and you will be surprised that they have more tender hearts. They are more loving people, more companionable. You can enjoy the company of the sinners, you cannot enjoy the company of the saints. If you put four saints together they will be constantly quarreling — quarreling about stupid things: how many angels can dance on the head of a pin, how many hells there are... Buddha says there is only one hell, Mahavira says there are seven Sanjaya Vilethiputta says there are seven hundred.

If you put a dozen saints in one house there will be no peace at all in that house; they will be constantly barking at each other. Sometimes I am fascinated by the idea that dogs may be reincarnations of saints — barking at anything, and particularly at few things. For example, all dogs are against uniforms. They will bark against the postman, the policeman, the sannyasin. Maybe they are angry at their own past life!

But sinners are very friendly for the simple reason... I am not telling you become sinners, I am simply making a point so that you can understand why sinners look so soft, loving, human, and why saints look so inhuman. The reason is the sinners are closer to their unconscious and man's unconscious is feminine.

The same happens with intellectual women, particularly the women who belong to Liberation Movement. They are harsh, ugly, hard, and constantly argumentative. They become unloving, they become very egoistic. They are a new version of female saints, for the simple reason again because they have gone against their natural unconscious spontaneity. They are living in their heads. They have dropped the very idea of the unconscious, they are not allowing their instincts. They are lopsided; they have lost their balance.

The balanced man is neither man nor woman; he is a mixture of both, a synthesis rather. His masculinity compensates his femininity. They are not at daggers with each other; they are dancing in tune, in deep harmony, together. There is great accord.

So the difference is not much; the difference is very little. Of course it has become very big because for at least ten thousand years man has dominated the scene. He has repressed the woman in himself and because of that he has repressed the woman on the outside too. He had to — both are part of one logic.

If you allow your own inner woman freedom to meet with the man inside you, to have a deep togetherness, an orgasmic quality, so that as far as your consciousness is concerned it is no more split as man and woman... It is one, it is human, it is whole. It is no more a conflict; it is a concord. It has attained to the highest synthesis possible. When this happens one is whole; whether one is man or woman does not matter.

But for centuries man has dominated, and the only way to dominate is to destroy the outer woman, to reduce her into a slave, to reduce her into a commodity, sellable, purchasable, something of the marketplace. This is the ugliest thing that has happened in the past. Because of this the whole past of humanity is rotten, unbalanced, insane. And if the man represses the woman on the outside, of course he cannot allow the woman inside either: he has to repress that too.

And the woman has been told that she has to be womanly; that means she has to reject all that is masculine in her. She has been forced to go to the very extreme of being a woman and the man has to be completely denied. And this has been taught as if it is something of great value — as culture, as religion, as civilization.

The woman has to be shy; the woman has to be in every possible way dependent on man. She has to be a servant, not a companion, not a friend.

This idea affected everything, even religion. And the people like Jesus, Mahavira, Gautam the Buddha, these great persons who are the very salt of the past humanity, the few people who had flowered, even they could not go against the social structure absolutely. I can understand why they could not go against the social structure — because they had to work with a society which was not of their making; it was already there.

Buddha had only forty years to work. Now you cannot transform everything in the society. He had to decide whether he has to work and create something or he has just to fight. If he was to fight for every single inch, then no work would have been possible. He had to compromise. He accepted many things which I know were accepted very unwillingly.

And the same is true about Mahavira, Lao Tzu, Zarathustra, Jesus, Mohammed. But they had to function in a particular society, which was given, already there, and it had existed for thousands of years. And they decided it is better to work silently and help few people to become enlightened rather than fight with the society and waste your whole time, and not help even few people to become enlightened. That was the choice before them.

Buddha was not willing to allow women to be initiated as sannyasins for the simple reason because the Indian society has been very repressive; it has created great walls between men and women. To destroy those walls would have been releasing a chaos. It would have released so much repressed energy that Buddha was not thinking that he will be able to help anybody; everything will go berserk. Hence he postponed as long as he could.

When the women became very insistent, and particularly when his own stepmother asked to be initiated, he could not refuse. He owed much to this woman, because his own mother died the very day he was born. He was brought up by this stepmother with such care, with so much love. He had never felt that she is a stepmother;

he had never missed his mother. And when this stepmother asked to be initiated — and she was getting very old, and death was coming close — he could not say no. Very unwillingly he said yes.

But when he said yes to his own mother, then other women also said, "Now you have accepted one woman as a sannyasin, then why debar us?" And it was logical. The door opened...

And Buddha said very sadly that, "My religion would have lived at least for five thousand years and helped thousands of people to become enlightened, but now it will exist only for five hundred years."

And that's how it happened, because once the women came in, the repressed male sannyasins started getting infatuated. They had lived in compartments and suddenly they were free — suddenly the women were there, and beautiful women. Almost from all royal families the first sannyasins had come. It almost always happens: when a man like Buddha arrives on the earth it is the most intelligent ones who come first to him. It is natural, because only they can understand.

You can see it here happening: the most intelligent people of the world from every nook and corner of the world, have arrived here. But the Indian masses go on ignoring as if it has nothing to do with them. They are not yet at the level of that intelligence where they can understand what is happening here. What to say about ordinary masses...

Just the other day the Poona magistrate has given his judgment concerning the case of one madman who had thrown a dagger at me, obviously intentionally to kill me. He has freed him, and the reason that he has freed him, the most basic reason that he has given, is really worth consideration. I laughed at it, I enjoyed it!

The reason that he has freed him is that if it was an attempt to murder me, then I would not have continued my discourse! Who can continue talking when somebody is trying to murder you? But he does not know me. I would have continued even if I had died — I would not have finished before ten!

But he cannot understand, and I can understand him — he cannot understand. When somebody is trying to kill you, can you go on speaking the same way? His argument seems to be very valid. So what to say about the ordinary masses? — even an educated magistrate thinks in the same way.

Once Buddha allowed women to enter in his commune, the repressed male sannyasins started losing their grip on their own consciousness. It happened because of repression. That's why Jesus and Mahavira were also of the same opinion.

I can allow for the simple reason that twenty-five centuries have passed and in these twenty-five centuries much has happened, particularly in the West. That's why my appeal will be far more in the West than in the East, because in the East nothing much has happened. Karl Marx has not happened in the East, Friedrich Nietzsche has not happened in the East, Sigmund Freud has not happened in the East, Carl Gustav Jung has not happened in the East, Albert Einstein has not happened in the East...

The West is far more ready. The West has gone through a great revolution about sex about the discrimination between sexes. The West has dropped the old nonsense. That's why it is possible for me to allow man and woman together to be here. And you can see the difference: when Indians come here they create trouble.

For these six years I have been here, at least more than three to four hundred thousand westerners have visited the place. Not a single westerner has tried to rape any Indian woman. What to say about rape — they have not even bothered about Indian women, they have not even thought about Indian women! But so many Indians have tried molestations, efforts to rape; all kinds of things they have done. And they go on asking me why Indians are not easily allowed in the ashram. They come for wrong reasons, even the well-educated.

Just a few days before the manager of the Ambassador Hotel came to see — rich, well-educated — and when he found Padma working in her department alone, he immediately grabbed her breasts! And the man had asked Sheela the first thing, that, "Why I don't see many Indians here?" And when he was caught red-handed Sheela told him, "Now you know the reason why so many Indians are not there in the ashram! We have to throw them, just as we are throwing you out!"

One government officer, one S.D.O. had come to investigate the morality of my sannyasins, and Sheela was showing him around the ashram. When he found that Sheela and he were alone he asked Sheela, "Can I kiss you?" And he had come to investigate the morality of the ashram! And because Sheela reacted and shouted at him he had written a very nasty and wrong report about the ashram, and he has been one of the causes that we could not get the Saswad land for the commune. He created every possible trouble. And he was sending messages that "If Sheela comes to me, then I will help you!"

Now these are the people...! Buddha had to work with these people, and Jesus, and Mahavira. They can be forgiven. They wanted to help man and woman both, but the trouble was the society.

To me there is a possibility. I can choose from all over the world people who are ready to drop this stupid division between sexes. Of course the approach will be different: the woman will start with love and end with meditation, and the man will start with meditation and end with love. Only this much difference will be there. To the man love will come as a consequence, as a fragrance of meditation. To the woman meditation will come as a consequence, as a byproduct, as a fragrance of love.

Rut whether the man or the woman when they reach to the highest peak of consciousness, to the Everest of consciousness, they will have both exactly balanced: meditation and love.

Question 3

OSHO,

How about telling us a little esoteric bullshit?

— *Prem Shraddhan*

Bullshit is simply bullshit! Even if you make it esoteric it does not change its quality — it still stinks! You can give it a beautiful cover, a beautiful packet, but the content will be the same. You can wrap around it something beautiful, but that will be only a wraparound. When you will dive deep into it, then you would know — you have fallen into a ditch full of bullshit!

A sannyasin and newly-arrived non-sannyasin are sitting together in Vrindavan. "Hey, Swami," says the non-sannyasin, "you have probably been around this place for a while. Can you tell me what Osho is teaching you?"

The sannyasin ponders over this for a while, then says, "It's like this: imagine two guys walking along a road; they both fall into a ditch. One of them gets dirty, the other does not — which one of them is going to have a shower?"

"The dirty one, of course!" says the non-sannyasin.

"No. The dirty one sees the clean one and he thinks himself to be clean. The clean one sees the dirty one and he thinks he is dirty, so the clean one is going to wash himself. Now imagine they fall into a ditch again — who is going to shower now?"

"Now I know," answers the non-sannyasin, "the clean one!"

"No. The clean one realizes while showering that he was clean, and the dirty one realizes while the clean one is taking a shower, so now the right one showers! Now imagine they both fall into a ditch again — who is going to shower now?"

"From now on, of course, always the dirty one!"

"No. Have you ever seen two guys fall into a ditch three times, and one always comes out dirty and the other always clean?"

A Catholic priest was walking along a cliff by the sea when he heard the shouts of someone in difficulty. He saw a man who obviously could not swim struggling for his life in the water.

"Save me, save me, father! I am drowning!" cried the young man.

"Are ye Catholic or Protestant, son?" asked the cleric.

"Protestant, father!" gasped the young man as he went under the water. The priest began to walk on.

"For God's sake, father, save me!" screamed the terrified boy surfacing again.

"What religion are ye, son?" shouted back the priest.

"Protestant, father!" spluttered back the answer. The priest again began to walk on as the unfortunate youngster went under for the second time.

"For the love of God, save me, father!" screamed the boy in desperation.

"What religion are ye, son?" came the demand again.

After a moment's hesitation the young man shouted, "I'm a Catholic, father!"

The priest immediately threw off his clothes, dived into the sea and swam strongly to the boy, catching him by the hair as he went under for the third and last time.

"What religion are ye, son?" asked the priest again, as he held the young man's head above the water.

"Catholic, father!" came the response.

The cleric smiled, let go the young man's hair, and as he sank said, "Good, die in faith!"

Question 4

OSHO,

Why the so-called authoritative scholars, theologians and philosophers on religion are against you?

— Pritama

It is natural. They philosophize about God, I know. They think about light, I see. They read the scriptures, I have read the universe. We cannot agree.

It is like a blind man collecting information about light. How he can agree with the man who has eyes? Although he collects information about light, but information about light is just information; it is not an experience. The experience is bound to be totally different. The experience is qualitatively different; it is not only a question of quantity. It is not that I know more than that they know or less than that they know; it is not a question of more or less. I simply know, and they have been collecting information from others. Their knowledge is borrowed, and of course the man who lives with borrowed knowledge, whose whole life depends on borrowed knowledge, is bound to be afraid of the man who has experienced it.

They have always been against; it is nothing new. If they were not against me, that would be surprising. That will be almost unbelievable! Their being against me simply proves that man has not learned anything, as if the evolution of man has stopped long before. They still behave in the same way they behaved with Jesus, with Buddha, with Krishna. Their behavior has not changed, and I don't see that it is going to change ever — because of their vested interest. Men like me are dangerous to their business!

It is a question of life and death for them. Their whole profession depends on borrowed knowledge, and my insistence is to help you to know it on your own. And the moment you know, all that is borrowed fades away, becomes irrelevant, meaningless, loses all significance. And with it disappear all the priests, all the theologians, all the philosophers, all the scholars, the pundits...

Right now you respect them, you honor them, because you feel ignorant and you think they know. And blind are leading the blind! You are far more honest — at least you recognize your blindness, your scholars are far more cunning; they don't recognize that they are ignorant. Deep down they know it, but they don't show it. They go on hiding it in every possible way. And people like me start exposing them — how can they tolerate it?

And it has always been a known fact that scholars are one-dimensional. They have to be one-dimensional if they want to be scholarly. If a man tries to know everything about God... and remember, "about". By knowing God he will become multidimensional, because God means the whole existence. By knowing God he will know the whole, but by knowing about God he has to become one-dimensional. He has to focus his mind, he has to go on narrowing his consciousness; he has to pinpoint it. Naturally he knows more and more about God, but less and less about everything else. His knowing becomes only inclusive about God and excludes everything else.

That's why authorities always behave foolishly. As far as their own field is concerned they are great experts. If you ask any question about something which is not part of their expertise they are at a loss — they are as foolish as no fool ever can be, because fools have a little bit of multi-dimensionality. But the scholars are absolutely one-dimensional, they are fixed on one point; they are specialized people.

In the beginning, just two thousand years before there was only one knowledge without any divisions; it was called philosophy. In the days of Aristotle it was called philosophy; philosophy meant all knowledge. So if you look in Aristotle's books — who is the father-figure of the western philosophy — you will find everything, things which have nothing to do with philosophy at all.

For example, how many teeth a woman has. Now what it has got to do with philosophy? And even about that he is wrong! And he had two wives, not only one — he could have counted very easily. And as far as a woman's teeth are concerned you need not even ask her to open her mouth — it is always open! You can count very easily; there is no trouble. And having two wives and committing such a mistake! He says that women have less teeth than men. The logic is: how women can have anything equal to men? He never bothered to experiment.

But his books contain everything. It contains biology, religion, philosophy, mathematics, logic, language, aesthetics — everything

Knowing Nothing About Everything

possible. It contains physics... That's how the name "metaphysics" was born, because in Aristotle's books, after physics comes religion. Metaphysics simply means "the chapter next to physics". After the chapter on physics there is a chapter on religion, hence it was called metaphysics.

If Aristotle comes back he will be absolutely puzzled. If he goes to Oxford there are three hundred sixty-five subjects taught. He would not be able to believe — three hundred sixty-five subjects! And they are every day growing more and more — branches of branches of branches.

I have heard a future story:

A man goes to his optician. He is suffering from pain in one of his eyes, and he tells the doctor.

The doctor asks, "Which eye, right or left?"

And he says, "Left."

And the doctor says, "Sorry, but I have specialized only in the other eye. You have to go to somebody else."

A man's son came back from the medical college, and he asked, "In what you have specialized?" He was an old physician, old kind of physician who used to treat every kind of disease.

The son said, "I have specialized about nose."

And the father asked, "Which nostril?"

Yes, it is going to happen one day — right nostril or left nostril, and you will have to go to different experts.

This is the way of specialization: one becomes narrowed, one starts knowing more and more about less and less. And a moment comes, is bound to come — at least logically it can be conceived that it will happen one day... If this is the process of science — knowing more and more about less and less — then one day somebody will declare. "I know all about nothing."

The process of experiencing is totally different: it is knowing less and less about more and more. And a moment comes: one knows nothing about everything. That's what Dionysius calls agnosia, that is the State of meditation: one knows nothing about everything. He has become absolutely multidimensional. He is simply aware, not a knower. There is no knowledge, he is simply wise.

Now how the expert can agree with the wise man? The expert cannot agree with the Buddha, impossible; their dimensions are totally different. One knows more and more about less and less, the other knows less and less about more and more. One reaches ultimately to know everything about nothing, the other reaches ultimately to know nothing about everything — they are following diverse paths. But the Buddha experiences and the expert only accumulates information.

A very pretty secretary, wearing a sweater and mini-skirt, passed through a chemistry lab.

"Get a load of that!" said one of the scientists to the other.

The other glanced at the well-stacked figure and replied indifferently, So what? She's nine-tenths water!"

"Sure," said the first, "but what surface tension!"

A great scientist riding on a bus had noticed a clock on a building that showed nine-thirty. Farther on he saw another clock; this one showed nine-fifteen. Good heavens!" he cried. "I must be going the wrong way!"

A story is told about a professor of English who was indisposed and stayed home one day. "What happened?" one of the students asked his daughter.

"He is terribly upset," she disclosed. "Last night an owl in one of the trees kept repeating 'To who? To who?' instead of 'To whom?'"

The newlywed wife was a professor of philosophy, and it always almost happens with the professors of philosophy, that she suffered from insomnia. She kept waking up her husband whenever she heard noises downstairs.

Finally he said, "Go to sleep, dear, please. Burglars don't make noises!"

So she started to wake him up every time she heard nothing.

That is logical! That is philosophical!

Before beginning a postmortem the doctor wanted to check the chest. The cadaver was wheeled into the X-ray department and placed properly in the apparatus by the pretty technician, then she put the photographic plate into the control panel. As she stuck her head out from behind it she said automatically, "Please take a deep breath and hold it!"

A technician is a technician! They function automatically. Experts function very unconsciously. They know not what they are doing, they know not what they are saying. They know nothing because their whole consciousness is full of dead facts and informations. They can talk about love, but they have never loved. They can talk about God...

And remember the meaning of the word "about': about means around. Around and around they go, but they never touch the center of it. It cannot be touched just by knowing about God. You can quote the Bible, the Koran, the Gita, the Vedas; that is not going to help, unless you can speak out of your own inner communion.

And Jesus said unto them, "Who do you say I am?"

And they replied, "You are the eschatological manifestation of the ground of our being, the charisma manifested in conflict and decision in the humanizing process."

And Jesus said, "What?"

Now this language! Even the Polack Pope would have understood- this is the language of the Christian theologian: "You are the eschatological manifestation of the ground of our being, the charisma manifested in conflict and decision in the humanizing process."

And Jesus said, "What?!"

You ask me, Pritama: Why the so-called uthoritative scholars...?

They are not authoritative; they are quoting others. What authority they can have? Authority should come from your own authentic experience. That is the only source of authority; there is no other source of authority.

A Ramakrishna can speak authoritatively, a Raman can speak authoritatively, but not Vivekananda; he is just a scholar. Mahavira can speak authoritatively, but not Gautam Ganadhara, his disciple, who is just a brahmin pundit collecting information, taking notes, compiling what Mahavira has said. Jesus can speak authoritatively, but not the popes.

And the irony is that these people are thought to be authoritative because they can quote exactly the words of the scriptures. But the words of the scriptures can be quoted by a computer more efficiently, more accurately! It can be done by a mechanical device; no consciousness is needed for that, no awareness is needed for that. One need not be a Christ to repeat the Beatitudes: "Blessed are the meek for theirs is the kingdom of God." This can be repeated by a record, a gramophone record!

Have you seen the most famous gramophone company, His Master's Voice symbol? — the dog wagging its tail. A gramophone record can do it, and that's what these popes are doing — His Master's Voice — the shankaracharyas are doing, ayatollahs, imams are doing — just repeating.

A small child was teaching to his parrot all the four-letter words. The mother when heard was shocked. She came running in and she said, "What are you doing? Have you gone mad? You are destroying the parrot — you are teaching him four-letter words!"

And the child said, "No Mummy, I am just telling him, 'Please remember, these words are not to be repeated by you!' Just the way you have taught my father and my father has taught me, I am

Knowing Nothing About Everything

teaching him and I am telling him, 'Remember to tell your children not to repeat these words. These are very ugly and dangerous words."

You can teach a parrot and he can repeat anything, but a parrot is not an authority. Machines can do computers can do even a far better way.

So, Pritama, don't call these people authorities — they are not. They are befooling others and perhaps themselves. They are not real philosophers; they are more "foolosophers" than philosophers! Philosophy, the very word, means love for wisdom, and they have nothing to do with wisdom at all.

Wisdom happens only through meditation; it never happens by collecting information. It happens by going through a transformation. Wisdom is the flowering of your consciousness, the opening of the one-thousand-petaled lotus of your being. It is the release of your fragrance, the release of the imprisoned splendor.

Real philosophy has nothing to do with thinking; on the contrary it has everything to do with transcending thinking, going beyond and beyond thinking, going beyond mind, reaching to the pure space of no-mind. Out of that space something flowers in you. You can call it Christ-consciousness, Buddhahood, or whatsoever you like. That is true philosophy.

The better word for philosophy will be philosia — not only love for wisdom but love for seeing the truth. Sia means to see, Philo means love — love to see. That's exactly the Indian word for philosophy, darshan; darshan means philosia. Don't translate it as philosophy. Doctor Radhakrishnan and others have done a great disservice to the East by translating darshan as philosophy. It is philosia.

In the East our interest has always been to see the truth, because by seeing the truth, as the Isha Upanishad says, you become the truth itself Only by becoming the truth you have authority; then the truth speaks through you. You are just a medium, a vehicle, a hollow bamboo flute, and God starts singing through you.

That miracle has to happen here to my sannyasins. That's what my only teaching is: become a hollow bamboo flute. Don't hinder. Let God flow through you naturally, spontaneously. And if you allow your nature and spontaneity, just as every river reaches to the ocean you will also reach to the ultimate ocean of God.

Question 5

OSHO,

You are talking and talking and I hear flowers and silence and laughter everywhere.

Come now! Admit it! Are not you in the tradition of Gautam Buddha's great italian disciple, maha-gossipa?

— Yoga Nishant

I am nobody's disciple, and I am nobody's Master either. I am not your Master, just a friend on the way, a fellow-traveler. And I am nobody's disciple, because nothing can be learned from anybody, and I am nobody's Master because nothing can be taught.

I can allow you to be with me. Something can happen which is neither done by me nor done by you. Nobody can claim that "I am the doer of it." It can simply happen, just as in the morning the sun rises and the flowers open and the birds start singing. The sun cannot say "I have opened the flowers." The sun cannot say that, "I have managed this whole orchestra of the music that suddenly has arisen on the earth." Neither the birds can say that, "It is because of our singing that the sun has risen."

You must have heard an old story of a woman who had a hen, and she believed that it is because of her hen that the sun rises, because early in the morning just before the sunrise the hen gives a joyous shout. And she was very proud because she was the only one who had a hen in the village.

And nobody seemed to be grateful to her, so one day out of disgust she said, "I am leaving this village, and then you will know!

The sun will never rise in this place because I am taking my hen away."

And she left the village, she reached another village, and of course when the hen shouted with joy in the morning, the sun rose there and the woman was tremendously happy. She said "Now, now those fools will realize. Sun has risen in this village, it cannot rise there! Now it will be always night there!"

Neither the birds can say nor the flowers can say that, "The sun has risen because of us," nor the sun can say. It is a synchronicity. This word is very beautiful; it is coined by Carl Gustav Jung. You understand the law of causality: in the law of causality one thing functions as a cause and the other thing happens as an effect. Wherever the cause is produced, the effect is bound to follow. It is a mechanical process. You heat the water to a certain degree and it evaporates; heating is the cause and evaporation is the effect.

Synchronicity is a non-causal relationship. Things happen, but you never know who is the cause and who is the effect. They happen simultaneously.

That's the beauty that happens whenever you are with a Buddha. The Buddha is not a Master, you are not a disciple; you are not learning anything from Buddha, the Buddha is not teaching anything to you. It is just being together. It is a love affair! Being together... and something happens, something which is beyond both. Something is triggered. At the most it can be said that the Buddha functioned as a catalytic agent, but whatsoever happens happens in you; he has not caused it.

Hence I say I am not anybody's disciple nor I am anybody's Master. But, Nishant, you have found the right name for me: I am an Italian, Maha-Gossipa! Remember me not as the man who has given you a great gospel but as a man who has given you many gossips. My gospel is my gossip!

At a local businessman's club four members got together after a few drinks and began to confess their secret vices.

"I must own up," said the leading banker, "that I gamble. Every week or so I place a bet on the horses, not too much, but I have been doing it for years."

"Well, I will come clean of my weakness," said the prominent executive. "No one in town has ever seen me drunk, but twice a year I drive to another town where I am not known, rent a motel room for a few days, get stoned, and return home feeling better than ever!

"I am not ashamed to admit that my weakness is women," said another important businessman. "I have to be very discreet, of course, but with a cautious secretary it can be managed easily enough. I have never yet been found out."

The fourth member of the group, who had been listening intently, said nothing. He was the rabbi of the village. The others expected him to reveal something, but he shrugged his shoulders as is the way of all the Jews of all the ages. He simply shrugged his shoulders.

"Well," asked one of them, "Rabbi, how about you?"

"I would rather not confess," he said shaking his head. They looked at him with suspicion. What could he be covering up? Each of them accused him of being a poor sport, especially since they had all opened up.

Finally the rabbi gave in. "All right," he said reluctantly, "if you must know my weakness, it is scandal — and I can hardly wait to get out of this place!"

9
Both And More

Into A Blinding Darkness Go They Who Worship Action Alone.

Into An Even Greater Darkness Go They Who Worship Meditation.

For It Is Other Than Meditation,
It Is Other Than Action.
This We Have Heard From The Enlightened Ones.

Meditation And Action —
He Who Knows These Two Together,
Through Action Leaves Death Behind And
Through Meditation Gains Mmmortality.

Into A Blinding Darkness Go They Who Idolize The Absolute,
Into An Even Greater Darkness Go They Who Dote On The Relative.

For It Is Other Than The Relative,
It Is Other Than The Absolute.
This We Have Heard From The Enlightened Ones.

Aum
Purnam adaha
Purnam idam
Purnat purnamudachyate
Purnasya purnamadaya
Purnameva vashishyate

Aum
That is the whole.
This is the whole.

From wholeness emerges wholeness.
Wholeness coming from wholeness,
Wholeness still remains.

P.D. Ouspensky has written a tremendously significant book, Tertium Organum. The fundamental of Tertium Organum is based and rooted in this sutra: From the whole comes the whole, yet the whole remains behind, intact. From that comes this. That is whole, this is whole, but even though it has come from the whole, the whole is not reduced in any way. It remains the same, as if nothing has been taken out of it.

This is a strange mantra, one of the most strange ones, because it goes against the very idea of arithmetic. It belongs to meta-mathematics. The ordinary mathematics will not agree with this. If you take something from anything, then that much is reduced in the original, and if you take the whole then nothing is left behind.

Ouspensky has done a great service to humanity by proposing a higher mathematics, a mathematics of the beyond. That's what the Upanishads are.

First: the whole is not a finite entity. If it is finite, then of course if you take something out of it it will be reduced, it will not be the same any more. The whole is infinite, so whatsoever you take from it, it remains still the infinite.

And where you can take? The whole pervades all, so the very idea of taking is just an idea. As far as reality is concerned nothing is taken out of it and nothing is added unto it; it is always as it has always been.

Secondly: in the ordinary mathematics the whole is the sum total of its parts; in the higher mathematics that is not so. The whole is not the sum total of its parts, it is more than that. That "more" is very significant. If you cannot understand that more you will remain absolutely unaware of the religious dimension of things.

For example, the beauty of a rose flower — is it just a sum total of its parts? It should be, according to the ordinary mathematics — it is not. The beauty is something more. Just by putting all the chemicals, the water, the earth, the air, and everything that constitutes the flower — even if you put all that together the beauty will not arise. The beauty is something more, hence in analysis it disappears.

If you go to the chemist, the scientist, to inquire about the beauty of a rose, he will analyze it. Analysis is the method of science. Analysis means breaking it into its parts so that you can know of what it constitutes. But the moment you break it into parts, the invisible "more" disappears. The invisible more exists in the organic unity; you cannot analyze it. It is synthesis, it is totality.

The same is true about all the higher values. A beautiful poem is not just the words that compose it; it is something more. Otherwise anybody who can put words together in a rhythmical form will become a Shakespeare, a Kalidas, a Milton, a Shelley. Then any linguist, grammarian will become a great poet. That does not happen. You may know the whole grammar of the language, you may be acquainted with all the words of the language, still to be a poet is a totally different phenomenon. Poetry comes first, then come the words, not vice versa — it is not that you arrange the words and the poetry arises.

A few of the students of Charles Darwin once played a trick on the great scientist — because he was continuously searching about all forms of life and he was always categorizing to what species a certain animal or insect belongs to.

It was his birthday and his students thought of playing a trick, just a joke. They dissected many insects and glued their parts — legs from one insect, wings from another, head from the third one, the body from the fourth, and so on. At least from twenty insects they managed to glue together a new insect which exists nowhere.

They brought it to Charles Darwin and they said, "Here is a great surprise for you, as a birthday present. You may have never come across this insect! And we have been hiding it for this day. Can you tell us to what species it belongs, what is its name?"

Darwin looked at the insect and he asked only one question to the students; "Does it hum?"

They said, "Yes, when it was alive it used to hum."

"Then," he said, "it is a humbug!"

You can put parts together, but you will create only a humbug; you will not be able to create life. You will not be able to create a new form, a new manifestation of something living.

The Upanishads talk about two trinities. One is called Satyam Shivam Sunderam. Satyam means truth; Shivam means good, virtue, goodness; Sunderam means beauty. Upanishads say these three are beyond ordinary mathematics.

And they also talk of another trinity: Satchitanand — Sat, Chit, Anand. Sat means being, Chit means consciousness, Anand means bliss. Upanishads say this trinity also belongs to the higher realm, the world of synthesis, wholeness. It is beyond ordinary logic, ordinary mathematics.

These two trinities are far more beautiful, far more meaningful than the Christian trinity of God the father and Christ the son and the holy ghost. Compared to these two trinities the Christian trinity looks very immature, childish. Sometimes even children have more insight than the Christian trinity.

When Sigmund Freud said that God the father is nothing but a deep desire of an immature person to cling to the father, the idea of father, it is a father-fixation, he was right. But he had never heard about Satyam Shivam Sunderam or satchitanand. He would not have been able to say anything derogatory about these ultimate visions.

The Christian trinity is certainly very childish, and I say to you, sometimes even children are far more intelligent.

A small child was asking another child, his friend... they were learning the alphabet and the first child asked the second, "Why it is so that B always comes before C?"

And the other child said, "Obviously, you can see only if you are. First you have to be and then only you can see! That's why C comes after B. How it can come before?"

Now even these two children are far more developed, far more perceptive than the Christian trinity — father, son, holy ghost — what nonsense they are talking about?

Higher values are truth, good, beauty, being, consciousness, bliss. And why they are called higher? — because they don't come within the realm of the lower mathematics. The lower mathematics means the whole is simply the sum total of its parts; that defines the world of the lower mathematics. And the higher mathematics, the meta-mathematics, means the whole is more than the sum total of its parts.

You cannot know beauty by analysis; it needs a different vision, a synthetic vision. The poet can understand the beauty, not the scientist. The painter can understand the beauty, but not the chemist. Truth can be understood only by a mystic, not by a philosopher. It can be understood by a lover but not by a logician. It can be comprehended by intuition but not by intellect. Intellect divides; intuition puts things together, and not only put things together — it creates an organic unity.

Life can be looked in two ways: the scientific, the analytical, or the religious, the synthetical.

Today's sutras are of such great value that they are incomparable in the whole religious literature. Even in the world of the Upanishads — there are one hundred eight Upanishads in all, these sutras are incomparable, unique.

The first sutra:

Into A Blinding Darkness Go They Who Worship Action Alone.
Into An Even Greater Darkness Go They Who Worship Meditation.

Action means that which is external to you, meditation which is internal to you. Action is outer, meditation is inner. Action is extroversion, meditation is introversion. Action is an objective approach; science is rooted in it, hence science insists on experimentation. And because science insists on action, experiment, it destroys all that is more than the external — it denies. It simply denies the world of interiority, the world of subjectivity. It is so absurd that science accepts the outer without accepting the inner. How the outer can exist at all without the inner? It is nonsensical.

If there is a coin it is bound to have two aspects; you cannot find a coin which has only one aspect to it, only one-sided coin; it is impossible. Howsoever thin you make it it will always have two sides to it; you cannot make it so thin that it has only one side.

But science goes on insisting on this foolishness: that the external is true and the internal is false. It believes in matter, but it does not believe in consciousness. It says matter has validity, and science asks for objective validity. Of course the world of subjectivity cannot have an objective validity — it is so obvious. The very asking is wrong. The inner cannot come and manifest itself as the outer, but science is blind about it And those who believe in science say that consciousness is illusory.

Karl Marx, who thinks he is creating a scientific communism, says that consciousness is an epiphenomenon, a byproduct of matter. It does not exist in its own right; it is just a combination of material elements, chemistry, physics. It is just a combination, nothing more than that. When a person dies the elements start falling apart and then there is left no consciousness. Hence there is no immortality, no soul. Man becomes just a machine with a wrong notion that it has a soul. Man is not a he or she but only an it.

This scientific approach has colored even the world of psychology. In fact, ninety percent of the psychologists should not use the word "psychology" at all; it is just wrong for them to use the word because they deny the psyche, and still they go on using the word "psychology".

Ninety percent of psychologists belong to the school called Behaviorism — Pavlov, Skinner Delgado and others. They say man is nothing but his Behavior; there is nobody inside him. The inside exists not; whatsoever man is, he is on the outside. Hence he can be studied just like any object, any other object, he can be studied like any other machine.

Isha Upanishad says:

Into Blinding Darkness Go They Who Worship Action Alone.

They are falling into a blinding darkness by only following the outer, the extrovert, the objective. They are losing all sense of the inner. They will exist like robots.

That's why it was so easy for a man like Joseph Stalin to kill millions of people. You see the strange world of logic? Krishna could say to his disciple, Arjuna, "You can kill, there is no problem, because the soul is eternal; it cannot be killed, it cannot be burned. No weapon can enter into it. Nainam Chhindanti Shastrani: there is no way — no sword, no spear can even touch it. Nainam Dahati Pavakah: neither the fire can burn it. The soul is immortal, eternal; only the body dies."

Hence he says to his disciple, Arjuna, "Don't be worried, don't feel guilty. You can kill because nothing is killed: Na hanyate hanyamane shareere. When you kill a body nothing is killed, because the body is already dead and the soul is immortal, so who is killed? The body was already dead, has always been dead; it is matter. And the soul has always been immortal, is still immortal. You are only de-linking them, and there is nothing wrong in de-linking them. You are just separating them — separating the essential from the non-essential. In fact, you are doing a great service to the person you are killing! He himself was not able to separate the essential from the non-essential. In fact, you are doing a great service to the person you are killing! He himself was not able to separate the essential from the non-essential — you have done it for him."

And Joseph Stalin could kill millions of people... the logic was totally different but the result is the same. That's why I say the world of logic is very strange. Joseph Stalin is a scientific communist, a fanatic follower of Karl Marx and Friedrich Engels.

He says there is not soul, so nothing is killed — you can kill! The body is only matter and the matter will remain. The air will remain in the air, the earth will go back to the earth, the water will go to water, and all the elements will be dispersed back. And there is no soul, so nothing is killed. Without any guilt he killed millions of people.

Arjuna also killed millions of people without any guilt, Mao Tse-tung did the same, but their approaches are very different. But it seems to deny one, either the external or the internal, is dangerous: its ultimate outcome will be destruction.

Hence the Isha Upanishad is right:

Into A Blinding Darkness Go They Who Worship Action Alone.
Into An Even Greater Darkness Go They Who Worship Meditation.

Meditation alone again leads to another extreme. Meditation means the internal, the subjective; it means introversion. And obviously the introverts start denying all external reality. They start saying it is maya, it is illusion.

Karl Marx says the inner is illusory, epiphenomenon. And Shankara and Berkeley, they say the external is illusory, the internal is the only truth. Both are incapable of accepting the totality. They choose, they are not choiceless people.

Religion is born out of choiceless awareness. The first, who has chosen action alone, becomes a scientist. The second who has chosen meditation alone, becomes a philosopher. But both miss the whole.

And remember one thing: the half truth is more dangerous than the untruth itself, the partial truth is more harmful than the untruth itself. Why? — because it is very difficult to refute the partial truth because it has something of truth in it. Although it is partial, but because of that presence it is difficult to deny it.

It is difficult to deny Karl Marx and it is difficult to deny

Both And More

Shankara. Both are believers of one aspect of reality? neither of them is religious. One is moving towards the external, the other is moving to the internal, and reality is both and more.

That's my approach here, the total approach to life. Therefore I don't say to my sannyasins, "Escape to the monasteries or to the Himalayan caves." I don't say, "Renounce the world." Renouncing the world means renouncing action. Then what will you be doing in your caves and in your monasteries? Then only meditation is left.

In the past this has been the case: either a person lived in the world... then he was very active but his action was superficial because there was no meditation in him, no depth, no inner world He was just his behavior he was just his outer garb, his periphery. Naturally he created a superficial world with no depth, with no height; he created a very poor world.

And then there was the other extremist who escaped from the world. Seeing its superficiality, seeing its peripheralness, he renounced it. Of course he started going deeper into himself, but his going deeper into himself became uncreative. He had depth, but that depth remains unexpressed. He was silent, but there was no song in it. And when a silence is without song it is dead; it has depth but no manifestation.

You may be a great painter but unless you paint, what is the point of being a great painter? You may be a great poet but unless you sing, what is the point of your being a great poet?

So on the one hand there were people who had chosen action, the world — the extroverts; and on the other hand were the introverts who had chosen their own being. Both were lopsided. Hence I agree with the Upanishads: life has to be total, not lopsided. Only then there is balance and in that balance is music; in that balance there is a center and a circumference. In that balance you are rooted in yourself, but you are not uncreative, you are creative.

The monks, the nuns down the ages have been absolutely uncreative; they have not contributed anything to the world. In fact, the superficial people have contributed far more, hence this emphasis. The Isha Upanishad says:

> Into A Blinding Darkness Go They Who Worship Action Alone.
> Into An Even Greater Darkness...

Remember the emphasis:

> Into An Even Greater Darkness Go They Who Worship Meditation — Alone.

The Upanishads are really courageous: they say the truth as it is, with no compromise. Nobody would have thought that the Upanishads will be so hard on meditation. It can be understood easily that they are hard on the extrovert mind but they are harder on the introvert for the simple reason that the extrovert was superficial but at least he has contributed something to the world.

You can see it: the East has lived with meditation alone and the West has lived with action alone. The West lives in a kind of blindness, but the East lives in a deeper darkness, in a deeper blindness. The western mind is superficial, but it at least has contributed much — technology, industry, scientific farming. It has given people a better standard of life; it may not have given them a better quality of life but at least it has given them a better standard of life. It has given them better houses, better roads, better cars, better airplanes. It may not have given them a better consciousness, but it has contributed, it has been creative — of course superficially. But the East which became escapist in the name of meditation, became basically a drop-out, has not contributed even that much.

What your so-called saints in the East have contributed? It is poor because of those saints, and it is going to remain poor unless those saints are no more respected. But people go on respecting the same old rotten traditions; they cannot see. Deeper is their blindness, darker is their darkness. They cannot even see who is the cause of all this misery.

Twenty-two centuries of slavery in India. Who is the cause of all this? Your saints, your mahatmas, your so-called sages who escape to the monasteries, who escape to the Himalayan caves, to the forests, to the jungles — and you have worshipped them, you have respected them. When you respect somebody it means deep down you would also like to be like him — that's what respect means.

The word "respect" is beautiful; it means seeing again and again —"respect". When you pass a beautiful woman, if she is really beautiful you will have to look again and again. That is respect: seeing again and again. You will walk slowly you will find excuses to go back, you will enter into the same shop the woman has entered, you will start asking for the same commodities she is purchasing so that you can be on the same counter. You will not be looking at things, you will be looking at her. This is respect — literal meaning of the word!

When you respect a person it means you are fascinated, infatuated. You would like to be like him. And the East still goes on respecting the same fools who are the cause of its misery, its starvation, its whole ugly state.

People are dying; sixty percent people in India are starving, and by the end of this century India will be the biggest country as far as population is concerned. It is going to surpass China; by the end of this century it will be the most populated country. Right now its problems are immense — what is going to happen by the end of this century? A great calamity is awaiting: at least half of the population will die through starvation, famine, floods. By God's grace something is bound to happen!

Who is responsible for all this? — the people who have insisted at least for three thousand years continuously that the real is inner and the outer is maya, illusory, why bother about it?

In the whole world things have changed, except in this unfortunate country. India is not yet part of twentieth century; it lags behind at least one thousand years. People in India have not been able yet even to provide themselves simple toilet facilities. The whole country is used as a vast latrine and nobody seems to be bothered about it! It is taken for granted. The whole country is living in unhygienic conditions, in illness, but that too is taken for granted. And we have found explanations and rationalizations for it — that it is because of our past karmas that we are suffering. That means all the sinners are born only in India and all the saints are born in the western countries — which are materialist! They should not go there at all! But these are ways to avoid seeing the truth. The truth is that you have praised the inner too much and destroyed the outer.

And I agree with the Upanishad: that if you have to choose between action and meditation, it is better you choose action. It will lead to darkness, but it will not be so dark as it will be if you choose only meditation alone. But there is no need to choose in the first place — you can have both! When you can have both, why choose?

For It Is Other Than Meditation...
The Truth Is Other Than Meditation.
It Is Other Than Action.

The truth is far more than action: it is both and more. And you will know the "more" only if you are capable of creating a synthesis between the outer and the inner, between action and meditation. Meditate, but let your meditation be expressed in action. Act, and let your action become a part of your meditation. There is no dualism, there is no antagonism between the two. One can act meditatively, one can dance meditatively.

When you dance meditatively your dance starts having a new flavor — something of the divine enters into it — because if you are meditatively dancing then the ego disappears, the dancer disappears. That is the whole art of meditation: disappearance of the ego, disappearance of the mind. The dancer become thoughtless, silent the dance continues and the dancer disappears. This is what I call the divine quality: now it is as if God is dancing through you, you are no more there.

One of the greatest dancers of this age was Nijinsky, and there must have happened, by coincidence, a certain synthesis between dance and meditation in him. He was not the master of it, because

Both And More

he had never learned the art of meditation. It must have happened. Just as a consequence of his total effort to go into dance, his total commitment.

And a miracle used to happen once in a while: Nijinsky will take such high jumps, leaps in the air, which are not physically possible because of the gravitation of the earth. And the spectators were simply mystified; they will miss few beats of their heart. It was a miracle to see Nijinsky moving, as if there is no gravitation — he will take such high leaps and so easily!

And the second thing was, when he will start descending back, he will come as a feather comes very slowly, as if there is no hurry, as if the gravitation is not pulling him like a magnet. It is, according to scientific rules, impossible, but what can you do when it is happening? Even scientists observed Nijinsky and they were puzzled.

Again and again Nijinsky was asked, "How do you manage it?" He said, "That I cannot say, because when it happens I am not there. I have tried to manage it and I have always failed. Whenever I try to manage it, it doesn't happen. Once in a while when I forget myself completely, when I am utterly abandoned, it happens. It happens on its own; I cannot manage. I cannot say that tomorrow it will happen. You are not the only one who is surprised. When it happens, I am myself surprised, utterly surprised, because I become weightless."

A meditator can be a dancer, in fact far greater a dancer than anybody else. A dancer can be a meditator, far greater meditator than anybody else. A painter can be a meditator, and then his painting will have a totally different fragrance, a different flavor, a different beauty.

And this is so about all the actions: whatsoever you are doing, don't renounce it — transform it through meditation. Action has to be transformed, not renounced. The world has to be transmuted, you are not to escape from it. It is a God-given opportunity.

And remember, the ultimate truth cannot be reduced either to action or meditation: it is both and more. Never forget the more, because if you forget the more you will miss the whole point — you will miss the higher mathematics. It is transcendental; it is surpassing all dualism and all polarities. It is not just the sum total of its parts, it is something more — like beauty, like music, like poetry.

This we have heard from the enlightened ones.

Remember, these Upanishads were not written by the Masters themselves; these are notes of the disciples. The Masters have always believed in the spoken word; there are reasons for it. The Masters have never written books. The spoken word has a lively quality to it; the written word is dead, it is a corpse.

When I am speaking to you it is a totally different thing than when you will be reading it in a book, because when you are reading in a book it is only a word; when you are listening to the Master it is more than the word. The presence of the Master is overpowering! Before the word reaches you, the Master has already reached; he is already overflooding you. Your heart is breathing with the Master, beating with the Master in the same rhythm. You are breathing in the same rhythm. There is a communion, an invisible link the presence of the Master, his gestures, his eyes... the words spoken by him are ordinary words, but when spoken by a Master they carry something of the beyond; they carry some silence, some meditativeness, some of his experience, because they come from his innermost core.

It is like passing through a garden: even though you have not touched a single flower, but when you reach home you can still feel the fragrance of the garden; your clothes have caught it, your hairs have caught it. The pollen of the flowers was in the wind. You have not touched anything, but the fragrance was in the air; it has become something part of you.

The Master simply means a certain noosphere. The word "noosphere" is coined by Chardin, one of the very strange men of this century. He was basically trained as a scientist — he was a geologist — but his whole heart was that of a mystic. It is very unfortunate that he belonged to the Catholic Church, and the Pope prevented him from publishing any of his ideas while he was alive. And he was such an obedient person, he followed the order, so while he was alive nobody came to know about him. His books were published only posthumously, but those books are of tremendous import, because he was a scientist and yet a meditator, a man of great prayer; there is a certain synthesis. His approach is very clear, like that of a scientist and yet full of poetry.

But the world missed a direct communion with Chardin. The Catholic Church is the culprit — they prohibited. They have always been against anything new happening in the world. So only when he died his friends started publishing his books. Now the people who have come across his books can see what the world has missed, because now they are only words — beautiful words.

Chardin coined the word "noosphere". We are acquainted with the word "atmosphere"; atmosphere means the air that surrounds you, the climate that surrounds you. Noosphere means the world of subtle vibes, thoughts, feelings, that surrounds you.

A Master carries a noosphere around himself; I call it the "Buddhafield". Jains have a very specific idea about it; they worked very hard to find it, exactly what it is. And I think no other tradition has discovered all the details about the Buddhafield that surrounds a Master like Mahavira. Jains have worked — they were a little bit scientific in their approach — and I agree with their discoveries about the Buddhafield.

They say a Master has a Buddhafield around himself extending in all the directions for twenty-four miles — a circle with the radius of twenty-four miles becomes a Buddhafield whenever a person becomes enlightened. No other tradition has worked it out with such scientific detail — even they have measured the length, how big is the circle that surrounds the awakened person.

Whosoever is a little bit open entering in the Buddhafield will start feeling something strange that he has never felt before. But it happens only if one is open.

Many people ask me, "If we come here and don't become sannyasins, will not we be able to receive your grace?" From my side there is no problem: I am not addressing my energy to anybody in particular, it is simply there. It is a noosphere; it all depends on you. To become a sannyasin simply means that you are dropping all your defenses, that you are withdrawing all your arguments, that you are opening your windows and doors to me — that's all! It is a gesture from your side that you are vulnerable, that you are receptive, sensitive, that you are available. I am available whether you are a sannyasin or not; it does not matter. I am available even to these poles of the Buddha Hall! But what can I do? — if they are not orange they will miss!

A sannyasin simply means a readiness to receive. The energy is there; if something is missing it is on your part.

All the Masters of all the ages have depended on the spoken word for the simple reason because the spoken word comes directly from their innermost core. It carries the fragrance of their inner world, the richness of their inner world, the beauty of their inner world. It is soaked with their inner being, it is full of their energy. By the time it is written it will be not the same thing.

The spoken word means a communion between the Master and the disciple. The written word is not a communion, it is a communication; anybody can read it. The student can read it, he need not be a disciple. The enemy can read it, he need not even be a student. Somebody can read it just to find faults in it, just to find something so that he can argue against it.

But with the spoken word it is totally different. Even if the opponent comes, the spoken word dances around him. There is every possibility that although he had come with a conclusion, a fixed idea, his fixed idea may become a little bit loosened, he may become a little relaxed. He may start looking again before he takes any decision. He may start putting his a priori ideas aside. The rumors that he has heard can be easily put aside if he comes in the contact of the spoken word.

That's why the disciple who has written these beautiful sutras, recorded them — they are his notes — says:

This we have heard from the enlightened ones.

He is not saying that, "This is my experience." He is not saying that, "I am the writer of these beautiful sutras." His humbleness... that is the sign of a disciple. It has disappeared from the world; the very phenomenon of the disciple has become more and more rare, it has become almost non-existential. Otherwise there was nobody to prevent him to sign these sutras. He could have said, "These are mine."

Just a few days before a book in Marathi was published from Bombay. He has stolen a whole chapter from one of my books — the whole chapter without any change; not even a single word is added or deleted. And he has used that whole chapter as an introduction to his book. It is one of my introductions to Ashtavakra Gita, and when it was found a letter was written to him that, "How it has happened?" He didn't reply. Then a notice was given to him — then he came running and he said, "I was not aware of the law." But he was told it is not a question only of law.

"Were you not aware that you are translating the whole chapter into Marathi without changing a single word? You have not mentioned from where you have taken it, you have not asked our permission, but that is not much important. You have not even mentioned... even that is not much important. We had written a letter to you; you have not even replied to that."

People have lost all sincerity, and this is not so with the ordinary people — even it happens sometimes with my sannyasins. When they go back to their countries and they start a center there, sooner or later, only a few of them — but that too should not happen — start functioning as if what they are saying is their own. They start pretending that they are enlightened people, that they are Masters. If you are enlightened people, there is no problem, if you are a Master there is no problem, but you are not! And they go on coming to me, and they go on asking the same stupid questions they used to ask before, but back in their own countries they start behaving as if they are enlightened or Masters in their own right. They repeat my words.

Just the other day I had seen a booklet of a commune in Spain. The commune is absolutely run on the same lines as my commune, even they call themselves "the orange people". They call themselves sannyasins, they use orange clothes, they wear a mala. The only difference is that there is no locket in the mala, instead of the locket they have this Hindu symbol aum. They do Dynamic Meditation, they do Kundalini Meditation, they do Nadabrahma. They change their names — they use Sanskrit names, Indian names — but they don't want to be known that they belong to me. A commune of thirty people behaving independently.

And the man who is the head has never been here, but he goes on sending his people. Many people have come here, they take sannyas here, and when they go back the only change that has to be done is to drop the picture from the locket and put aum, and everything is okay!

In their brochure they have used my words, my statements, without mentioning me, just translated into Spanish, and it has become their own. And you will be surprised: they run a mala shop, a boutique, a Vrindavan. It is a true carbon copy!

People have lost all truthfulness. The person who has taken these notes has not even given his name, but he again and again repeats:

This we have heard from the enlightened ones.

And remember, he does not say, "This I have heard" even we have heard. He is simply representing the whole world of the Masters' disciples. He is not even using the word "I", that this I have heard.

This we have heard from the enlightened ones.

"Those who have known, we have heard it from them." He does not bring himself in at all.

Just the other day I have received a letter from Sudha. Few days before she wrote a letter that, "Osho, I am in a great conflict: I cannot leave you, I cannot live without you, and yet when I am in the commune I don't feel absolutely surrendered to you. That makes me feel sad. I want to be absolutely surrendered, to drop all my mind and all my ego. That I cannot do, and because I could not do it you have sent me to the West. But I cannot live in the West either! I hanker for your presence, I want to be back home as soon as possible."

She talked this with one of our sannyasins, Gunakar, who runs a beautiful center in Germany, Karuna. She talked to him on the phone and Gunakar wrote her a letter that, "You come to me and I will help you to get rid of Osho, I will help you to go beyond this attachment."

Now he runs a center for me — helping people to get rid of me! He was here. Twice he tried to become enlightened and failed! He will declare he has become enlightened and then he will come to his senses again. Now running a center he is imitating; now he is trying to help people to get beyond the attachment.

Sudha has done a good job of writing a letter to him that, "I don't want to get rid, I want to get rid of myself, not Osho! And I don't need your help. First you help yourself Physician, heal thyself first!"

But Gunakar is getting into stupid ideas... just few days before he wrote a letter to all the members of UNO that, "I represent Osho, I represent the hierarchy of the esoteric Masters, and I want you to do these things. Unless these things are done, the world is not going to be saved."

Now he is trying to save the world — he has not even been able to save himself!

But these egoistic ideas are bound to happen because deep down the ego has lived for so long that it does not want to leave you. Even when you think you have dropped it, it simply hides somewhere, in some dark corner of your unconsciousness, and it starts functioning from there.

This is the true way of a disciple to say:

This We Have Heard From The Enlightened Ones.

Meditation And Action —
He Who Knows These Two Together,
Through Action Leaves Death Behind
And Through Meditation Gains Immortality.

Words which should be written in gold, far more precious than any diamonds can ever be. This is my whole approach:

Meditation And Action —
He Who Knows These Two Together...

It is so clear! And in India people go on reciting the Isha Upanishad, but I don't think that they ever ponder over what they are reciting. They are all escapists, they are all renouncers of the world — they have left action behind. If they have understood the Isha Upanishad and its message they will be my sannyasins, not the old, traditional ones.

My sannyasin represents togetherness of action and meditation He is in the world and yet not of it. He is like a lotus flower coming out of dirty mud, but transforming the mud into the beauty of a lotus, living in a lake yet untouched by the water, absolutely untouched.

A true sannyasin should be in the world, in action, and deeply rooted in meditation. Your roots should be in meditation, your branches should be in action. You should be like a tree: its branches go high in the sky, they are longings for the stars; it goes on rising high. But remember, a tree goes high only if its roots go deep, in the same proportion: deeper the roots, higher the branches; higher the branches, deeper the roots. They balance each other. Roots have to be in meditation and branches in the world — in the full sunlight, dancing in the wind, whispering with the clouds — and deep inside you, in the inner world, growing roots into meditation. Then you will be a full tree.

Up to now two types of people have existed: a few have existed without roots — of course, without roots a tree is bound to be false — and few people have existed just as roots without trees, and just roots are ugly. Have you seen beautiful roots? Flowers are beautiful, but flowers need foliage, branches, the sun, the moon, the stars, the rain, the wind — they need the whole world — then those colorful flowers... these both have to be together; only then you will be an integrated, whole being.

The worldly has only branches but no roots, hence he is dull, juiceless, dry, dead, a corpse, just somehow dragging, out of old habit. And your monks, your nuns — Catholic Hindu, Jain, whatsoever their denomination — they are just roots, ugly, not worth looking at. No question of respect, not even worth looking once — the question of twice does not arise — and without any flowers.

My sannyasin has to be both: with roots in the interior world and with flowers in the exterior world. My sannyasin has to be both: capable of intellect and also capable of intuition. There is no need to choose: whatsoever God has given has to be used to its fullest.

> Through Action He Leaves Death Behind
> And Through Meditation Gains Immortality.

It is only through action, through creativity, that you go beyond death. Action functions as negative: it is the art of removing hindrances. For example, you are digging a well: Action means removing all the layers of earth and the rocks — if sometimes needed, dynamiting the rocks, drilling so that you can find the water sources. The function of action is negative: it is removing hindrances, obstacles, obstructions. And the function of meditation is realization of that which is. When the water starts coming up, meditation is drinking of the water to quench the thirst. Both are needed: action to remove the rocks and meditation to make you capable of drinking the ultimate, the wine of the ultimate.

> Through Action Leave Death Behind
> And Through Meditation Gain Immortality.

And these are two aspects of the same phenomenon. If you

don't leave death behind, how you can enter into the world of immortality? Leave time behind so that you can enter into the timeless, into the deathless.

Into a blinding darkness go they who idolize the absolute.

Philosophy idolizes the absolute. Bradley, Hegel, Shankara, they idolize the absolute and they deny the relative. The relative means it is illusory; absolute is true and whatsoever is relative is illusory.

Into an even greater darkness go they who dote on the relative.

Science emphasizes on the relative. Albert Einstein discovered the theory of relativity. Jainism has a little bit of scientific attitude, hence Jains were the first to contemplate on the theory of relativity. Albert Einstein without knowing it is a Jain! Before Albert Einstein, twenty-five centuries before him, Jains have discovered sayadvada; sayadvada means the theory of relativity. Einstein says everything is relative. Sayadvada can literally be translated as "perhapsism": everything is just a perhaps; nothing is absolutely certain, just a perhaps.

If you had asked Mahavira, "Does God exist?" he will say, "Perhaps." If you ask him, "Are you absolutely sure about it?" he will say, "Perhaps." He will never budge from his perhaps. Everything is only a perhaps, because everything is relative. Nothing can be said absolutely, certainly, categorically. It depends, and one thing can be looked from many standpoints.

Sayadvada — "perhapsism" — has seven standpoints. If you ask about God, Mahavira will give you seven statements. He will confuse you more than you were ever confused before! He will say, "Perhaps God is" — his first statement. "Perhaps God is not" — his second statement. "Perhaps God is both" — his third statement. Fourth: "Perhaps God is and inexpressible" — his fourth. "Perhaps God is not and is inexpressible" — fifth. "Perhaps God is and is not both, and also is inexpressible." You may have come to him with a little bit of understanding for or against, but he will destroy all your standpoints. He will give you the whole perspective, from all the standpoints.

That's what Albert Einstein has done, of course in a more scientific way; Mahavira's way is far more philosophical. Albert Einstein used to say that, "Only at the most one dozen people in the whole world understand what I am saying." Not that there are not many more intelligent people in the world, but the very idea of relativity has something fundamentally wrong about it.

Something can be relative only if you accept the absolute. If you don't accept the absolute, then what do you mean by relative? Even the meaning of the word "relative" loses all significance; it loses meaning. Relative simply means that which is not absolute, but what is absolute? According to Albert Einstein there is nothing absolute, all is relative. And according to the absolutists there is nothing relative, all is absolute. Then what do you mean by absolute? The very term has meaning only in contrast to the relative.

Upanishads are very clear. They say:
Into A Blinding Darkness Go They Who Idolize The Absolute.

Because they have chosen again one side of the coin: the unchanging, the axle. And:

Into An Even Greater Darkness Go They Who Dote On The Relative.

They have chosen the other side, the wheel, the moving, the momentary, the temporary, the changing. But change is possible only on the foundation of no-change. The wheel cannot move without the axle. And what is the meaning of axle if there is no wheel? They are together and they are meaningful only in their togetherness.

Isha Upanishad is trying to make it clear that: never choose, remain choicelessly aware and accept life as it is don't impose any choice of your own. The absolute is there, the relative is there. Your mind is relative, but your consciousness is absolute. Your body changes, your mind changes — they are like a wheel — but your witnessing consciousness is like an axle; it remains always the same, never changing. It is on that axle that the mind-and-the-body wheel moves. And they are not against each other; they are supporting each other, they are complementary to each other. This high synthesis is the message of the Upanishads

> For It Is Other Than The Relative,
> It Is Other Than The Absolute.
> Because It Is Beyond Both And More.
>
> This we have heard from the enlightened ones.

The disciple again and again repeats it so that you don't forget that he is not speaking on his own authority, he is simply recording the words of the Master. This sincerity is part of disciplehood, and only through this sincerity a disciple one day can become enlightened.

Enlightenment happens only if you become more and more sincere and authentic. And you have to be very alert because the ways of the ego are very subtle: it would like to claim that which you don't have. Beware of the ego!

> *Aum*
> *Purnam Adaha*
> *Purnam Idam*
> *Purnat Purnamudachyate*
> *Purnasya Purnamadaya*
> *Purnameva Vashishyate*
> *Aum*
> That Is The Whole.
> This Is The Whole.
> From Wholeness Emerges Wholeness.
> Wholeness Coming From Wholeness,
> Wholeness Still Remains.

10

The Eternal Religion

Question 1

OSHO,

We Indians know that we have been caught in serious diseases for centuries, but when such a great doctor like you refuses us, what will become of us?

— *Prem Vinod*

I am not refusing anybody, but I have to refuse your diseases, certainly. I cannot accept your diseases — no physician can do that. And those who accept your diseases are your enemies. Your diseases have to be mercilessly destroyed, whoever you are — Indian, German, English. Diseases come in all forms, sizes and shapes. You may be a Hindu or a Christian or a Jew; it does not matter.

The whole past of humanity has been full of many fundamental errors, but they have existed for so long that they have become almost part of you. Hence the feeling, Vinod, that I reject you. I am simply rejecting the disease. but you are identified with the disease. You think your diseases, the sum total of your diseases, is what you are. That's not true — you are not just your diseases. You are something beyond all that has happened to you in the whole past. All that has happened is only a conditioning; it can be dropped, it has to be dropped. Hence I condemn it, but your ego feels hurt. I cannot help; I cannot have any compassion for any kind of disease.

But when diseases exist tor a long time and they are given from one generation to another generation they become very respectable. You forget that they are diseases; you start thinking that they are specialties to you.

For example, T.M. Ramachandran has asked: "OSHO, why do you say that nothing has been happening in the east? Great, great things have been happening in the east as well. Is not hinduism and its way of life the greatest religion in the world?"

And what is this hindu way of life? It is utterly life-negative! Even to call it a way of life is not right. It can be called a way of death, but not a way of life. How anything life-negative can become a philosophy of life?

Hinduism teaches you to reject life, to renounce life. You worship the escapist people; you call them saints, mahatmas. Those who have gone against the world, those who have rejected the world, those who have condemned the world and all that it contains, they are thought to be people of God.

God exists in the manifest world as the unmanifest center of it all. The moment you reject the flower you also reject its fragrance; if you escape from the flower you are escaping from the fragrance too -- and God is the fragrance of existence. Those who go against life are going basically against God.

You have heard the proverb: Man proposes and God disposes. Hinduism does just the opposite: God proposes, man disposes. It is God's proposition — this existence, this life, but man disposes it.

George Gurdjieff, one of the greatest Masters of this century, used to say that, "Your mahatmas are all against God" — and he is absolutely right, one hundred percent right, because your mahatamas are denouncers. They negate. They make you feel guilty of love, of life, of laughter. They make you feel guilty if you are joyous, if you are cheerful. They make you feel guilty if you enjoy food, if you enjoy friendship, if you enjoy any kind of relationship. They make you feel guilty for all that you enjoy and they impose things upon you for which there is no enjoyment in you.

All that you can do with these negative attitudes is nourish your ego. Hence your mahatmas are the most egoistic people in the world. But when one starts thinking of diseases as if they are something great, then it becomes very difficult for him to listen to the physician.

I don't reject anybody, Vinod. To me it is all the same whether you are a Hindu or a Mohammedan or a Christian. Your diseases are a little bit different but not basically, because all the religions that have existed in the past have used one similar strategy, and that is to create guilt. That has been the technique of the priest to dominate you: make people feel guilty of small joys — and of course those joys are natural and spontaneous.

And when a person becomes guilty of his own nature he starts rejecting himself, he starts dying. It is a slow kind of suicide. He becomes sad, he becomes drained off His life loses flavor. And then of course, trembling, he has to go to the priest, because the priest knows the way how to go beyond this guilt. The priest creates the guilt in the first place — it is his trade secret — and then you have to go to the priest because there is nobody else who can guide you. That is the business of the priest: to guide you about spiritual affairs. And you are feeling so sad, so miserable; you need help, you need somebody to support you. You need somebody to teach you ways, means, methods so that you can get rid of your guilt.

But the priest goes on creating more guilt in you. He creates so much fear of life in you that Hinduism became obsessed with the idea how to get rid of birth and death, how to get rid of aavagaman — coming and going into existence.

Life is so beautiful!

Rabindranath, one of the great poets of all the times. was on his deathbed. A friend told him — a very religious friend. of course — that, "Pray to God that this should be your last life, you should be freed."

Rabindranath opened his eyes... his last moments but he became angry and he said, "Shut up! I am praying to God that 'Your life has been such a beautiful gift to me that give it to me again and again. I would like to come back to see the sunrise, the sunset, the starry night, the flowers, a bird on the wing, the green trees, your rivers, your mountains, your people... I would like to come again and again and again! It is so vast and inexhaustible, and it has not been a misery to me."

Rabindranath is against your whole tradition of the so-called Hinduism. He is one of the most insightful persons that was born into this unfortunate country. He lived joyously, he lived a life of celebration. He loved poetry, created poetry He loved painting, he created many paintings. He sang, he danced.

This is true prayer! And because of this I say Rabindranath is not a Hindu. He was so much against renunciation that he dared even to write a poem against Gautam the Buddha. The poem is of immense beauty and of great meaning too.

Buddha has left his young wife and a child who was just one day old. Buddha was only twenty-nine years of age and he escaped — that was the ancient Hindu way. He escaped into the forest to find out God.

Rabindranath describes his renunciation and describes that when he become enlightened he came back home to share his experience.

Yashodhara, his wife, asked him one question which he could not answer. He stood before Yashodhara with his eyes looking at the earth, ashamed. Only Rabindranath could have dared such a poem. What was the question that Yashodhara had asked? She had asked a very simple question: that, "Now that you have become enlightened, please answer one of my questions that has been haunting my days and my nights for all these years that you have been away. Since you left I have been tortured by this question and I have been waiting, because only you can answer it.

"The question is: whatsoever you have found in the deep silence of the forest, was it not possible to find it here in the palace with me, with your child, with your old father who has almost gone blind crying and weeping for you? And just look at me! I have become so old within these six years, just waiting every moment for you, waking up in the night again and again, maybe — you had left in the night, you may have come again — dreaming about you. Ask your son; he has been continuously asking me, 'Where is my father?' The whole kingdom is sad, the palace is sad; it has become a cemetery. Just answer one of my questions: Whatsoever you have found in the forest, was it not possible to find it here?"

And Buddha stood ashamed. He could not answer.

This is a parable invented by Rabindranath, but has great significance. Rabindranath is saying God can be found now and here. There is no need to go into the forest; there is no need to renounce the wife, the children, the old parents. There is no need to go against life. Going against life is like trying to go upstream, fighting with the river — an unnecessary fight. Relax, rest, enjoy... and God can be found any where because he is everywhere.

Hinduism is life-negative; that's why it has respected the ascetics. Now, the ascetics are nothing but masochist people, absolutely ill, psychologically ill. The ascetic is the person who enjoys torturing himself, and Hindus have respected the ascetics. The more you torture yourself, the greater a saint you are. So if you lie down on a bed of thorns, thousands will gather to worship you. If you fast for months, then your name and fame will spread to all the corners of the country.

And one of the strangest things is, nobody ever asks, "What this man has contributed to life?" Lying on the bed of thorns is not a contribution; it does not make life more beautiful. it does not enrich existence in any way. Just by fasting for months is not any creative act — it is destructive, it is really suicidal.

Hinduism is suicidal. That's why it was possible for twenty-two centuries for this country to remain in slavery — for the simple reason nobody is interested in life, so what does it matter who rules it? It is all dream, it is all maya. Let anybody rule it!

This country has lost its soul, because only people who love freedom can have souls. This country only talks about the soul, but slaves can't have souls. But slaves can always rationalize; in fact they have to rationalize, just to console themselves.

And Hindus have become great rationalizers; they rationalize everything: "It is late, nothing can be done about it. God has decided so. Not even a leaf falls from a tree without the will of God, so how can the country be a slave without the will of God? He must have chosen; we have simply to accept the fate."

And when one starts accepting the fate one becomes lazy, sloppy, lousy, because then nothing is left for you to do.

It was the morning after, and he sat groaning and holding his head.

"Well, if you hadn't drunk so much last night you wouldn't feel so bad now," said his wife tartly.

"My drinking had nothing to do with it," he answered. "I went to bed feeling wonderful and woke up feeling awful. It was the sleep that did it!"

You can always rationalize. You are not responsible — whatsoever had to happen had to happen. What can you do about it?

India has remained the poorest country in the world, and nobody thinks that Hinduism is the cause of it. If you believe in fate you will not endeavor to become rich, you will not make any effort to be scientific, you will not create technology, industry. You will simply wait: whenever God changes his will, things will change. As far as you are concerned, nothing can be done about it.

A newly-rich dame had bought a summer place in the Himalayas and hired a village woman to do the housework.

"I am a person of few words," she haughtily told the old woman. "If I beckon with my finger, that means 'come'."

"Very well, madam," replied the old Indian woman. "I am a person of few words myself. If I shake my head from side to side, that means 'I am not coming.'"

Just watch — what you are talking about? A great religion, the

The Eternal Religion

greatest religion, and what it has given to you? Poverty, starvation, illness. The whole country is living undernourished, sixty percent of people are starving, and nothing is being done. Problems go on increasing, and Hindus simply go on sitting, worshipping the elephant god, Ganesha, or the monkey god, Hanuman, or the holy mother cow, and hoping that these elephants, monkeys and cows are going to help! It has become now so deep-rooted that something drastic is needed.

That's what I am trying to do. Naturally I will offend the unintelligent crowds; I can only be understood by the very intelligent few.

Barfly: "What's that drink you are mixing?"

Bartender: "I call it a rum overture."

Barfly: "What's in it?"

Bartender: "Sugar, a dash of clam juice, and rum."

Barfly: "How is it?"

Bartender: "Stimulating. The sugar gives you energy and the clam juice gives you drive."

Barfly: "And the rum?"

Bartender: "Ah, that! That gives you ideas about what to do with all that energy and drive."

I am mixing a rum overture! You need some drive and you need some ideas what to do with that drive and energy.

I am not rejecting anyone, Vinod, but I have to reject all these life-negative attitudes.

India has become a country of hypocrites for the simple reason: whenever you deny nature it is bound to happen because the nature will assert, is bound to assert. You can repress it for a time being but not for ever, and whatsoever is repressed will take revenge with you. It will come back. with vengeance it will come back.

So on the one hand you will see the Hinduist morality the puritanism, and on the other hand you will see the Hindu obscenity.

The Kamasutra of Vatsyayana was the first book on obscenity in the whole world. Only in this century Havelock Ellis, Sigmund Freud, Kinsey, Masters and Johnson, these people have started thinking about sexual postures, sex energy and what it is all about and what can be done about it. But Vatsyayana's Kamasutras are three thousand years old. Vatsyayana was a Hindu, and Hindus have respected him. They have called him Maharishi, the great seer. On the one hand the so-called moralists and on the other hand the Kamasutras of Vatsyayana and the Kokashastra of Pundit Koka. Pundit Koka was a Kashmiri Hindu brahmin of the highest caste and his book is fifteen hundred years old, and one of the ugliest in the world. And he was an ordained Hindu.

And who has created the temples of Konarak, Puri and Khajuraho? On the one hand Hindus have been teaching Brahmacharya, celibacy, as the highest goal for humanity on the other hand they were making sculpture so obscene that it is incomparable. Nowhere else in the world exists any temple like Khajuraho temples. And it was not only one temple, it was a whole city of temples. At least one hundred temples still survive; there must have been a thousand temples — ruins are there — and each temple has thousands of obscene postures. They must have taken hundreds of years to make. And if you see Khajuraho you will not believe...

These people who publish magazines like Playboy and Playgirl should come and learn from Khajuraho! Whatsoever they are doing is just ordinary. They cannot compete with Hindu fantasy — for the simple reason because they cannot compete with Hindu repression! Once you repress something natural then it starts coming into your mind, it starts moving towards your head. It may disappear from the sex center, which was a natural phenomenon, but now it enters in your head.

This has driven the whole Hindu culture towards a very schizophrenic existence. It seems almost impossible how to relate these two phenomena going together.

Pundit Koka of Kashmir... and he is not alone. In the name of Tantra almost ninety-nine charlatans have been bringing sex from the back door. In the tradition of Tantra you will find only one percent authentic Masters; ninety-nine percent are just pseudo, tricky people. In the name of Tantra they are bringing the whole sexuality from the back door.

Pundit Koka says that if you really want to move deep into the phenomenon of sex then you have to find a woman of the lowest caste. She has not to be your wife, because with your wife you will not be able to enter into a really fantastic world of sexuality. Her topography is known to you, her geography is known to you; there is nothing to explore. So find a woman who is not your wife.

Secondly, the woman has to come from the lowest caste because they are more alive people. The higher the caste, the people are more and more bloodless. If you go to the lower castes then people are more alive, more wild. Hence I say to you that Coca-Cola must have originated with Pundit Koka — Cola must have been his girlfriend. That's why it is so juicy! It is a discovery of the great tantrikas — Coca-Cola!

I am not rejecting Hindus, Jews, Jains or anybody. I have no antagonism with anybody. I don't belong to any tradition, hence for me all the traditions are the same; but because I don't belong to any tradition I can see clearly the diseases. When you belong to a tradition you cannot see; your eyes are clouded, you are prejudiced.

Repression brings hypocrisy, and you can see it in India everywhere. People will talk that the world is illusory and the same time they will be as greedy about money as nobody else in the world is. This is strange — but not really. If you go deep into it, because they are denying something natural... The world is given to you by God. If you deny it you will have to become obsessed with it; every denial becomes obsession. "Renounce the money!" these people go on saying...

If you go to Vinoba Bhave, who represents Hindu tradition, and you take a few notes in your hand, he will immediately close his eyes — he does not see money. Now poor paper, just printed, and makes the Hindu mahatma so afraid that he closes his eyes! It cannot be the currency notes; it must be some deep fear, some greed. He does not touch money.

On the one hand these people go on saying that gold is nothing but dust, but they will not touch gold.

I had asked Vinoba when I met him... He was very eager to meet me, so I said, "Okay, now it is your responsibility. If you want to meet me then I am no more responsible. Whatsoever happens, transpires, transpires!"

I asked him, "If you say that gold is just dust, why don't you touch gold? You touch dust!"

In fact, Vinoba Bhave believes in naturopathy — mud packs, mud baths. He is very at ease with mud, enjoys it! Then what is wrong with gold? I take gold baths, gold packs! If It is the same, why bother? But it is not the same. If he is afraid of touching gold and is not afraid of touching dust, then he is being cunning, deceptive — not only to others but to himself too. Then don't call gold just dust; then gold has some speciality which dust has not got.

You will find Hindus more greedy than anybody else, more full of sexuality than anybody else, more full of sexual fantasies than anybody else, more full of attachment than anybody else. And still you go on saying that Hinduism is the greatest religion in the world? What nonsense you are talking about? Hindus are the most dishonest people for the simple reason they have not been honest to accept the realities of life.

A man met a friend he had not seen for years and asked him how he was feeling.

"Awful," replied the friend. "In addition to my high blood pressure I have got arthritis and bronchitis."

"I am sorry to hear it. What about your job?"

"Oh, I'm still at the same thing I've been doing for the past twenty years — I'm selling health foods."

This man must have been a Hindu! — selling health foods, and suffering from high blood pressure, arthritis and bronchitis.

We all know the legend how Diogenes, the great Greek mystic, used to go about with a lantern looking for an honest man, even in the bright daylight. Some modern cynics ask why the cynic philosopher didn't go about in broad daylight without his lantern. Others ask why he didn't look in a mirror. Naturally enough, the legend appears in jokelore. One story tells how Diogenes had spent several hours after dark searching crime-ridden New Delhi for an honest man, and was very weary. A passerby, recognizing him, asked, "What luck?"

"Everything considered, not so bad," reported Diogenes. "I still have my lantern!"

In Delhi that is really luck if you can save your lantern, even in the bright day! Some politician is bound to grab it!

The Indian politician is the worst kind of politician in the world, for the simple reason because he belongs to a very ugly, ill, canceric civilization. Hinduism is on its deathbed, or maybe it is already dead and people are worshipping a corpse, because it stinks!

I would like to change this whole situation. Hindus, if they are courageous enough, will disconnect themselves from their past; that will be a resurrection. And they can prove, certainly, a great blessing to the whole world, because for centuries they have not worked; their potential has remained unactualized. It is like a farm which has not been cultivated for centuries. If you cultivate it right now it will give you the best crop possible, because for centuries it has been accumulating potential.

Hindus can assert a new era in the world. If they resurrect, if they drop out of their old past, if they disconnect themselves from their tradition, if they can have a new birth then they may prove the greatest intelligent people in the world. Their contribution can not only transform this country, it can be a boon, a blessing to life on earth, because they have genius — gone wrong — they have intelligence — gone astray. If it comes to the right dimension it will be good for their own health, it will be good for the health of the whole world.

And the same is true about other races too. Any race that remains clinging with the past remains clinging with corpses. One has to live in the present because the future is born out of the present. And India is living in the past. Out of past nothing is born; clinging to the past is wasting your time.

Everything in India is past-oriented. People are reading the story of Rama, and these are the days all over the country they will be playing the drama of Rama. Every year they go on playing the same drama; for thousands of years they have been doing it. They are not even bored by it! It seems they have lost all intelligence. They go on seeing the same thing, repeating the same thing, as if there is nothing else to do. And they go on talking about the golden age — in the past, it is always in the past.

Remember this: a child always thinks good days are to come; the old man always thinks good days, golden days are past. The child is future-oriented, the old man is past-oriented, and the young man, if he is really young — which is very rarely so... Physically there are so many young people in the world; they constitute the majority. But many of them either are still in their childhood psychologically, and many of them have already passed into old age psychologically.

If somebody is really young he lives in the present. Now is the only time for him and here is the only place for him. He does not waver between past and future, because both are non-existential; that which exists is the present. The young person lives in the present, and the same is true about civilizations.

The young civilization lives in the present, and if a civilization continuously lives in the present it remains young. That is the whole secret of remaining young. The new civilization, just born,

The Eternal Religion

immature, childish, lives in the future, and the old civilization lives in the past. You can immediately see and decide and categorize any civilization, to what category it belongs.

India lives in the past; it is getting old, shrinking. It has lost the joy of life, the youthfulness, the freshness. Countries like Russia, China live in the future. Their golden age is to come, when the classless society, the utopia conceived by Karl Marx will happen, when there will be no class, no poor, no rich, no one dominated and no one dominating, no bourgeoisie, no proletariat. When the classless society and the stateless society will be born, somewhere far away in the future, then humanity will have a golden age.

Countries like India live in the past; the golden age has passed long before. Man is falling down. There is great enthusiasm in China because the future seems to be very alluring; there is no enthusiasm in India. India became free before China, but China has been able to solve many problems which are of a vaster dimension than Indian problems because China has the greatest population in the world. But it has been able to solve those problems, it has been able to become a strong country.

India has remained poor; its problems have increased, and there seems to be no possibility that it can solve its problems the way it is moving. Its golden age has passed; there is no enthusiasm, there is no spirit. People are simply dragging.

America is young, lives in the moment, hence there is great exploration going on about everything: science, religion, philosophy, art, new forms of art, new methods, new ways to reach to the moon, to the Mars and finally to the stars, new methods, quicker methods to enter into meditation, into samadhi. In every dimension America is interested to explore; the young man's adventurous spirit is there. They are going to the farthest corners of the world to explore all possibilities.

India is old, dying; China is still born, just now growing towards a future; America is young.

Future can give you better possibilities than the past, but still future is non-existential; sooner or later you will get tired of it.

Russia is more tired than China because for sixty years they have been waiting and waiting, and now the hope is turning into a hopelessness. Now it is becoming more and more clear that that stateless society is never going to happen. In fact, the state has become more powerful than ever before. Even czar was not so powerful as Joseph Stalin was. Czar was thrown by revolution but in Russia now there is no possibility of any revolution. The state has become such a vast, powerful, technically equipped organization that nobody can revolt against it, nobody can organize any revolution against it. Even to talk anything against it is dangerous, even to think may be dangerous in few years, because now they are discovering that every child can be fixed with an electrode in the head and that electrode will go on informing the government computer what the person is thinking, what he is trying to do in his brain. Even brain waves can be traced, subtle indications can be discovered, and before the man has even uttered a single word he will disappear.

And those electrodes can do another work also: they can implant any idea in the person and you will never be aware that you are carrying an electrode inside your brain, because within your skull there is no sensitivity. If a stone is inserted inside your skull you will not feel that there is a stone. There are no sensitive nerves in the brain.

A person carried a bullet in his brain for nine years, absolutely unaware. By accident, through X-ray, it was discovered that in the First World War he had got hit by a bullet, and then the wound healed and the bullet remained inside for nine years, and he was not aware at all.

And electrodes are very small things; just they can be inserted when the child is born in the hospital. And of course in Russia every child is born in the hospital, so every child can be inserted with an electrode and that electrode will function in two ways — it will inform the government what the person is thinking, and it can do one thing more: the government can manipulate the person through the electrode; it can insert through radio waves, through remote control — ideas. And the person will think, "These are my

The Eternal Religion

ideas"; he will never think that these ideas are coming from some other source.

In Russia revolution is absolutely impossible, hence people are becoming more and more hopeless seeing that Marx had said state will wither away — once capitalism is gone there will be no need for the state — but the state has become more and more stronger. Marx' prediction has gone absolutely wrong: just the opposite has happened.

The same is going to happen to China. Right now they are very enthusiastic, but soon they will settle into the same slavery as Russia has settled.

The people who are past-oriented like the Hindus are living with a long, long dead past — and carrying it. It is a mountainous weight; they are crushed under it. And there is no hope in the future. The Hindus think that the best days were in the beginning; they don't believe in evolution, remember — they believe in involution. Evolution means we are reaching to higher peaks. Hindus believe we are deteriorating, coming lower, every day, the highest age was in the beginning; now we are at the lowest, kali yuga, the last. This is the very low state of humanity and there is no hope.

A country to be really alive, to be really adventurous, exploring, enjoying, celebrating, has to be constantly young, neither in the past nor in the future. I am against both the Hindu approach and the communist approach. I would like the whole humanity to be young and to remain young forever, and the way to remain young is to go on dying to the past and don't bother too much about the future. Future will take its own course. When it comes, if we are here we will respond to it; otherwise our children will respond to it. Why bother about it too much?

Live right now. Live as deeply and passionately as you can, because that is the only way to discover God. That's the only source to uncover the hidden secrets of life. God is not against life, God is the innermost core of life. Hence I teach a life-affirmative religion. I don't teach Hinduism, Mohammedanism, Christianity; I only teach a kind of religiousness. The world is fed up with all these isms".

There are three hundred religions and at least three thousand sub-sects of those religions. The world needs one universal religiousness.

My sannyasins don't belong to any religion at all; they simply belong to a new phenomenon: a religionless religiousness. The essential of religion, of all the religions, will be saved, but the peripheral will have to be dropped, the non essential will have to be simply burned.

And the non-essential has grown too much in Hinduism it is ninety-nine percent non-essential. And the same is true about other religions too, more or less, because Hinduism is the oldest one. Christianity is only two thousand years old, Mohammedanism only fourteen hundred years old Sikhism only five hundred years old — of course, they are not that old so they have a little more life. But Hinduism, Jainism are very ancient — Jainism perhaps even older than Hinduism, hence more dead, hence more in the grave, not even on the deathbed Hinduism is on the deathbed at least Jainism is already in the grave!

We need a rejuvenation, not of something old but of the essential which is eternal. I call that eternal religiousness Sanatan Dharma: Ais Dhammo Sanantano — the eternal religion. It has nothing to do with Hinduism; it is non-temporal. Meditation is the most significant part of it, and out of meditation, the transformation of your whole character.

I am not against anybody but I have to say the truth as it is. I cannot compromise — truth is always uncompromising. I cannot be polite either, because that politeness will not help. I have to be mercilessly hammering, continuously, on all that is wrong and all that is ill. Chunk by chunk all the non-essential, ritualistic religion has to be destroyed. When only the essential is left you will see the youngness of it, the freshness of it the fragrance of it.

And the world is now in a great need, because man as he exists

The Eternal Religion

now cannot exist any more. Either he has to commit a global suicide or he has to come out of the past like a snake moving out of the old skin. He has to be reborn.

Only a new man can survive; the old man is incapable of survival in the future. Science has grown so much that unless we bring religion also to the same par there will be no balance. Religion is lagging far behind and science is growing every day so speedily that if we don't bring religion also to the present, science and religion cannot meet. And in that meeting is the only hope.

The meeting of science and religion will create the new man, the new synthesis.

Question 2

OSHO,

You have spoken many times about Zen Masters, and today you said that J. Krishnamurti is Zen and Zen means no teaching. Can you explain this point?

— Anand Alok

Zen certainly means no teaching at all, no doctrine. That is what J. Krishnamurti has been saying for fifty years or more. He never mentions the name Zen, but that does not make any difference; what he says is exactly, essentially the same.

But on one point there is a great difference. Zen says there is no teaching, truth cannot be taught. Nobody can give you the truth; truth has to be discovered within your own soul. It cannot be borrowed from the scriptures. It is not possible even to communicate it, it is inexpressible; by its very nature, intrinsically, it is indefinable. Truth happens to you in a wordless silence, in deep, deep meditation. When there is no thought no desire, no ambition, in that state of no-mind truth descends in you — or ascends in you. As far as the dimension of truth is concerned both are the same, because in the world of the innermost subjectivity height and depth mean the same. It is one dimension: the vertical dimension.

Mind moves horizontally, no-mind exists vertically. The moment the mind ceases to function — that's what meditation is all about: cessation of the mind, total cessation of the mind — your consciousness becomes vertical; depth and height are yours.

So either you can say truth descends as many mystics like Patanjali, Badnarayana, Kapil and Kanad have said. It is avataran — coming from the heights to you. Hence whenever a person becomes self-realized he is called an avatara. Avatara means truth has descended in him; the word avatara simply means descending from the above, from the beyond.

But the other expression is as valid. Adinatha, Neminatha, Mahavira, Gautam Buddha, these mystics have said that truth does not come from the beyond, it arises from the deepest source of your being. It is not something coming down but something rising up, welling up.

Both expressions are valid to me, two ways of saying the same thing: that the dimension is vertical. Either you can talk in terms of height or in terms of depth. But truth never comes from the outside, so nobody can teach you.

As far as this point is concerned, Krishnamurti is absolutely Zen. Truth cannot be taught, cannot be transmitted. Zen Masters — Bodhidharma, Lin Chi, Bokuju, Baso — they all have been emphasizing one point: that Zen is transmission beyond scriptures, beyond words. On this point J. Krishnamurti is in absolute agreement with Zen.

But there is one thing more in Zen which is missing in J. Krishnamurti, and because of that he has utterly failed. He could have been of great help and upliftment to humanity, but he has utterly failed. In fact, I don't know another name in the whole history of humanity who has so utterly failed as J. Krishnamurti. No other enlightened person has been such a failure. The other thing that is missing is the cause; it is a little bit delicate and you will have to be very attentive about it.

Zen says truth cannot be transmitted, hence it can only happen

The Eternal Religion

in a Master-disciple relationship. It cannot be taught so there is no question of a relationship between a teacher and a taught — because there is no teaching so there is no teacher and no taught. But it is a transmission. Transmission means heart to heart: teaching means head to head.

When the disciple and the Master meet, merge, melt into each other, it is a love affair, it is a deep, orgasmic experience, far more deeper than any love, because even lovers go on carrying their egos and egos are bound to clash, conflict. The Master and the disciple exist without egos. The Master's ego has evaporated — that's why he is a Master — and the disciple surrenders his ego to the Master.

And remember, by surrendering the ego the disciple is not surrendering anything in particular, because ego is just an idea and nothing else. It has no substance; it is made of the same stuff dreams are made of. When you surrender your dreams, what are you surrendering?

If you come to me and you say, "I offer all my dreams to you," you are offering, but I am not getting anything! And you may be thinking that you are offering great dreams of golden palaces and beautiful women and great treasures... you are offering great dreams, but I am not getting anything.

When you offer your ego to the Master you are offering something as far as you are concerned, because you think it is very substantial, very significant. When you surrender you think you are doing something great. As far as the Master is concerned he is simply laughing at the whole thing, because he knows what is your ego — just hot air! nothing much to brag about.

But device, a simple device, can help immensely. It is a device. The Master says, "Surrender the ego." When he says, "Surrender the ego," he is saying, "Give me that which you don't have at all but you believe that you have. Give me your belief — I am ready to take it. Let this excuse help you." You may not be able to drop it on your own, but in love with the Master you may be able, you may gather courage to risk. Love encourages you to risk. In love you can go to any lengths. When you are in love with the Master and he says, "Give me your ego," how can you say no?

To be with a Master means in a state of saying yes, yes, and again yes! It is an absolute yes, unconditional yes. So when he says, "Give me your ego," you simply give your ego to the Master. To you it is very important; to him it has no meaning, no substance, no existence, but he accepts it.

The moment you drop your ego the meeting starts happening. Now two zeros start moving into each other. Two lovers enter into each other's bodies; that is a physical phenomenon and the orgasm that happens is a physical thing. The Master and disciple are lovers of the spiritual plane: two zeros, two egoless beings enter into each other. In that merger something is transpired. Not that the Master gives you something, not that you take something, but because of the meeting something happens, out of the meeting something happens — something which is greater than the Master and greater than the disciple, something more than the meeting of these two, something transcendental.

That part is missing in Krishnamurti. He says truth cannot be taught, but he has missed the other point. Yes, it cannot be taught... but he is a logical person and that is his problem. He is trying to put his enlightenment very logically; he does not want to bring any illogicality in it, any paradox in it.

Now Zen people don't bother about logic; they live the ultimate paradox. They go on saying there is no teaching and truth cannot be taught, and still Zen Masters are there and Zen disciples are there. And people have raised questions, skeptical people have always raised questions that: "What is this? On the one hand you say truth cannot be taught, and on the other hand why you initiate, why you accept people?"

And the Zen Masters have always laughed, because this paradox cannot be explained. If you want to know it really you have to become a disciple, you have to become a participant, you have to become part of the mystery; only then you will have the taste of it. It is a taste; no explanation can help. If you have tasted sugar you

The Eternal Religion

know it is sweet, but no explanation can give you the idea of sweetness. If you have seen the light you know what it is, but to the blind man you cannot explain; it is utterly futile.

Zen Masters have never bothered, hence their statements are very paradoxical.

One Zen Master, Ikkyu, was staying in a temple, just an overnight stay, but it was a cold night and he was shivering. In the middle of the night he got up and found one of Buddha's statues, a wooden statue, and burned it, and was very happy with the fire and the warmth.

The priest of the temple, seeing the light and the fire inside the temple, could not believe what is happening. He was a little suspicious when he had allowed this Ikkyu to stay for the night in the temple, but he had not thought that he will do such a thing — "He will put the whole temple on fire!" He rushed in and he found he had burned one of the most beautiful statues of the Buddha. And he was, of course, angry and he shouted at Ikkyu that, "What have you done? And you think you are a Buddhist? And you are wearing the yellow robes of the Buddhist monk! And I have even heard that not only that you are a Buddhist monk, you are a great Master and you have many followers! And what have you done?" The statue was completely burned!

Ikkyu took his staff and started searching in the ashes for something. The priest asked, "What are you looking for?"

He said, "I am looking for Buddha's bones."

In the East we call the bones "flowers". When a man dies we collect his bones after the body is completely burned; those bones are called "flowers".

So he said, "I am looking for Buddha's flowers."

Even the priest could not resist laughing. He said, "You are crazy! How can you find flowers in a wooden statue?"

Now was the turn of Ikkyu to laugh, and he laughed and he

said, "Then you are not so stupid as I thought! Bring... there are two more statues in the temple and it is still a long night. And why don't you also join? It is so warm, and we will burn those other two statues also. When there are no bones in it, certainly it is not a real Buddha — just wood."

The priest became so much afraid of this madman, he threw him out. It was dangerous to keep him inside the temple — he may burn other two statues! The temple had only three statues.

In the morning when the priest opened the doors he saw Ikkyu bowing down just in front of the temple before a milestone. He had put a few flowers — must have gathered some wild flowers — he has put those flowers on the milestone and was doing his morning prayers and meditations. And he was repeating the famous Buddhist mantra: "Buddham Sharanam Gachchhami — I go to the feet of the Master, Buddha. Sangham Sharanam Gachchhami — I go to the feet of the commune of my Master. Dhammam Sharanam Gachchhami — I go to the feet of the ultimate truth that my Master realized."

The priest came, shook him and said, "What are you doing? You are really absolutely mad! This is a milestone, this is not Buddha! You have burned a Buddha statue in the night, and now before a milestone you are doing your prayers and saying: Buddham sharanam gachchhami, sangham sharanam gachchhami, dhammam sharanam gachchhami?"

Ikkyu said, "It is not a question whether it is a statue or not; the question is my heart. It is morning time, I am doing my prayer. Any excuse will do. In the night I burned one excuse — that was only an excuse, it was not Buddha. This is another excuse, and this is far simpler because I can find the milestone anywhere. I need not be dependent on any temple, on any statue."

The priest said, "You are very illogical!"

And that's what has been told to the Zen Masters down the ages — since the days of Mahakashyap; the first Zen Master, the first Patriarch, it has been again and again said that, "You are

The Eternal Religion

paradoxical. On the one hand you deny: that there is no teaching, on the other hand you become disciples, Masters. On the one hand you say there is no prayer, on the other hand you pray to Buddha."

You have to be very very alert to understand the paradox. The prayer has to be out of your overflowing love; it has nothing to do with the statue or the stone. Those are just excuses. And Buddha is everywhere — to Buddhists Buddha means God. The stone is as much Buddha as the statue. The whole existence is full of Buddhahood, godliness, and the Master has experienced it.

The disciple accepts the Master so that he can come closer to him. In saying yes to the Master he becomes attuned to the Master. The word "attunement" is beautiful; it means "at-onement". He becomes one with the Master. In that oneness something that cannot be given through words is transpired through the being — something like bringing an unlit candle close to a lit candle. There is a certain point when the unlit candle comes within that limit — suddenly the flame from the lit candle jumps into the unlit candle. The lit candle loses nothing at all, but the unlit candle gains infinitely.

Now the reverse process is happening: when the disciple comes to the Master he gives his ego and thinks he is losing much — and the Master gets nothing. When the Master gives something he gives infinitely, he gives his light, but he loses nothing; his light remains the same. From one lit candle you can light millions of candles, and the lit candle loses nothing at all although the unlit candles gain infinitely.

This point is missing in J. Krishnamurti, hence whatsoever he is saying is Zen, but he is not doing Zen — saying but not doing.

I am saying and doing both, and only doing can bring fulfillment, flowering. Just saying is not going to help. Whether you say positively something about truth it is useless, or you say something negative about truth. Even saying that truth cannot be told is meaningless. What is the point for fifty years saying again and again that truth cannot be told? Then why bother? Say once "Truth cannot be told" and every day repeat "Ditto" — that's enough — and go home! There is no point in saying it again and again, unless by saying it you are encouraging the people towards some other phenomenon.

Truth cannot be said, this is one part. The second part is: but truth can be transpired. It can be shared — not told but shared. And for that sharing the love affair of the disciple and the Master is a must; without it it is not possible.

Question 3

OSHO,

What do you have up your sleeve?

— *Prem Shraddan*

Nothing much just few jokes for you! The first:

A man who had lost all his money at the gambling tables in Las Vegas begged a dime from another patron to use the men's room. One of the stalls was not locked, so he saved the dime, and then used it to play a slot machine. Luckily he hit the jackpot.

With the money he tried another machine, and again he won. Fortune continued to smile on him as he went and played the crap tables and roulette wheels, running his winnings up to a million dollars.

He told his extraordinary story all over Las Vegas — at bars and parties. Always expressing gratitude to his benefactor, he said he would split the million with him. After several weeks, among a group of men at a bar, one of them exclaimed, "I am the man who gave you the dime!"

"I am not looking for you," the lucky man answered. "I am looking for the guy who left the door open!"

The second:

Jim Smith ran into an old friend on the street who was sporting two black eyes. After greeting each other, Jim asked, "Say, where did you get those shiners?"

"At church," was his friend's reply.

"How?" Jim asked, somewhat astonished.

"Well," began his friend, "I was sitting behind a big, fat lady in church. When she stood up I noticed her dress was caught in the crack of her butt. I reached over and pulled it out and she turned around and socked me in the eye!"

"Wow!" said Jim, amazed. "But how did the other eye get black?"

Sighing, his friend said, "When I realized that she did not like what I had done, I put it back!"

And the third:

Johnny the Sperm and all his little friends were preparing for their big thrust out into the world. They were exercising and building up their strength. Johnny said to the other sperms, "Listen, fellows, I want to be number one — I want to be the first to become a human being!"

They were all hanging around when suddenly the bells of Jerusalem rang, "Gong!... Gong!... Gong!" Johnny took the lead — he was number one! But suddenly all the other sperms saw him turn around and start racing back towards them.

"Hey, Johnny!" they yelled. "What's wrong?"

"False alarm, boys," Johnny called out to them. "It's a blowjob!"

11

No Mind At All

Question 1

OSHO,

When answering the following you would be speaking to about half a million radio listeners in Europe; most of them may not have heard anything about you yet.

If one of the listeners to this program is devoted to socialism, what would you tell him?

If one of the listeners is a practicing Catholic, what story would you have for him?

If one of the listeners is a potential seeker, what message would you have for him? However, if your message is silence, how would you convey this silence on radio?

— *Gotz Hagmuller*

First: I am not for socialism, because to me freedom is the ultimate value; nothing is higher than that. And socialism is basically against freedom — it has to be, it is inevitable, because the very effort of socialism is to bring something unnatural into existence.

Men are not equal, they are unique. How can they be equal? All are not poets and all are not painters. Every person has unique talents to him. There are people who can create music and there are people who can create money. Man needs absolute freedom to be himself.

Socialism is dictatorship of the state; it is a forced economic structure. It tries to equalize people who are not equal; it cuts them in the same size, and they have different sizes. Naturally to few people, to very few people it will fit, but to the majority it will be a crippling phenomenon, paralyzing, destructive.

I appreciate freedom in every sphere of life so that everybody is allowed to be himself The society is not the end but only a means; the end is the individual. Individual has a greater value than the social organization. The society exists for the individual, not vice versa. Hence I believe in laissez-faire.

Capitalism is the most natural economic structure; it has not been forced, it has grown. It has not been imposed, it has come on its own. Certainly I would like poverty to be eradicated from the world — it is ugly — but socialism cannot do it. It has failed in Russia, in China; in every country it has failed to eradicate poverty. Yes, it has succeeded in one thing: it has made everybody equally poor; it has distributed poverty.

And man is so foolish that if everybody else is also as much poor as you are you feel more at ease; you don't feel jealous. The whole idea of socialism has arisen out of jealousy. It has nothing to do with understanding man, his psychology, his growth, his ultimate flowering; it is rooted in jealousy. Few people become rich; those few people are targets of everybody else's jealousy — they have to be pulled down. Not that you will become richer by pulling them down; you may become even more poor than before because those few people know how to create money. If they are destroyed you will lose all capacity to create richness.

That's what has happened in Russia: the rich people have disappeared, but that has not made the whole society rich; everybody has become equally poor. Of course people feel happier in that way because there is nobody who is richer than them. Everybody is equally poor, all are beggars; it feels good. Somebody rising higher than you, and your ego is hurt.

People talk about equality, but something fundamental has to be understood: men are not psychologically equal. What can be done about it? Albert Einstein is not equal to any Tom, Harry, Dick — he is not! You can sooner or later start equalizing people as far as intelligence is concerned; Shakespeare, Milton, Shelley are not equal to other people; they have a dimension of their own.

One thing I agree: that there should be freedom for everybody, and equal freedom for everybody, to be himself To put it more precisely: freedom means that everybody is free to be unequal! Equality and freedom cannot go together, they cannot coexist. If you choose equality, freedom has to be sacrificed and with freedom all is sacrificed. Religion is sacrificed; genius, the very possibility of genius, is sacrificed; man's higher qualities are sacrificed. Everybody has to fit with the lowest denominator, only then you can be equal.

It is like you are going to climb a mountain — if all have to be equal, then the person who is the laziest will become the criterion; everybody has to move according to the laziest. The first will not be the criterion but the last. This will be a great calamity. If the last becomes the decisive factor, then what about those who are like Everest?

And my observation is that every individual is born with some specific talent, some specific genius to himself He may not be a poet like Shelley or Rabindranath, he may not be a painter like Picasso or Nandalal, he may not be a musician like Beethoven or Ravi Shankar, but he must have something. That something has to be discovered. He has to be helped that he can discover what he has brought to the world as a gift from God.

Nobody comes without a gift; everybody brings a certain potential. But the idea of equality is dangerous, because the rose has to be the rose and the marigold has to be the marigold and the lotus has to be the lotus. If you start trying to make them equal then you will destroy all; the roses, the lotuses, the marigolds, all will be destroyed. You can succeed in creating plastic flowers which will be exactly equal to each other, but they will be dead.

And that is what is going to happen if socialism becomes our way of life in the whole world: man will be reduced into a commodity, he will be reduced into a machine. Machines are equal. You can have millions of Ford cars exactly equal to each other. They go on coming through the assembly line, absolutely the same as the other. But man is not a machine, and to reduce man to be a

No Mind At All

machine will be destroying humanity from the earth.

Do you think in Soviet Russia Gautam Buddha is possible, Jesus Christ is possible, Lao Tzu is possible? And what to say about Buddha, Jesus and Lao Tzu? I ask you: is even Karl Marx possible? Even Karl Marx is not possible, because Karl Marx has an intelligence of his own and he will not be tolerated. He is not an ordinary person; certainly he is not a part of the so-called proletariat. He was part of the most refined bourgeoisie.

His whole life he never worked. From morning to evening he was sitting in the British Museum studying. In fact, British Museum has never come again across another scholar of the same caliber. He was so much intrigued with his studies, so much fascinated, that when the closing time will come he had to be forcibly thrown out every day,. because he will insist, "Just wait a little more — let me finish this book! Don't disturb me! What does it matter if you close the museum half an hour late? If I don't do this work, tomorrow I may have completely lost the track of it. Let me finish it!" He had to be forced, physically forced

And it happened many times that he was found almost in a state of coma; studying continuously he will become so dizzy he will fall unconscious, he will fall in a swoon, and he had to be carried on a stretcher to his home.

Now this man is no more possible. In the first place British Museum is not possible in Russia.

I have heard:

An American journalist — must be somebody like Gotz Hagmuller — was visiting Russia. He asked a professor... thinking that a professor will answer him intelligently, but whatsoever he asked the professor always started his answer, "Yes, just the other day I read in pravda..."

The Russian word pravda means the truth. What irony! It should mean the lie! The pravda is the most lying newspaper in the world, but it means the truth.

He will always start. "I have read in the pravda..."

Disgusted, the journalist finally asked, "Have you not got any opinion of your own?"

The professor said, "Yes, I have got my own opinions, but I don't believe in them!"

In Russia there is no freedom of thought, because freedom of thought means the beginning of inequality. Freedom of thought means man is not a machine, and then two men cannot be equal.

The idea of equality is absolutely unpsychological. I can accept it only in one sense: that everybody should be given equal opportunity to be himself — and that means to be unequal. You have to understand this paradox: everybody has to be given equal opportunity and freedom to be himself, and that simply means everybody has to be given equality to be unequal.

The poverty can be destroyed — there is no need for socialism — the poverty can be destroyed only by a higher capitalist system. Karl Marx has predicted that the first country to go communist or socialist will be America; his prediction proved absolutely wrong. He had never thought that a country like Russia or China is ever going to become communist; Russia and China are economically very backward. In the days of Karl Marx, Russia was living in the world of feudalism; even capitalism has not happened there.

If Karl Marx comes back he will be absolutely unable to understand how it happened that Russia became the first communist country, the first socialist society. He was hoping America will become the first communist country. Why he was hoping that? — because if capitalism grows and reaches to a peak of producing wealth to the maximum, poverty will disappear naturally, because when wealth is too much nobody wants to hoard it. You don't hoard air — it is available. It is freely available, it is so much there. You don't hoard anything which is not in scarcity.

People are money-minded, greedy, because money is scarce. If you don't hoard it, if you don't cling to it, somebody else will snatch it away from you. Before somebody else does it you have to do it. Otherwise you will be a loser. And the only way to destroy poverty is to create so much wealth that greed becomes irrelevant. When wealth is enough, the poverty will disappear. Of course there will be still people who will have more wealth and people who will have less wealth, but that is natural and nothing is wrong in it. Somebody will be more intelligent and somebody less intelligent, and somebody will be more healthy and somebody less healthy, but we can create a society where everybody can attain to his maximum. Even then inequality is bound to remain, and there is no need to destroy that because that creates variety and variety brings richness. It is good that people are not equal.

Poverty should go, but the only way for it to go is to produce more wealth, to industrialize society more scientifically, to bring more and more technology, and with a deep understanding of nature so your technology and industry don't destroy nature. They should become part of ecology, they should not go against it. That is the highest scientific development. It cannot happen through socialism; it can happen only through capitalism.

The word "capitalism" has become very derogatory, but I am not worried about that. I believe in capitalism and not in socialism, because to me capitalism is the only hope for freedom, for growth, for individual uniqueness. It is a respect for the individual; socialism is disrespectful of the individual. Socialism does not believe in the soul of man; it cannot believe because if you believe in the soul of man then you cannot behave as if man is a machine. You have to give respect to the uniqueness of every individual. Not to give that respect means committing suicide.

The second thing you ask: If one of the listeners is a practicing catholic, what story would you have for him?

It is good to be a Christ, it is ugly to be a Christian — Catholic or Protestant, it doesn't matter. It is good to be a Buddha, but ugly to be a Buddhist. When you can be a Christ, why settle for less? When Christ-consciousness can flower in you, when you can become a Buddha in your own right, when you can experience what Buddha and Christ have experienced, then why just be a follower, an imitator, a carbon copy? I am against carbon copies.

My effort here is to help you to discover your original face, so whether you are a practicing Catholic or a Protestant or a Hindu or a Mohammedan, it is all wrong. Love Christ, but don't be a Christian. Love is a totally different phenomenon. If you become a Christian you are addicted with Christ, you become dependent on Christ. If you are a Christian you are bound to be anti-Buddha, anti-Mahavira, anti-Lao Tzu, anti-Zarathustra, anti-Patanjali. Just choosing Christ and becoming anti to all the other great awakened individuals who have walked on the earth is becoming poor, unnecessarily poor. When you can claim the whole heritage of humanity, when all the Buddhas, all the awakened ones can enrich your being, why narrow down your consciousness? Why become focused and obsessed with Christ or Buddha or Mahavira or Krishna?

A Catholic means he is obsessed with Christ, a Hindu means he is obsessed with Krishna, a Jain means he is obsessed with Mahavira, and obsession is a psychological disease.

One should be open, one should be available, to the stars, to the sun, to the moon, to the wind, to the flowers, to the birds. One should be available to all, because this whole belongs to us.

Love Christ, because love is not excluding others; love is an inclusive phenomenon. If you love Christ you have to love Buddha too, because that is another aspect of being a Christ. If you love Christ you have to love Mahavira too, because that is again another aspect of the same fulfillment. Buddha, Christ, Mahavira, Mohammed, Bahauddin, Kabir, Nanak — different aspects of the truth.

Truth is multidimensional. Why choose one dimension? Why become linear? Why be so miserly, even in your spiritual love? Why not be open and available, vulnerable to all, so they can all dance in your being?

I would like my sannyasins to be lovers of all. Enjoy all kinds of flowers! Don't become addicted with the rose, because the lotus has its beauty just as the rose has its beauty. And where is the problem? Cannot you enjoy the rose and the lotus together? Just one thing has to be understood: if you love beauty you can enjoy all, if you love truth you can enjoy all the awakened ones.

But a practicing Catholic does not love truth — he believes. No believer is a seeker of truth; all believers are non-seekers. They have already believed without inquiring, without going in the exploration, without adventuring into the unknown territory. They have already become prejudiced.

And what do you mean by "a practicing Catholic"? What you can practice in the name of Catholicism? Whatsoever you do will be nothing but an effort of conditioning yourself according to your belief It will be a state of autohypnosis, and autohypnosis is not going to help you to become awakened.

Religion is not a question of practicing at all. If you practice you will miss religion and its beauty. Religion is the experience of a spontaneously flowing consciousness. Practicing means imposing something upon yourself, cultivating a character. Religion has nothing to do with cultivating a character. It is an inquiry into "Who am I?" It is going inwards, reaching to the very rock bottom of your being, to the ground of your being, discovering your center. And from that discovery an explosion happens and your old character simply disappears like a nightmare, and a new quality arises in you. You are more alive, more rejoicing, more full of love, more full of celebration. And this state of celebration makes you aware that existence is not dead. Because you are alive you can contact the living sources of God is not a person but only the experience that the whole existence is an alive phenomenon; it is not matter alone. It is throbbing with life! It is overflowing with life; that it has a heartbeat. The moment you know that the universe has a heartbeat you have discovered God. But first, please, discover your own heartbeat, discover your own center.

Religion is not a question of practicing, it is a question of discovering. It is not a question of belief. Beliefs are all against truth; they make your mind prejudiced. Belief means you don't know, still you pretend to know. Belief is a lie, it is hypocrisy.

So whether somebody is a practicing Catholic or a Hindu or a Mohammedan, all practicing people are dangerous. They are false, pseudo; they are not authentic, they are not real. The real person is a seeker.

And the third thing you ask: If one of the listeners is a potential seeker, what message would you have for him?

My whole message is only for him, the potential seeker. These are the qualities of a seeker. First: he will not be a Christian, a Hindu, a Mohammedan, a communist; he will not be an atheist or a theist. To seek, this basic requirement has to be fulfilled: you have to put aside all your beliefs, because if you carry your beliefs then your beliefs will distort your vision. Beliefs are like colored glasses: they will make the whole existence of the same color as your glasses. It will not be the true color of existence; it will be imparted by your glasses. You have to put aside all your glasses. You have to contact reality directly, immediately. There should be no idea between you and existence, no a priori conclusion.

A real seeker has to be in the state that Dionysius calls agnosia — a state of not-knowing. Socrates said at the very end of his life, "I know only one thing, that I know nothing." This is the state of a true seeker.

In the East we call this state meditation: no belief, no thought, no desire, no prejudice, no conditioning — in fact, no mind at all. A state of no-mind is meditation. When you can look without any mind interfering, distorting, interpreting, then you see the truth. The truth is already all around; just you have to put your mind aside.

The seeker has to fulfill only one basic thing: he has to drop his mind. The moment the mind is dropped, a great silence arises — because the mind carries your whole past; all the memories of the past go on hankering for your attention, they go on crowding upon you, they don't leave any space within you.

And the mind also means future. Out of the past you start

fantasizing about the future. It is a projection out of the past. You have lived a certain life in the past: there have been a few moments of joy and many many dark nights. You would not like to have those dark nights; you would have your future to be full of those joyous moments. So you sort out from your past: you choose few things and you project them in the future, and you choose a few other things and you try to avoid them in the future. Your future is only nothing but a refined past — a little bit modified here and there, but it is still the past because that's all that you know.

And one thing very significant to be remembered: those few moments of joy that you had in the past were basically part of those long dark nights, so if you choose those moments those dark nights will come automatically; you cannot avoid them. The silver linings in the dark clouds cannot be chosen separately from the dark clouds. In the dark night you see the sky full of stars; in the day those stars disappear. Do you think they evaporate? They are still there, but the context is missing. They need darkness; only then you can see them. In the night, you will be able to see them again. Darker the night, the more shining are the stars.

In life everything is intertwined with each other. Your pleasures are intertwined with your pains, your ecstasies mixed inevitably, inseparably with your agonies. So your whole idea of the future is sheer nonsense. You cannot manage it, nobody has ever been able to manage it, because you are trying to do something which cannot be done in the very nature of things. It will be simply a repetition of your past.

Whatsoever you desire is not going to make any difference. It will be again and again a repetition of your past, the same past, maybe a little bit different, but not because of your expectations — a little bit different because life goes on changing, people go on changing, existence goes on changing. So there will be few differences but not basic differences, only in the non-essential parts. Essentially it will be the same tragedy.

Dropping the mind means dropping the past, and with it of course the future disappears. Dropping the mind means you are suddenly awakened into the present, and the present is the only reality there is. Past is non-existential, so is future. Past is no more, future is not yet, only the present is. It is always now — only the now exists. And the meditator starts merging and melting with the now.

And that's what silence is. It can be conveyed, Gotz Hagmuller, to your radio listeners. Just these pauses... these wordless moments... when you start feeling the now, the here... when suddenly you become aware that five thousand people are sitting here, but as if there is nobody at all. The Buddha Hall is absolutely empty.

When we are in the present... silence descends. You can hear the birds chirping, but they don't disturb the silence — they enhance it, they beautify it.

Take my message to your people. First: freedom is the ultimate goal and socialism goes against it, hence I favor a state of laissez-faire. Secondly: nobody can practice religion. Religion really means your spontaneity, your nature. You cannot practice it, you have to allow it. You have to remove all the barriers that prevent the flow of your nature. It is like a stream prevented by rocks: remove the rocks. There is no question of practicing; it is already there. It is your nature! When the hindrances are no more there you start flowing, just like a river moving towards the ocean.

Each consciousness moving towards God, towards the ultimate ocean, is religious. Religion is neither Christian nor Hindu nor Mohammedan. These are all political games played in the name of religion. A religious person is simply religious, natural, spontaneous, living out of his own light.

Buddha said to his disciples, and this was his last message on the earth: "Be a light unto yourself" — live according to your own light, not following and practicing somebody else's light, because that will make you only a carbon copy, and howsoever beautiful the carbon copy is it is still a carbon copy.

Discover your originality, and it cannot be done by practicing.

No Mind At All

Practicing means imposing some ideas from others, trying to act as others would like you to act. Act as you would like to act. Take the risk — it is dangerous.

To be religious is to live in danger — it is not security. To live in religion means constantly exploring the unknown and ultimately the unknowable.

And thirdly: be a seeker, never be a believer. If you cannot say, "I know God," please don't say, "I believe in God," because that is falsifying. That is even not being true about God, not even being sincere with God. With whom you are going to be sincere then? If you don't know, say, "I don't know." At least that is true. Don't pretend that you know because pretensions are dangerous. They will deceive others and they can deceive yourself too.

And only a seeker can become a meditator. Meditation means absolute silence. It is only in silence that one comes to know, one comes to love, one comes to dance in tune with existence.

Question 2

OSHO,

What are you trying to do here exactly?

— Govind Narayan

It is a very difficult question to answer. In the first place I am not trying to do anything; the very word "trying" does not fit with me. If somebody asks you, "Are you trying to love this woman?" what you will say, Govind Narayan? Trying to love? Either love is or love is not. Trying to love simply means you don't love, hence you are trying. But what can you manage by trying? Empty gestures. You may say to the woman "I love you" thousand and one times in thousand and one ways, but deep down you will know that it is only an effort; your heart will not be with it.

I am not trying to do anything, I am just being myself. Then whatsoever is happening is happening — it is a happening. What is happening here, remember, it is not being done by me. You cannot make me responsible for whatsoever is happening here — I am not responsible at all! It is happening, certainly, but neither I am doing anything nor my sannyasins are doing anything. But in this non-doing something transpires.

But Govind Narayan is not a sannyasin; he must be a casual visitor, hence the question has arisen to him. And he will not understand what I am saying, but he may understand this:

Tu jism ke khushrang libason pai hai najan
Tu jism ke khushrang
Tu jism ke khushrang libason pai hai najan
Main ruh ko mohtaje kafan dekh raha huin
Kya puchhte ho hal mere karobar ka
Aaine bechta hun main andhon ke shahar main.
Tu jism ke khushrang libason pai hai najan
Main ruh ko mohtaje kafan dekh raha huin
Kya puchhte ho hal mere karobar ka
Aaine bechta hun main andhon ke shahar main.

Roughly it can be translated:

Don't ask me, sir, what I am doing here.
You are proud of the dreamlike psychedelic colors
Of the body and the mind,
But I can see death knocking at your doors.
You are lost in a dreamworld, and I can see
Death approaching every moment closer and closer.
Don't ask me, sir, about my business here.
I sell mirrors in the city of the blind!

Aaine bechta hun main andhon ke shahar main.

I sell mirrors in the city of the blind!

And this is certainly a city of the blind! This whole earth is full of blind people — blind because they cannot see death approaching, blind because they cannot see that life is evaporating every moment, blind because they cannot see the momentariness of all that they are accumulating, blind because they don't know from where they come, why they come, to where they are destined, blind because they are not even aware who resides at the innermost core of their being.

When Alexander the Great came to India... and he came at a very right, ripe moment... Buddha had left his body only three hundred years before; his vibe was still alive. People were still filled with the joy, with the silence that they have experienced in Buddha. He had gone, the flower has disappeared, but the fragrance was still in the air, still lingering. It lingered on at least for five hundred years.

Alexander was very much surprised; he had never felt such quality. He came across many people he had never come across in his whole life. They were strange — they talked a strange language, they lived a strange life. He was mystified.

He met a naked fakir and he was so much impressed by the man's beauty, his grace, his silence, his bliss, that suddenly he felt his own poverty. And he was the conqueror of that time, the conqueror of the then known world, the greatest conqueror ever. And he felt his beggarliness before this naked beggar, because he could see he was empty. And this naked man was overflowing with meaning, with joy, with splendor.

Alexander begged from this beggar that, "Give me some gift that can be of help to me!"

The beggar pulled out a small mirror — so goes the story — from his bag, and gave the mirror to Alexander the Great. Seeing that it is just an ordinary mirror, and very cheap too, Alexander said, "Do you think this is such a great gift? From a man like you I was expecting something really miraculous!"

And the naked fakir laughed and he said, "It is more than you could have ever expected. Keep it safe for the day when the question arises in you 'Who am I?' and then look into it."

Alexander could not resist the temptation. That very night when he was alone, he looked into the mirror and he was surprised: he saw his original face.

This must be a story, because no mirror can show you your original face — unless that mirror means meditation. Meditation can show you your original face. The story simply says that the beggar gave him the secret of meditation; it is a metaphorical way of saying. Meditation is a mirror. All the mirrors can only show the physical face, but meditation can show you your spiritual face.

And that's what I am doing here:
Aaine bechta hun main andhon ke shahar main.
I am selling mirrors in the city of the blind.

And it is really a city of blind people, mad people, dead people; all kinds of strange people have gathered on the earth. It seems the earth must be a dumping place of the universe because scientists say at least there are fifty thousand planets on which life exists, so they must need some place to dump. They must be using earth as a dumping place — because it is so full of mad people, so full of dead people, so full of mediocres, stupids...

A couple of jazz musicians, real gone, were watching a crater erupt.

"Man," cried one, "dig that crazy cigarette lighter!"

A young woman who had been completely broke for many weeks found a ten-dollar bill in the gutter. Overjoyed, she rushed into the nearest supermarket and spent it all on groceries. As she was walking out with her parcel she collided with a drunk and landed on the pavement amidst a mess of milk, coffee powder, broken eggs and tomato sauce.

Seeing her dream of a feast shattered, she burst into tears and began sobbing bitterly. The drunk staggered to his feet and gazed in fascinated silence at two eggs floating in a pool of tomato sauce. Then he looked at the woman and spluttered, "Don't worry, lady, it would not have lived anyway — its eyes were too far apart!'

A drunk was staggering down the road in the middle of the day, obviously much the worse for wear, and almost collided with a Catholic priest who was on his way to visit an elderly parishioner.

"Scuse me, Revrend," slurred the drunk, "but can you direct me to Alcoholics Anonymous?"

The priest's contemptuous expression brightened visibly and he shook the drunk warmly by the hand. "My son," he intoned, "I am pleased to see that even in your intoxicated state you can see the error of your ways, and have had the good sense to go and join Alcoholics Anonymous."

"Join? The hell!" said the drunk. "I am going to resign!"

A young boy was chasing crows away from some young plants in a field, shouting, "Fuck off! Fuck off!"

A priest was walking by, called the boy over and remonstrated with him for the use of bad language.

"Remember," he pontificated, "God is everywhere and hears every word you utter. Do not offend his ears with such language! Besides, if you shout, 'Shoo, shoo!' loudly enough, they will fuck off just as quickly!"

Question 3

OSHO,

It is said that Zarathustra had loudly laughed when he was born. Is it true?

— *Narendra*

It must be true, because a man like Zarathustra comes in the world with great insight. He must have seen the world immediately — he must have seen the whole crazy scene! It depends how much intelligence you have got. Few people take their whole life to realize that they have been living in a madhouse. He must have seen at the first moment that "This is a crazy place I am entering into!"

And it is not only Zarathustra — every child, the moment the child becomes capable of focusing properly, he starts smiling, because he is then able to see what his father looks like!

A recent story tells about a baby who was giggling and laughing minutes after he was born. The obstetrician noticed he had unusual muscle control, his tiny left fist being tightly clenched. When the doctor pried it open he found a contraceptive pill.

Zarathustra must have laughed! Whether he laughed or not... I am not concerned about history, but to me his laughter is very significant. The world is in such a mess! Ordinarily children are born crying — that too is their judgment! They are saying, "My God! So this is the world I am born into?"

Zarathustra has a different attitude, from the other extreme — he laughed. He must have been a man like me, hence I have very deep love for Zarathustra.

A rabbi and a Hindu monk, who was obviously a teetotaler, happened to be seated together in the dining car of a train. When the rabbi ordered a martini, the Hindu monk was shocked.

"I would rather commit adultery!" he scoffed.

"I didn't know they gave you a choice here," replied the rabbi.

The army recruit from the country was being given his physical examination. "Well, that's everything but the urine test," said the doctor. "I want a specimen of yours in one of those little bottles on that shelf down at the other end of the room."

"What did you say, Doc?" asked the young man.

"Just urinate in one of those little bottles down there," repeated the doctor.

The recruit still looked doubtful. "Do you mean all the way from here?" he asked.

A rambling man thought up a new scheme for winning sympathy. He rang the doorbell, then got down on his knees and started nibbling on the grass. "What are you doing there?" asked the lady when she opened the door.

The tramp rose weakly to his feet, clutched his stomach in mock pain and moaned, "Ma'am, I am so hungry I just had to take to eating grass."

"Why, you poor man, stop eating that dry old grass!" cried the woman sympathetically. "Go around in the back where the grass is greener and longer!"

A man won a turkey in a raffle and brought it home, but his wife was annoyed. "Who wants the bother of plucking it?" she said in a huff.

"If that's the way you feel," he replied, "I will pluck it and cook it myself."

So he busied himself plucking it and when he was finally through he trussed it and put it in the oven. But he forgot to light the gas. After washing up he settled down to read. Half an hour later he heard a muffled voice say, "What are you going to do about it?"

Without taking his eyes off the newspaper he said, "Do about what?"

The voice answered, "I am getting cold. Either put my feathers back or light the gas!"

If Zarathustra laughed, what is wrong in it? He must have seen the whole stupidity, that he has to live with these people, and he started with a laughter.

The noted agnostic lecturer, Robert G. Ingersoll, said once: "No man with a sense of humor ever founded a religion."

He is wrong — Zarathustra did. Of course, about ninety-nine percent religions Ingersoll is right; his statement is significant. He says, "No man with a sense of humor ever founded a religion." It is true about Jesus, about Buddha, about Mohammed, about Krishna — it is absolutely true; these people don't seem to have any sense of humor — except about Zarathustra. Maybe Ingersoll had never heard about Zarathustra.

He is the only man known who started his life with laughter — must have had an immense sense of humor. To begin your life with laughter is not an easy matter. He must have prepared for it for many lives; he must have come ready.

Christians say Jesus never laughed in his whole life; maybe they are right. I don't want to believe it because that means a great condemnation of Jesus, but if Christians say, then, of course, who am I to disagree with them? They are the authoritative people, at least about Jesus — they own Jesus!

Protestant Church in Germany has banned my books in the churches, in the churches' libraries. It has been given to all the priests, to all the churches, that my name, even my name, should not be mentioned in any sermon. Nothing should be quoted from my books, even to refute it, because people become interested!

This may be one of the reasons why Jesus has succeeded to change almost half the humanity to Christianity, because people are sad. Zarathustra has not found many followers, you know? His followers are only confined in Bombay — just only few thousand. Why Zarathustra has failed? Maybe that laughter is the cause: he has the sense of humor.

People are serious, sad, miserable, hence the cross of Jesus seems to be very appealing, because their life is also on the cross. They can understand Jesus and his agony — they are passing through it. Their whole life is nothing but carrying a cross. They can find a deep affinity with Jesus, his crucifixion — they are also crucified. But what affinity they can find with Zarathustra? Why Zarathustra failed?

Buddhists have found millions of followers; the whole Asia is Buddhist. Christians have found millions of followers; half the earth is Christian. Mohammedans are next to Christians — and Mohammed has no sense of humor at all. With a sword in his hand he is very serious, really serious. He is much concerned about your welfare — if you don't listen to him he is ready to fight with you, but he is determined to convince you because he is determined to save your soul. Even if he has to use the sword he has to save you. How can he allow you to fall into hell? It is for your own sake.

Zarathustra is the only person who has not been able to find followers. I can see the point: with a sense of humor, who is

No Mind At All

going to listen to you?

I am trying again something like Zarathustra. My effort here is to prove Ingersoll wrong. I am trying to found a religion based totally on the sense of humor!

Shakespeare and others have punningly described the foolish pretender to philosophy as foolosopher. By the same wordplay the philosophy of foolosophers is called foolosophy.

Bertrand Russell was always critical of foolosophers, for their lack of both common sense and a sense of humor. He tells how he was once near death with pneumonia delirious for three weeks. After he revived, the doctor said to him, "When you were ill you behaved like a true philosopher: every time you came to yourself you made a joke."

Russell wrote afterward, "I never had a compliment that pleased me more."

He himself was a serious man. In his delirious state he must have forgotten all his philosophy and seriousness, must have become more relaxed, must have forgotten that he is a philosopher and he has to be serious — must have joked.

To me sense of humor should be the foundation stone of the future religiousness of man. There is no need to be so serious. Man is the only animal who has the sense of humor. You have never seen buffaloes laughing, or the donkeys. Only the man can have the feel of the ridiculous, of the absurd. It needs great intelligence to have sense of humor; on the lower planes it does not exist and even all human beings don't have it; those who exist on lower planes of intelligence are bound to be serious — serious like the donkeys. Donkeys are very serious people, always thinking about serious things, it seems, much disturbed with all the problems of the world.

I have watched donkeys very closely; from my very childhood I have been very much interested in donkeys. If Pavlov could find many things about man by studying dogs, if Skinner can find many things about man by studying white rats, if Delgado can find many things about man by studying monkeys, I feel why these people have missed the donkey? He comes closest to human beings — a serious philosopher, a pundit, a scholar, a theologian! Who has ever heard a donkey laughing?

Zarathustra seems to be of the highest caliber, of the most refined intelligence At the first sight of the world he laughed He could not contain himself, he could not resist the temptation seeing where he has landed.

The old professor of philosophy who was retiring addressed his class: "Men, I have two confessions to make before I go," he said "The first is that half of what I have taught you is not true The second is that I have no idea which half it is!"

A pious old gentleman heard a tough kid on the street swearing at his playmate "Don't you know," he admonished the youngster, "it is wrong to use such four-letter words? God will punish you."

The youngster looked at the man with scorn. "God can't hear me," he said. "He's way up in heaven."

"Young man, God is everywhere."
"Is he over in my house?"
"He certainly is."
"Is he in my yard?"
"Of course."
"You're crazy — we haven't got a yard!"

Children are far more clear: you cannot befool them so easily. And at the first moment when the child opens his eyes his clarity is absolute. No priest has come in, no politician has corrupted him yet. He has not been conditioned by Catholics and Protestants and Hindus and Mohammedans. He has not been told all kinds of lies and beliefs and superstitions. His eyes are clear, he can see through and through.

Zarathustra did the right thing — that he laughed.

Once Diogenes asked alms from a man with a philosophic bent of mind. "Before I give you a drachma," said the man, "convince

No Mind At All

me why I should do so."

"If I thought you were amenable to reason," Diogenes told him, "I would recommend that you go and hang yourself."

Who is amenable to reason? It is an irrational world, and Diogenes is right the man was asking, "Convince me — why should I give you anything? Why? Diogenes answer is right that: "If I thought that you can understand reason, then the only thing I would suggest for you will be go and hang yourself, because what you are doing in this irrational world? Such a reasonable man!"

The laughter of Zarathustra looks irrational, but it is not irrational. Seeing the irrationality all around he must have been perceptive, very perceptive.

The story is strange. There are many miracles talked about people like Jesus, Buddha, Mahavira, Krishna, but they are almost the same. The miracle of walking on water is repeated in thousands of stones; it is nothing special to Jesus. The miracle of curing the people from their incurable diseases is nothing new to Jesus. It is the same miracle being done by so many people around the world, in every tradition, in every religion. Even the miracle of raising the dead is not new; that too is a common miracle attributed to many people.

But this miracle of Zarathustra is simply unique; no other person has been attributed with this miracle. Nobody has ever thought about it. And it is far more significant than raising the dead, because raising the dead is not going to help. Lazarus has to die finally, has to die sooner or later, so what does it matter — this week or the next week? He may have lived few years more — so what? Curing a man from his illness does not matter much, because still death will come, other diseases will come. Even if he starts seeing — he was blind before — what does it matter? So many millions of people have eyes — what has happened to them?

In fact, there is a Sufi story about Jesus, not related by the Christians in their scriptures They must have all avoided it The

Bible is not exactly true; much has been edited out of it Anything that was going to create trouble for the theologians, for the priests, for the popes, has been edited out, left out But there are always few people who will not miss such an opportunity; they will collect all those rejected parts — because they are far more important than the accepted ones.

This story is a rejected story by the Christians, but the Sufis have preserved it, and they have done a great service to humanity.

Jesus enters a town and he comes across a man who is lying in the gutter shouting ugly words, completely drunk. Jesus comes close to him to help him, looks at his face and recognizes that this man is well-known to him. He was very ill, Jesus saved him, dragged him almost from the door of death.

He shook the drunk and asked him, "Do you recognize me?"

He said, "Yes, I recognize you perfectly well. You are the man who created the trouble! I was going to die — why you saved me? And now why you have come again? Are you gong to do something more?"

Jesus could not believe the way the man was behaving, as if Jesus has done something wrong to him. Jesus said, "Why you are so angry?"

The man says, "I am angry because I was going to die and the whole thing was going to be finished, and you saved me! Now I don't know what to do with my life. You see, I am lying down in the gutter — you are responsible! Now I am simply trying to forget myself and my problems and my anxieties by drinking as much as I can. And I know it is poison, but what else to do? Why you saved me? I have been looking for you — it is good that you have come by yourself Answer me!"

And Jesus could not answer him. The man is asking a relevant question: "Why you saved me? For what? For this gutter? For drinking and trying to forget my miseries?"

Jesus moved, very humiliated, shocked.

He saw another man who was running after a prostitute He prevented the man — he forgot the first man — just old habits! He prevented the second man and said, "What are you doing? Has God given you the eyes just to lust after women? Even to think of lust is sin — you will suffer in hell!"

And the man said, "Stop all this nonsense! It is you who cured me of my blindness! I was perfectly happy with my blindness because I had never seen a woman, so I was never disturbed I never cared who is passing, man or woman, it was all the same It is you who cured me Now what should I do with these eyes? These eyes feel attracted towards beauty And remember, at the last moment on the day of judgment, I will point you — that you are responsible I was an innocent blind man. You gave me eyes, and I had not even asked! I was just sitting, you came and touched my eyes and you cured me! You did not even ask me!"

Jesus was now really shocked. He didn't go into the town. he left the town. When he was coming out he saw a man preparing to hang himself by a tree. Again he forgot — old habits die hard! He reached to the man and said, "What are you doing?"

And this man was nobody else but Lazarus! He said, "So you have come again! Get lost! I am committing suicide — enough is enough! And how you came to know? Last time my sisters invited you, Martha and Mary, they invited you. And I was dead — at last I was dead, resting at peace, and you came and resurrected me and now again you are back! You won't allow me any peace? How long I have to live, and why should I live? What is the point of it all?"

All these miracles are meaningless, but Zarathustra's miracle of laughing at the moment of his birth is really significant.

A great Zen Master lay critically ill. As his doctor prepared to leave he said cheerfully, "I will see you in the morning."

Although the dying Master knew his hours were numbered, he could not resist quipping, "Of course. But will I see you?"

12
A Mystery To Be Lived

◻ Question 1

OSHO,

For days now I have been on fire inside. I feel the unknown in part of me, and I am afraid to jump. Everything is cuckoo, and it's beautiful and scary at the same time.

Push Me, Osho!

On Fire,

— *Vivek*

Crazy, baby, crazy! That's what I am here for, to put you on fire. And once it starts happening, nothing else is needed to be done. Then it goes on growing by itself, in spite of all your fears; they cannot prevent the fire. They are natural — they come from your past, but the past is impotent when it confronts the present. The fire is present, the fire is now, and the fears come from the past; they are already dead. They belong to the non-existential, and the non-existential cannot do anything to the existential.

They are like darkness. The darkness can be very old, ancient, millions of years old, but just a small candle is enough to dispel it. It cannot say that, "I am very ancient, so how you can dare? You are just a small candle and you have come into existence this very moment, and I am so old, so ancient." But there is no time for darkness to say all that. The moment the candle is lit, the darkness starts disappearing. The problem is how to light the candle; once it is there, then there is no problem at all. If the candle is not there then darkness is very real, too real —although it exists not. It is only an absence.

A Mystery To Be Lived

Vivek, once the fire is inside, even just a small part of you is on fire, that will do — it will spread. It is not a fire that dies. Once it is there it is going to consume you totally; that is inevitable.

My work ends the moment the fire is on. Then the fire will do...

You say: For days now I have been on fire inside. I feel the unknown in part of me, and I am afraid to jump.

It is natural to be afraid to jump. And to jump in fire is like killing yourself In a sense it is suicide: the ego is going to die. Hence the fear, because we have existed as an ego; that is our identity. To drop it means death. The mind cannot conceive what else will be left once the ego is gone. The mind knows only the ego; it knows nothing behind, beyond. It knows nothing of the transcendental. The mind is part of ego, and when the ego starts dying the mind starts dying, and it creates all kinds of fears, anxieties. It is just a self-defense.

But once the fire is on, the mind is finished. It may take a little while for the fire to spread to the whole jungle of your being, but the mind cannot do anything to prevent it.

The moment the mind becomes impotent, the work of the Master is finished. Then he simply watches. Then he enjoys the disappearance of your ego, your mind, your whole so-called personality.

You say, Vivek: Everything is cuckoo.

In the beginning it will look like that, because mind is our logic and the fire is going to destroy our logic — because life is more than logic. In fact, life is illogical; it has to be because it contains contradictions. Logic is a choice; you go on choosing that which is consistent with your idea. Life is far more than that.

If you believe that life consists only of days, then you will ignore the nights. You will not take any note of the nights because they will create confusion. Then what will happen to your idea, your prejudice, that life consists only of days? You have to cling to your idea; the nights seem to be confusing. You have to deny, you have to keep closed to the nights. You have to say they are illusory, they are dream-stuff, they are unreal; the real is the day. This is how mind tries to be consistent and logical. If it accepts the night, then the logic starts disappearing then the contradiction has happened, then the consistency is lost.

If you accept only the flowers or only the thorns you will avoid the opposite, and life consists of polar opposites. Life cannot be consistent, remember it; only death is consistent. Hence logic is more in tune with death than in tune with life. Life is vast, it is so vast it can easily take in the contradictory; in fact, it rejoices in contradictions. On the same rose bush it grows flowers and thorns. How can it be logical? Logic will say, "Either grow thorns or grow flowers."

Logic means either/or, and life means both/and. Hence the moment the mind starts slipping, dying, one feels as if one is going mad.

In the East we have continuously observed the phenomenon; we call it a kind of spiritual madness. In Bengal the mystics have been called bauls; baul means the mad one. In the Sufi tradition the mystic is called a mast; mast means a mad one. And Jesus, Bahauddin, Francis, Eckhart, Kabir, Chuang Tzu, these are all mad people — for the simple reason because they have not chosen; they have accepted life as it is in its totality.

Science up to the time of Albert Einstein remained very consistent, very logical. Albert Einstein is the first mystic in the world of science; a scientific mysticism he introduced, and he disturbed the whole edifice of the old science. After Albert Einstein, science, particularly physics which was his field of work, is no more the same — because he accepted contradictions. In fact he said that, "When I had started my work I had thought that life and logic are synonymous — my work was to solve problems logically — but as I went deeper I became aware that life is not synonymous with logic: it contains contradictions. And in fact because of those contradictions it is beautiful, because of those contradictions it has a certain tension; that tension gives it aliveness, it gives it possibilities to be dynamic, moving."

And at the end of his life he said, "Now I cannot say that life is a problem. To call life a problem is a logical statement, because a problem means something that can be solved through logic, if not today then tomorrow. Sooner or later logic will find a way and the problem will be dissolved."

Einstein said, just two days before he died that, "Life is no more a problem for me, it is a mystery."

And the difference between mystery and problem is immense, qualitative. A problem can be solved logically; a mystery cannot be solved logically or in any other way. A mystery has to be lived, accepted as it is; there is no way to solve it. Life is a mystery; it is a mystery because it is contradictory. And thousands of contradictions are there, but those contradictions give it variety, vastness.

So in the beginning when mind starts losing its grip upon you, it feels as if one is going cuckoo. But to be a cuckoo is really far more beautiful than to be a pundit, a professor, a theologian, a priest, a politician. Have you not heard the distant call of the cuckoo, how beautiful it is? And cuckoo is crazy! The beauty of the cuckoo's song is transcendental. It should not be so — looking at the mundane life, looking at the ordinary life. The cuckoo goes on singing as if it lives in another world.

My sannyasins all have to be cuckoos! They have to learn the song: the Song of Solomon, the song of love, life, laughter.

The only thing beautiful in the Old Testament is the Song of Solomon; everything else is ordinary. Of course Jews and Christians are very much embarrassed by the Song of Solomon; they would like it not to be in the Old Testament. It does not look religious: it praises life, it is very fleshy, it is very alive. It praises love — it is sheer poetry. But they cannot deny it — it is there. All that they can do is either ignore it or give it some esoteric meanings, which are all nonsense.

It is a very simple song; it is not a parable and it is not metaphorical. It is very direct, immediate. It says exactly what it says; it is like two plus two are four.

Vivek, read the Song of Solomon — it will help your inner fire. It is one of the greatest documents in the world, one of the most beautiful. Even the Bhagavad Gita, compared to the Song of Solomon, has not that beauty. It sings the song of the earth; it is rejoicing in the ordinary. And the moment you rejoice in the ordinary you transform the ordinary.

There are two things in the Old Testament: one is the Song of Solomon and the other are the Ten Commandments. About the Ten Commandments, Vivek, remember this:

Two men were wrangling vehemently about something when one of them said, "The trouble with you, Bill, is that you don't agree with anybody on anything. I'll bet you don't even accept the Ten Commandments."

"That's not true," disagreed the other. "If you make only one small change in them I'll agree with all of them."

"That's certainly surprising," said the first man. "What's the small change you want made?"

"Just strike out the word 'not' all the way through."

And that's what the Song of Solomon is: the small word "not" has been striked out all the way through.

And you ask me, Vivek: Push me, Osho! on fire...

That I am doing without ever taking anybody's permission! I never come from the front door because nobody would allow me from the front door. I never knock, I never ask, "May I come in, sir or madam?" I enter as a thief, I enter from the back door. And certainly I have to enter as a thief because you are asleep; knocking on the door won't help. You will rationalize in your sleep, "It must be the wind, or an airplane passing by, or something else." You will rationalize, turn over, go under the blanket and start dreaming again. Maybe knocking on the door can trigger a few dreams in you; that's all it will do. You are so fast asleep, I have to come from the back door.

A Mystery To Be Lived

In India we have one thousand names of God; one whole scripture is devoted just only to the names. Nothing else is written in that scripture: Vishnu Sahasranam — One Thousand Names of God. Just names are counted from one to one thousand. The most beautiful name that I love is Hari; Hari means the ultimate thief.

Just two days ago I was giving sannyas to a beautiful sannyasin. I have given her the name Haridasi — surrendered to the ultimate thief And when I told her that, "Your heart is stolen," for a moment she was transported into another world. Her hand suddenly went on her heart and I said, "It is not there!" And she understood the point immediately. She lost few heartbeats; tears of joy came to her eyes. She could not speak a single word; her voice was choked. It is bound to happen when your heart is gone!

I go on doing things in my own way. And with you, Vivek, I am not worried. You are on fire, your heart is stolen long before. And I am pushing you, and I am absolutely certain that the thing that you are all here for is going to happen to you. Fortunately you are not a Polack, otherwise there was a danger...

Have you heard about the new Polish parachutes?

They open on impact... but they are having great difficulty with them because most Polacks miss the ground!

Question 2

OSHO,

Years ago you seduced us, the blind, into buying your miracle mirrors. We bought them, thinking they were cheap and good-looking. But soon they showed us our ugly faces and we were scared. But before we broke those mirrors, you encouraged us to go on looking, to go on watching, to go on witnessing, and in bargain, you extracted from us the price of our very life.

However, looking back, Osho, I find I have not paid a thing to you. It has all been a gracious gift from you — for nothing. How shall I say thank you, Osho, for all this, and for persevering with us and making us stick on until we really saw our original faces in the miracle mirrors of meditation?

Still I cannot keep wondering, Osho, why and how so many keep on missing you. Are they scared of the super-salesman?

Osho, what are they waiting for? Whom are they waiting for, when this gift of gifts is incessantly showering all over?

— *Ajit Saraswati*

The work of a master is really the work of seduction: he seduces you into the unknown. There is no other way, only seduction can be helpful. You cannot be convinced of the unknown; whatsoever you can be convinced about is bound to be the known. The unknown is unknown. You have not tasted of it, you have not even heard anything about it, you have no idea what it is.

I can convince you of that which you have already some idea, but the unknown is absolutely unknown — and not only unknown, it is unknowable too. There is no way to know it because it is the intrinsic quality of the knower himself It never becomes the known; at no point it becomes the known. The deeper you go into it, the more and more you realize that it is not only the unknown but the unknowable because it is the center of the knower himself How the knower can himself become the known? That is impossible; the knower will always stand beyond the known, surpassing the known.

Hence the work of a Master is actually of seduction. He allures you, he fascinates you; he promises you bliss, truth, freedom — he gives it many names. He makes you afire with longing. A moment comes when the longing is intense and passionate, that you take the jump. It is really mad! No logical person can do it.

Hence I have to destroy slowly your clinging with logic. I have to shift your energy from the head to the heart, because the heart is illogical and from the heart there is a possibility, a bridge, a rainbow bridge towards the unknown and ultimately towards the unknowable.

Hence the word "seduction" actually describes the whole work of all the Buddhas. But the people who are too much clinging to

A Mystery To Be Lived

logic cannot be seduced. If they ask first to be convinced, then there is no way. If they ask for proofs, then there is no way. If the Master himself is a proof, then there is a way. If the presence of the Master is enough to give you the joy that can take you into the adventure, if the very presence of the Master gives you courage to go into the uncharted, only then the journey ever begins.

One thing is certain: once the journey begins you cannot come back. A journey begun is already half the work done; once it begins it has to reach to its climax. Only the beginning part is the most difficult part.

Hence I have to talk about the miracle mirrors and I have to praise those miracle mirrors of meditation; I have to go on saying what great ecstasies they are going to give to you. You are not interested in meditation, you are not interested in looking at your original face, but you are certainly interested in being ecstatic.

But when you for the first time take the mirror in your hand it gives you agony, not ecstasy, because you have to encounter all that is ugly in you, because the ugly is on the surface. But once you have seen the ugly you cannot rest at ease with it. That's the only hope, because nobody can rest at ease with his ugliness. Once seen, you have to destroy it, you have to remove all the masks that are ugly, you have to peel the whole skin that is ugly. And behind the surface there is tremendous beauty. Behind the masks — and there are many masks — your original face is nothing but God's own face. In your originality you are not separate from God; in your personality you are separate.

"Personality" comes from the Greek word persona; it means the mask. In your individuality you are one with God. Then you have the beauty of a Buddha, Krishna, Christ, the same grace. But before one can reach to it one will have to peel one's ugly layers like one peels an onion. And when you peel an onion tears come to your eyes, it is painful. And your false masks have remained with you so long that they have almost become your faces. Removing them is not like removing clothes, it is actually like peeling your skin — it hurts. Hence only the courageous can be interested in inner transformation.

You ask me, Ajit Saraswati: Osho, why and how so many keep on missing you?

They are cowards, they don't have any guts. They don't want to risk anything, and without risk nothing can be gained in life. The higher the peak you want to reach, the greater the risk.

The way of inner search belongs only to the gamblers, not to the businessmen. And people are very calculating, they are constantly calculating, they are always thinking in terms of calculation. Not even for a single moment they are ready to risk anything. They want every kind of security, guarantee, safety, then only they will budge an inch. And in the spiritual inquiry there is no safety, no security. In fact, that's why it has such tremendous beauty: it is an adventure.

The adventure cannot be secure; it is going beyond the boundaries of the known. When you are living within the boundaries of the known, things are secure; you know everything, you are efficient. When you move beyond the known you are taking a risk. You may lose the known, and who knows whether you are going to gain anything in this adventure or not?

You ask me: Are they scared of the super-salesman?

They are simply scared of truth. Because they have lived in so many lies for so long they are afraid: if truth comes in all their lies will collapse. And they have invested not only this life but so many previous lives in those lies. Their investments are great, and truth is going to shatter. They are not bold enough to allow the truth to come in, to accept the fact that if truth destroys the lies it is better that those lies should be destroyed sooner than later, because if you don't destroy them today then tomorrow one more day is lost, then next life one more life is lost, and your investment becomes bigger and bigger with the lies. It is better to finish it quickly; the sooner you do the better. But for that a certain kind of youthfulness is needed.

And in this country particularly there are only two categories Or people: children and old people, the youth does not exist. From

A Mystery To Be Lived

childhood people simply move into old age. The time of youth, youthfulness, rebellion, adventure, never happens.

And with me only young people — young in the spirit, I mean — can have any communion. And not only with me: it has always been so. With Buddha, with Jesus, with Lao Tzu, it was always the case: only very few youthful adventurers went with these dangerous people. They attained great treasures, but those treasurers are not certain, not guaranteed; there is no insurance.

You say:... Before we broke those mirrors, you encouraged us to go on looking, to go on watching, to go on witnessing, and in the bargain, you extracted from us the price of our very life. However, looking back, Osho, I find I have not paid a thing to you.

There is no need to pay anything to me, because whatsoever I am giving to you is not mine, it is God's. It is as much yours as it is mine. What I am giving to you has been given to me. This is the way I am thanking God — by giving it to you.

And, Ajit Saraswati, the only way to feel thankful is to share it with others. Spread it far and wide. Whatsoever you have experienced, share it. And don't be worried about what people will think of you — they will think you are mad! But If you talk to one hundred people at least there is a possibility of one person coming along with you. That's more than enough; it is a great reward. If you can transform one person even, that is enough. Millions are bound to remain in darkness; nothing can be done about it because that is their choice, it is their freedom. If they decide to remain in darkness; who are we to force them into light? We can go on trying, but ultimately it is going to be their decision.

The only way to show our gratitude to the Master is to help others. If it has been a gracious gift to you, give it to others as a gracious gift. Give it without any idea of giving only then is it gracious. Give it without any idea of reward only then is it gracious. Simply give it for the sheer joy of giving It.

You also say: How shall I say thank you, Osho?

It has not to be said. You need not say it, but I am hearing it. Your very silence is enough. It can be said only through silence; there is no other way to say it. Words are very inadequate.

And lastly, you ask: Osho, what are these people waiting for? Whom are they waiting for, when this gift of gifts is incessantly showering all over?

Ajit Saraswati, this world has been driven crazy — crazy not in the sense of a spiritual madness, crazy in the sense that people have become split, people have become schizophrenic, people have been reduced to the lowest state of intelligence, because all the oppressors, the exploiters the leaders, the gurus, they all wanted it in this way. Man should not be allowed to be free, man should not allowed to be rebellious, man should not be allowed to be intelligent. Intelligent people are dangerous for the status quo, for the establishment. The establishment wants people to be slaves, machine-like, robots, and they have succeeded. They start destroying a child the moment the child is born; they start crippling him, paralyzing him.

It is a very strange world: first they cripple you, then they provide crutches for you. And when they provide crutches for you they say, "Look what great service we are doing you!" First they make you blind and then they give you glasses so that you can see a little bit. First they make you dependent and then they start telling you how to be free.

We are living in a very strange world. Up to now humanity has lived in an insane way. It is ridiculous and absurd, and it is time that this should be finished.

That's what my effort here is: through my sannyasins to bring a new kind of man in the world, which will be divinely mad but not schizophrenic — a new man centered in his being. That is the meaning of the word "individual": he will be indivisible; you cannot split him.

A woman approached a psychoanalyst and asked him, "Can you split me into two?"

The psychoanalyst could not believe his ears. People had been coming to him who were suffering from a split personality, and this woman was asking, "Can you split me into two?"

He said, "What is the matter with you? Why do you want to be split in two?"

The woman said, "I feel so lonely!"

If you watch around yourself you will be surprised how an insane humanity we have created.

After several rounds of drinks at the cocktail party, a woman turned to her husband, "Henry, don't you dare take another drink. Your face is getting all blurred already!"

A big three-hundred-pound man was being led to the gallows. He looked at the trap and asked the hangman, "Are you sure that thing is safe?"

A researcher in sociology making a survey of homosexuality rang the bell of an apartment. The man who answered the door responded to his question, "Homosexual? I never heard of that word. Wait, I will ask my wife."

Turning his head, he called, "Ernest!".

The morning after she left on her honeymoon, a bride returned home. She related: "I took off my clothes. Then he took off his clothes. Then he put on my clothes and left!

A rabbi was telling a story:

"One day a poor woodcutter found a baby in the forest, but he didn't know how to feed him. So he prayed to God and a miracle happened — the woodcutter grew breasts and could feed the baby."

"Rabbi," interrupted a listener, "I don't like this story. Why such a weird thing like breasts on a man? If God is almighty he could have just dropped a bag of gold to give the woodcutter enough money to buy food for the baby."

The rabbi meditated on this for a while, then said, "Why should God spend such a lot of money when he can just do a miracle?"

In a deserted bar two people were seated at opposite ends of the room. The Jew and the Jap had been drinking for some time without noticing each other, when suddenly the Jew got off his stool, walked over to the Jap, and punched him on the nose. The dazed Japanese, struggling to his feet, asked the Jew why he did that.

"That was for Pearl Harbor," replied the Jew, and walked back to his stool.

After a few more drinks the Jap got off his stool and walked over to the Jew. He punched him very hard on the nose. The Jew, from his crumpled position on the floor, asked what that was for.

"That was for the Titanic," stated the Jap.

"But that was an iceberg!" complained the Jew.

"Well," responded the Jap, "Iceberg, Greenberg, Silverberg... they are all the same!"

When the flood was finally over and the animals were going out of Noah's ark, the elephant turned around to the flea who was behind him and said, "Stop pushing me!"

This is the world we are living! People have been driven to the lowest intelligence possible, and to raise their intelligence back is an arduous task.

It is a miracle if somebody listens to me, understands me and starts transforming himself. It is happening to you, Ajit Saraswati — you are blessed. Very few are so blessed in the world.

Question 3

OSHO,
What is nostalgia?
— Sahajo

A Mystery To Be Lived

Nostalgia is the longing to go back to the good old days when you were neither good nor old.

Question 4

OSHO,

Aren't you ever afraid that instead of the creation of a new kind of man, this is the creation of a new kind of sheep?

— Dick

I am not afraid at all, because even if a new sheep is created it is better than the old sheep — at least it will be new! And to be new is good, to be new is fresh, to be new opens new possibilities. Hence I am not afraid.

But you must be attached with the old kind of sheep, hence you are afraid. I can only try to give birth to a new man, but the birth cannot be absolutely guaranteed. I will do my best. It does not matter to me whether I succeed or fail. What matters is whether I tried my best or not — and I am trying my best. And that's all that I am interested in.

I am enjoying my work. Who cares about the result? The people who care too much about the result simply waste their energy, because caring about the result takes much of their energy. Then they become worried about the result — that is a distraction — then the end becomes far more important than the journey itself.

To me the journey itself is enough, the search itself is more than enough. To me the means and the ends are not separate, they are inseparable. Hence what I am doing I am enjoying; what happens, that is not at all a question to me.

But why are you worried? You must be interested in keeping people in their old traps. I can do only one thing... You have heard the old proverb — this is a new edition of that old proverb:

You can lead a hippie to water, but you cannot make him bathe.

I will lead the hippie to the water — that much I can do — I will persuade him, but then it is up to him to take a jump into the river or not. And who am I to throw him into the river? I can show him the way to the river, I can even lead him to the river, then it is his freedom. If he chooses to remain the same I am not going to disturb his freedom, I am not going to do anything against him.

I love every person as he is. I love my work; it is not work to me at all because I love it — it is just a play. But with you, Dick, there seems to be some problem inside you. Your question has nothing to do with my work, it has something to do with your prejudices.

You ask me: aren't you ever afraid that instead of the creation of a new kind of man, this is the creation of a new kind of sheep?

I am trying to create the new man. Even if out of one hundred, one new man is created, that will bring the whole consciousness of humanity a step forward, a step upward. There is a possibility many will become only new kind of sheep, but then too it is not bad, that too is a gain. It is better to be alive, young, fresh, new, even though you are a sheep.

But you must be somehow deeply interested in keeping people in their old patterns; your investment must be there. Your prejudices must be those of a Christian, a Jew, a Hindu, a Mohammedan.

Two musicians were walking in a street when a large bell from a building being demolished fell nearby with a loud clang. "What's that?" asked one.

"I'm not sure," said the other, "but I think it was B flat."

People have their own languages, their own prejudices, and they cling to their prejudices. Even though their prejudices have been a sheer misery for them, still they cling.

If you are an old sheep, Dick, at least become a new sheep — orange! It will not be a very great revolution, but even a little change is good. Just for that little change... and a little change may open doors for greater changes.

A Mystery To Be Lived

Two hobos sat with their backs against an old oak tree. Before them flowed a rippling stream. It was a delightful day, yet one of them was disconsolate.

"You know, Slim," he said, "this tramping through life is not what it used to be. Things are getting tougher every year. I used to hop a freight chugging up a steep grade very easy, but these diesels go like mad. And I'm getting tired of spending my nights in a cold barn and on park benches, wondering where my next meal is coming from. And odd jobs are getting scarcer all the time..." His voice trailed off as he sighed.

His companion turned to face him. "If that's the way you feel, why don't you hang it all up and find yourself a real job?"

The first tramp raised his head and opened his mouth in amazement. "What!" he cried. "And admit I'm a failure?"

Even a tramp, a hobo, a beggar does not want to accept that he is a failure.

Dick, the way you have asked the question simply shows that you are an old sheep — Catholic, Protestant — and you are afraid of the new sheep. You are not concerned about the new man. The old sheep is worried, because what is going to happen to the old prejudices, the old conclusions, the old ideology? It seems as if it will be a deep discontinuity with the past, as if one dies and is reborn.

But those who are ready to drop the old are not sheep. The very courage to drop the old is enough to prove that they are lions! The very courage that they are ready to come out of their old skins their old prejudices old idiologies, religions, philosophies, shows one thing very clearly, categorically: that they are not sheep. And that very courage is the hope for the birth of a new man.

You just put your old prejudices aside, and then try to understand what is happening here. Get a little bit involved, participate in what is happening here. You have lived according to your old beliefs. If you are contented, I will be the last person to disturb you; but if you are contented, why you are here?

For what? You must be discontented.

This is one of the strangest things about man: even if he is discontented he goes on believing, pretending that he is contented. And whenever there is an opportunity to change — and he is looking for an opportunity to change, this is the strangeness — when he finds the opportunity to change, he clings with the past.

A doctor was consulted by a prizefighter who was troubled with insomnia.

"Have you tried counting sheep?" asked the doctor.

"Yes, but it doesn't help. Every time I get up to nine I jump up!"

An old prizefighter! The moment he gets to nine he cannot resist. Instead of giving him a good sleep it will disturb him — he jumps up. People function mechanically, unconsciously. Your question has come out of your unconsciousness, Dick.

The tavern was near an army camp, and the pretty barmaid was popular with the enlisted men, especially since she preferred them to the overbearing officers.

One night a polite young private was sitting next to a cocky first lieutenant who tried to date her. When the lieutenant went to the men's room she put her face close to the private and whispered, "Now is your chance, soldier!"

The private looked at the tempting red lips and then cried, "That's right!" And he hastily drank the officer's beer.

You are here but not really here. And the way I talk must be so difficult for you to understand. If you have been listening to the sermons by the priests in the churches or in the temples or in the mosques, then what I am saying here will look very irreligious, will look very strange to your ideas of what spirituality should be. But I cannot talk the way your are accustomed to hearing. You may be waiting for some esoteric bullshit!

Kohn was home from seeing his doctor and meets his friend who asks, "Wha-wha-what is wrong wi-with you?"

"I've got prostatitis," replies Kohn.

"Wha-what... wha-wha-what is that?"

"I piss the way you talk!"

The new man can only be created with everything new: the way I talk, the way my people live, the way they behave, all has to be totally different from the old man. The new man cannot believe in your rotten morality — your morality has only created hypocrites. The new man can live only authentically; he cannot be concerned with your moral and immoral ideas. He can live only meditatively. He cannot be thought as a man of character, the way you have become accustomed to think of religious people.

The new man will not be a man of character, the new man will be utterly characterless. But when I say "characterless" please don't misunderstand me; I am not talking the way you understand. To me the characterless man is the only man who has character. Characterless I call him because he does not follow any dictates from the outside. He lives according to his own light, he lives meditatively. His character does not come from his conscience.

Conscience is an agency implanted in you by the society, it is not yours. Don't call the conscience as yours — it is not yours. It belongs to the Christian church, it belongs to the Hindu religion, it belongs to the Jain philosophy, it belongs to the communist ideology. It has nothing to do with you; it is implanted by others in you. It is a very subtle strategy to dominate you from within. On the outside they have put a policeman, the magistrate, the court, and in the inside they have created a conscience.

The real man, the new man, will live according to consciousness, not according to conscience. Of course, whatsoever his consciousness feels right he will do, whatsoever the risk, whatsoever he has to pay for it. Even if he has to pay with his life he will be ready to pay it, because there are higher things than life itself. Consciousness is far more higher than life. But he will not follow conscience.

The man of conscience is known as a man of character —

that's why I call the new man characterless, because he will not have any conscience, he will function out of consciousness. His commandments will be coming from his own center, and when they come from your own center they give you freedom. And out of freedom life takes a new flavor, a new beauty. You do the right, but now the right is not decided by others. It is no more a slavery, it is absolute freedom.

The new man will live out of meditation, out of consciousness, out of his own inner light. The new man will be an individual, not part of any collectivity.

My sannyasins here are not a collectivity. Each of my sannyasins is related to me directly. It is not a church, it is not an organization: it is a love relationship. And because they all love me, of course they start feeling love for each other too; that is secondary. Their love towards me is primary, then their love for other sannyasins is secondary; they are fellow-travelers. But nobody is bound to follow me or to follow anybody else. It is a commune of fellow-travelers. fellow-seekers.

There is no qualitative difference between me and my sannyasins. The only difference is a very slight one, very small one: I am aware of my inner world, they are not aware, but they have the inner world as much as I have it. I don't have it more, they don't have it less. They have the whole kingdom of God within themselves. I am not special in any sense. I am not claiming that I am the son of God, I am not claiming that I am an avatara of God, I am not claiming that I am a teerthankara. I am simply saying one thing: that I was asleep, now I am awake; you are asleep and you can be awake also. I have known both states — the state of being asleep and the state of being awake — and you know only one state, of being asleep.

But remember, the person who is capable of sleeping is capable of awakening. The very fact he can sleep is an indication that he can be awake! There is no difference at all.

I will go on trying to help people to be awake. The awakened man will be the new man. He will not be Christian, he will not be Hindu, he will not be Mohammedan; he will not be Indian, he will not be German, he will not be English. He will be simply an awakened being.

But, Dick, it is possible that there may be a few people who will only turn into a new kind of sheep, but that too is not bad. As far as being the old sheep is concerned, it is better than that. So if your are an old sheep, become a new sheep, and from there the journey starts, a possibility. If the old sheep can become a new sheep it is a radical change. The sheep deciding to be new — it is a revolution. And if this much is possible, then much more is possible too.

Question 5

OSHO,
What is your definition of a politician?
— *Nartan*

If a man dodges cars, he is a pedestrian. If he dodges taxes, he is a businessman. If he dodges responsibilities, he is an executive. And if he dodges everything, he is a politician.

And the last question:

Question 6

OSHO,
Once you told a joke for purna who was Leaving. I am staying will you tell a joke for me too?
— *Anand Donna,*
— *Okay,*

A jewish rabbi decided to sit in with the priest in his confessional box to learn the principles of the Catholic religion. Two women came, one after the other, and confessed to having had intercourse with their boyfriends, not only once but three times. For penance the priest told them to say three Pater Nosters and put ten dollars in the poor box.

The priest was called away urgently to give last rites to a dying man. He told the rabbi to stay and hear the confessions for the rest of the people. "Just remember to get the ten dollars," he said before leaving.

The first confessor was a young girl who told the rabbi that she had had intercourse with her boyfriend.

"Three times?" questioned the rabbi.

"Oh no, Father, just once," replied the girl.

"Are you quite sure it wasn't three times?"

"No, Father, only once," insisted the young girl.

"Well," suggested the rabbi, "I tell you what just say three Pater Nosters, put ten dollars in the box, and the church will owe you two fucks."

13

Prayer Simply Happens

I Absolute And Relative —
He Who Knows These Two Together,
Through The Relative Leaves Death Behind
And Through The Absolute Gains Immortality.
The Threshold Of Reality Is Veiled By Golden Light.
Reveal It, O Lord, For My Dharma Is To Know The Truth.
O Lord Of Light, The Knowing One,
The Golden Guardian, Giver Of Life To All,
Spread Apart Thy Rays, Gather Up Thy Brilliance,
That I May Perceive Thy Finest And Most
Splendrous Nature,
That Cosmic Spirit Which Lies At Thy Heart.
For I Myself Am That!
Let My Breath Merge With The Cosmic Breath,
May My Body Be As Dust,
Remember, O Mind, Remember What Has Been Done.
Remember, O Mind, Remember What Has Been Done.
O Agni, Show Us The Right Path,
Lead Us To Eternal Freedom,
Thou Who Knowest All.
May We Not Be Diverted From Our Goal,
For With All Devotion We Submit Ourselves To Thee.

Aum

Purnamadah
Purnamidam
Purnat Purnamudachyate
Purnasya Purnamadaya
Purnameva Vashisyate.

Aum

That Is The Whole.
This Is The Whole.
From Wholeness Emerges Wholeness,
Wholeness Coming From Wholeness,
Wholeness Still Remains.

The greatest contribution of the seers of the Upanishads is that they have made this world and the other world synonymous. They have dropped the idea of the mundane and the sacred that represents the absolute, the ultimate, the further shore; this represents the immediate, the herenow, this shore. Both are one because: that is the whole, this is the whole — there is no distinction at all.

The ordinary religions live on condemning this world; by condemning this world they praise the other world. The Upanishads have a totally different approach: they praise this world with all its beauty, splendor; through praising this world they praise the other world. This approach is life-affirmative.

The Upanishads are in tremendous love with life. They don't teach renunciation, they teach rejoicing. They would have agreed with Jesus when Jesus says again and again to his disciples, "Rejoice! Rejoice! I say again to you rejoice!" The Upanishads have a very aesthetic approach towards life — not the approach of an ascetic but the approach of a poet, a painter, a musician, a dancer. Their approach is in no way pathological.

But that vision has completely disappeared. Instead of that ecstatic vision of life, for three thousand years humanity has lived with a very sado-masochistic idea: torture yourself and teach others so that they can also torture themselves, because that's the only way to make God rejoice. This is really a condemnation of God, as if God is a torturer, as if he enjoys people being in pain and anguish.

Even today we go on praising the ascetic attitude. The person who tortures himself becomes a great saint. If he fasts starves his body, lies down on a bed of thorns, stands naked in the cold, sits in the hottest season surrounded by fire, then we have great respect for him.

This respect simply shows that our minds are in a very ill state. We are not for health, for wholeness, for joy, for bliss. We are suicidal, murderous. And in the name of religion great suicide has been committed. The whole humanity has become suicidal.

To understand these last sutras of the Upanishad remember one thing: to the Upanishads the beyond is not against the world, it is an intrinsic part of it. The beyond is also the within of the world; it is not far away, it is deep down here and now. Just as a river needs both the banks, life needs both this and that.

When you look at a river you see two banks, but if you dive deep into the river you will find those two banks are not separate; underneath the river they are joined together, they are one. In the same way this and that are one. They appear divided, but that is only an appearance; don't be deceived by it. Dive deep so that you can find the ultimate unity.

The so-called masochists, ascetic saints have been talking of advaita, oneness, but that seems to be only talk, just lip-service, because the way they behave, the way they live, simply shows duality. They renounce the world. If the world is illusory, why renounce it? What is there to renounce? Nobody renounces one's dreams. When you wake up in the morning you don't make a great declaration to the world that: "I have renounced all my dreams of the night!" When you wake up you simply know those dreams were not part of reality; they were just fantasies of the mind. There is nothing to renounce; they have evaporated by themselves. And if you insist in renouncing the dreams, that simply shows that you are still dreaming. Now your dream is that of renouncing the dreams — a new dream. The old dreams are replaced by a new dream.

Somebody is trying to conquer the world — a man like Alexander — and somebody else is trying to renounce the world — the man like Shankara. But both are agreed upon one point: that the world exists. Shankara says it is unreal. If it is unreal, then where are you going? Then why you are renouncing it? Then why this insistence, this emphasis? The whole emphasis proves just the contrary of what is emphasized.

When I was a student, one of my professors in the university always used to talk about his bravery, fearlessness, so much so that not even a single day passed by when he will not mention in some way or other that he is a brave man. I listened at least for two, three months, and then I stood up and asked him, "Insisting every day that you are a great, brave man, simply shows that there must be some cowardice in you. Otherwise why this insistence? Whom you are trying to prove? We are not asking whether you are a coward or a brave. We have not come here to inquire about your bravery or your cowardice, whatsoever it is — we are not interested in it. Why you go on insisting?" And from any reference, from any context he will jump to the conclusion, as if he was just always looking for any excuse to prove that he is a brave man.

He was shocked. He called me home in the night and told me that, "You are the first person who has made me aware of a certain fear in me. I am really a man who is full of fears. I am not trying to convince you — in fact, by talking to you I am trying to convince myself. And I am thankful," he said, "although when you said it for the first time before others I was shocked, angry, enraged. But later on when I thought about it calmly, quietly, I realized the fact of it."

The people who go on emphasizing the world is illusory are simply trying to prove to themselves that it is illusory but they know it is not. They are trying to create a great smoke around themselves that it is illusory, worth renouncing: "It is worthless, there is no meaning in it!" But why this insistence? If there is no meaning in it, there is no meaning in it. If it is illusory, it is illusory. You need not say it. And these so-called saints have written so many books proving that the world is illusory.

These saints have been talking about the illusoriness of the female body, that it is ugly, it is not beautiful: "Just look within the skin: it is nothing but bones, blood, pus, mucus." Whom they are trying to prove these things? And why this continuous insistence?

There seems to be a great attraction in them for the woman's body. They are trying to create defenses.

Upanishads never say a single word against the world; that seems to be a more truthful vision. The world is there, it is real. Of course its reality is relative, and that's a fact everybody knows its reality is relative. You love a woman today, tomorrow you may not love. Today it had seemed to you that you will love her forever, and tomorrow all that idea has simply evaporated. Just a day before you were ready to die for her, and a day afterwards you are ready to kill her!

It is a relative world, nothing is permanent here, that is true. Everything is changing, fluxlike; it is momentary. But that does not mean that it is unreal, that it is illusory. Even though it is momentary it is true, it is real. It has a relative reality.

The other world, the beyond, the absolute, has a totally different kind of reality; it is non-relative. But both are real. The relative and the absolute are two aspects of the same reality. Watch a river: in one way it goes on changing, in another way it is the same river. Watch your mind: the mind goes on changing — every moment something new comes something old dies — but in another way your consciousness your watcher is the same. You can experience both these things within you: the mind is a relative reality and your consciousness is an absolute reality.

You go to see a movie. The screen remains the same, but the scenes on the screen go on changing. Both are real. The scenes are for a moment there and then they are gone, but the screen remains the same. Because of the scenes you cannot see the screen. When the scenes stop, the projector stops, suddenly the screen is there utterly empty. That is the experience of absolute: it is emptiness, just a white screen; nothing moves, nothing changes. It is eternal, timeless. But the world of time, the world of change is also part of it.

Remember the metaphor of the wheel and the axle: the axle is absolute and the wheel is relative. But the wheel needs the axle; without the axle the wheel cannot move — on what it will move?

And the axle needs the wheel; without the wheel it won't be an axle at all. They are complementary not antagonistic.

This and that are two aspects of the same coin. The sutras:

> Absolute And Relative —
> He Who Knows These Two Together,
> Through The Relative Leaves Death Behind
> And Through The Absolute Gains Immortality.

See the point: One who knows these together... The Upanishad is not saying know the absolute and renounce the relative. It is saying know them together in their togetherness. Then only your knowing is whole, then only your knowing is total. The person who turns away from the world remains lopsided as much as the person who remains in the world and forgets the beyond. Both are partial, and to be partial is to be ill because then you cannot have your whole being, only a fragment. And to have a fragment only is to suffer, is to be miserable.

Hence my observation is: the worldly people suffer in one way and your so-called spiritual people suffer in another, but both suffer. Suffering comes from the partial truth. Bliss is the fragrance of the whole.

Bliss comes only when you live life in its totality. The totality includes this and that and it does not make any hierarchy that is not higher than this; that is hidden in this. This is the visible part of that, and that is the unmanifest part of this. This is the body of that and that is the soul of this.

And you can see within yourself: the body and the soul are living in absolute harmony. In the same way the God and his existence are living in deep harmony there is no conflict. The conflict is created by your so-called religious people; they have created all kinds of unnecessary struggles.

Hence true religion will be closer to the Upanishads than to Shankaracharya, than to Mahavira, it will be far closer to the Upanishads. And this Isha Upanishad is the very essence of the whole Upanishadic philosophy of life.

Prayer Simply Happens

> Absolute And Relative —
> He Who Knows These Two Together
> Through The Relative Leaves Death Behind
> And Through The Absolute Gains Immortality.

The absolute cannot be known by any method, it cannot be known by any teaching, it cannot be known by any scripture. The absolute cannot be known as an object of knowledge because it is the very center of your innermost core, it is the foundation of all your knowing. Hence it cannot be known as the known. No method will help, no teaching will help, no philosophy will be of any support in fact, they will hinder. To know the absolute, one has to drop all doctrines, all philosophies, all ideologies, all methods.

Just the other day somebody had asked: "Is it possible to find God by practicing Yoga?" God cannot be found by practicing anything — neither Yoga nor Tantra nor Zen nor Tao. God cannot be known by practicing anything whatsoever. Who will practice? All practices are confined to the mind and the mind practicing something means the mind is strengthened more and more through the practice, the mind is exercising and becoming stronger. Every practice strengthens the mind, and the mind belongs to the relative; It is the very foundation of the relative.

You can practice Yoga: you will have a better body, a better mind, you will have a better memory, you will have a longer life; all these things are possible. If you go deep into practicing Yoga you may even start having few miraculous powers siddhis, because you will discover subtle forces of the mind and the body which are not ordinarily available, which are not functioning. You will come across many new energies which you had never suspected.

Psychologists say major part of the brain is not functioning, and they are puzzled because if it is not functioning then why it is there? It seems to have no purpose and nature never creates anything without any purpose — it must have some purpose. But psychology has not yet been able to find any purpose and psychology may not be able to find. Unless Yoga, Tantra, Zen, Tao and all these methodologies of reviving subtle energies of the mind are included in scientific research work, psychology may not be able to find out any function

Even physiology has not found functions for few things, hence they are every time ready to remove your appendix because it has no function. The doctors are ready to remove your tonsils any moment because they don't seem to have any function — as if nature can grow something in you which has really no function. Then why your appendix should exist at all? Ordinarily — physiology is right and psychology is right — they don't have any function; but if you enter into the world of Yoga you will be surprised: even your appendix has a function, your tonsils have a function, and the major part of the brain which is non-functioning starts functioning.

You can start reading other people's thoughts. This will be done by a new center in the mind; the old centers cannot do it. You can start even projecting your thoughts into other people's mind; they will think they are thinking those thoughts. In fact, you are flooding their minds by your thoughts. You can have great powers of deceiving; they will not be able to see how you are doing it — how you are materializing a Swiss watch out of the air they will not be able to see. Just you know one simple technique: how to prevent them from knowing what is being happening just in front of their eyes.

But all these things have nothing to do with knowing God the ultimate; all these thing are part of the relative. Magicians can do it, hypnotists can do it, mesmerists can do it and there are many ways to find out these secrets These are not very spiritual things, in fact; only non-spiritual egoists become interested in these things.

Absolute is found only when you have dropped all knowledge; all scriptures are burned, all theories are rejected, the mind itself is put to sleep. Then the absolute emerges. It is your very nature. When all the clouds have disappeared the sun shines forth.

But methods can help to get rid of the relative. They can help you to become more powerful as far as body is concerned, mind is concerned. They can also help you to get rid of the relative, they can help to remove the barriers when I am talking to you, that's exactly the purpose of my talking to you: to help you to get rid of the relative. All the methods of Yoga, Tantra, Zen and Tao are negative — negative in the sense they don't give you the absolute, but they help you to be finished with the relative.

The sutra says:

Through The Relative One Leaves Death Behind
And Through The Absolute One Gains Immortality.

You can see the point: death represents all that is relative and immortality represents all that is absolute Death represents time, change, and absolute represents eternity.

In Sanskrit we have the same word for both time and death. We call death kaal and time also kaal. Sanskrit may be the only language in the whole world which has the same name for time and death. That's why it can be said truthfully that Sanskrit is the only language transformed by the insight of the seers; all other languages have remained ordinary. For ten thousand years thousands of people in the East have become enlightened, and they have changed the very structure of Sanskrit language. They have given it a color of their enlightenment, they have made words luminous; they have given those words new meanings which cannot be given by unenlightened persons. Now to call time and death by the same name is a great insight. It is not a question of knowing linguistics, it is a question of experiencing something tremendously valuable. Time and death are the same; to live in time means to live in death. And the moment time disappears, death disappears. So when you are utterly silent, when no thought moves in your mind, time disappears; you cannot have any idea what time it is. And the moment time disappears and the clock of your mind stops, suddenly you enter the world of the timeless, the eternal world, the world of the absolute. Jesus is asked by a seeker... it is not reported in the New Testament, but it is part of the Sufi tradition. A seeker asks Jesus: What will be the most significant thing in your kingdom of God? And the answer is amazing. Jesus says: "There shall be time no longer. That will be the most significant thing in my kingdom of God — there shall be time no longer. There will be no past, no future; there will be only present."

And let me tell you that present is not part of time. Of course ordinarily in the schools, colleges and the universities you have been told and taught and your dictionaries go on saying again and again that time has three tenses: past, present and future. That is absolutely wrong — wrong according to those who know. Past and future are time, but present is not time present belongs to eternity. Past and future belong to this — the world of the relative, change. Between the two penetrates the beyond, the transcendental, and that is the present. Now is part of eternity.

If you live in time, death is bound to happen. In fact, to say "bound to happen" is not right — it is already happening. The moment a child is born he starts dying. It takes seventy, eighty years to die, that's another matter. He dies, slowly, miserly, in installments, a little bit every day, every hour. He goes on dying, dying, dying... then the process is complete after seventy years or eighty years. When you say that somebody has died today, don't be misguided by your statement: he has been dying for eighty years, today the process is complete.

There is an ancient Chinese tradition in the Taoist school it seems to be the only tradition in the whole world where when a child is born the family cries, they weep because the birth is nothing but an arrow moving towards death. They don't celebrate it, they feel very sad. another being has entered into the world of death — how can you celebrate it?

If one wants to celebrate, then death is the right thing to celebrate: one person has completed the process of dying and perhaps he may not be born again; perhaps he has entered into the beyond, or at least this death process has ended. Maybe he will start another death process, but that is in the future and we don't know anything about it. Celebrating birth is ignorance: celebrating death is understanding.

Through The Relative One Leaves Death Behind...

If you use the methods of meditation you will leave the mind behind, and mind is the source of time and death both. Mind is time, mind is death. One aspect of mind is time, another aspect of mind is death. Through meditation, through watching the mind, you can leave death behind.

But this is only a negative process; the Upanishads call it neti neti — neither this nor that — the process of elimination. I am not this — the body, the mind. Then who am I?" First eliminate the non-essential, put it aside, and go on eliminating all that is non-essential until only the essential is left. And what is essential? How will you decide that only the essential is left? When there is nothing left to be denied nothing left to be eliminated... go on emptying your house throw all the furniture out. When there is nothing left to be thrown out, then a great revelation happens: you gain immortality; the absolute arises in you in all its beauty and splendor, in all its ecstasy. It overfloods you, it starts radiating; it starts reaching even to others who are available, receptive, vulnerable.

The Threshold Of Reality Is Veiled By Golden Light.

Now the Isha Upanishad reminds the seeker that: be aware. When you enter into the world of absolute reality you will come across a golden veil, very beautiful, so beautiful that many have become enchanted and stopped there.

The Threshold Of Reality Is Veiled By Golden Light.

All darkness disappears and there is such a golden light, so psychedelic... you have never experienced anything like it. You think you have come home. Wait, beware: this is just the light that surrounds the reality. You have to penetrate this light to reach to the very center of reality. When you come close to a flame, the flame is surrounded by golden light. Remember, the golden light radiates from the flame, but the golden light is not the flame itself. When you look at the sun you see a golden light radiating from the sun. We are far away from the sun; it takes for sunlight to reach to us ten minutes, and ten minutes for light is long distance because light travels by tremendous speed, ultimate speed Scientists say that that is the last, more speed is not possible. Light travels in one second, one hundred eighty-six thousand miles — in one minute sixty times more, in ten minutes six hundred times more. It is far away, but we can see the light; the rays are reaching us.

Remember, these rays are coming from the sun, but these rays are not the sun itself. If you want to reach to the sun you will have to go beyond these rays. And this sun is nothing compared to other suns which are far bigger. Even this sun is not a small sun; it is sixty thousand times bigger than the earth, and this is a very mediocre sun in the universe. There are greater suns than this, millions of times bigger.

In the night when you see stars you think they are very small — you are wrong. They are very far away that's why they look small; they are far bigger than the sun, but their distance is almost unbelievable. The closest sun next to this sun is four light years away; the rays from that sun reach to us in four years; from this sun it takes ten minutes, from that sun it takes four years, and that is the closest. There are suns from where it takes millions of light years for the sunlight to reach to us, and there are few suns conceived by the physicists whose light has not reached to the earth yet, since the earth was made. And there is a possibility that there may be suns even farther away whose light will never reach to the earth, because meanwhile the earth will disappear. It came into being, for millions of years it existed, the light was traveling and traveling with that tremendous speed of one hundred eighty-six thousand miles per second. By the time the light reaches the earth would have died; that light will never reach to the earth.

But all these suns, great suns, are nothing compared to the ultimate reality. Kabir says, "The moment I penetrated into my innermost core I found as if suddenly millions of suns had risen" — not one, millions of suns. Naturally, the Upanishadic seers are making you aware:

›The Threshold Of Reality Is Veiled By Golden Light.

And the light is so beautiful, so blissful, that you can be caught in the net of it and you can start thinking you have arrived. Many scriptures of the world say: God is light. The people who have said that have misunderstood: they have thought the golden light as God itself.

God is neither light nor darkness; he is both and beyond. Unless you reach to that ultimate which is always beyond the duality, transcendental to duality, go on remembering: you have not come home yet. Go on inquiring, go on exploring.

The Upanishadic seer prays to God:

Reveal It, O Lord, For My Dharma Is To Know The Truth.

Upanishads start in meditation and end in prayer. This is the right sequence. Nobody can start by prayer because if you start by prayer your prayer will be false, it cannot be true. You will be asking for some ordinary things — money, power, prestige — because that is where you are. Your prayer will be part of your mind, and mind is full of desires, hence your prayers will be full of desires and demands.

Go and listen to people who are in prayer in the churches, in the temples. What they are asking?

Even a man like the great Emperor Akbar used to pray for more money, more power. Once a great Sufi mystic, Farid, went to see him. He had never gone to Akbar; Akbar used to come to see him. Farid lived very close to Delhi, and Akbar had tremendous respect for Farid. He had asked him to come to the palace, but Farid will laugh at the whole idea and he will say, "You can always come whenever you want why bother me?"

But one day the villagers where Farid lived asked him that, "We don't have even a school in our village, and the great emperor comes to you. You can just give him a hint and immediately it will happen. You can just say that we need a school"

Farid said that, "If I have to ask something from him, then it is better I should go" And he went to see Akbar.

When he reached Akbar's palace he was well received; everybody knew about him. Akbar was in his small prayer house that he has made inside his palace. He ritually did all the five prayers every day, as a Mohammedan is required to do. He was doing his morning prayer. Nobody was allowed to enter in the shrine when Akbar was praying, but the guards did not prevent Farid; they could not think of preventing him.

He went in; he stood behind Akbar. Akbar was one of the greatest emperors who has ever lived on the earth. India has known only two great emperors: one was Ashoka, another was Akbar. They had the greatest kingdoms possible — the richest men of all the ages. And Farid was shocked. Akbar was not aware that Farid is standing behind — nobody, not even his wife, was allowed to enter in. So he was just praying to God, talking to God, unaware of the fact that somebody is listening.

As he ended his prayer he raised his hands towards the sky and said to God, "Give me more money, more power, more kingdom."

Farid was shocked: "This man has so much, and still he is asking for more he was going down the steps, Akbar saw him. He rushed, fell unto his feet and said, "Why you came? You could have asked me to come! And now why are you leaving?"

Farid said, "I had come to make a small request, but seeing that you are still a beggar I thought it is not right to make the request, because my villagers had asked you for a small school, but now I cannot ask because that means you will become a little less richer than you are; a little bit of money will have to be put for the school. No, I cannot ask you. Moreover, if you are asking God, I can ask God myself. Why I should ask through you, through your agency? But," Farid said, "I had never thought of asking anything from God, that's why I am such a fool that I came to you. But you have opened my eyes. I have been praying my whole life, but the idea never happened to me that one should ask anything."

Prayer can be of two types. One: the ordinary prayer that is being done all over the world; Hindus, Mohammedans, Christians, all are doing it. They have not transcended the mind, so their prayer is full of their desires.

To attain to real prayer first you have to become silent, first you have to pass through the alchemy of meditation. Meditation helps you to get rid of the mind, and when there is no mind you can pray, but that prayer will have a totally different quality to it.

This is the prayer:

Reveal It, O Lord, For My Dharma Is To Know The Truth.

The seer is saying that, "I have done whatsoever I could do: I have meditated, practiced Yoga, watched my mind, I have dissolved the mind, eliminated all that was stupid in me, mediocre in me, unintelligent in me. But from all that effort I have attained only to the golden light, your veil. Now unless you remove it, nothing is possible. Whatsoever I could do I have done — my doer is finished, my doing is finished. I have come to the very end of my tether; now my road ends here. Now only you can take me further ahead."

Prayer begins only when you have done everything that you can do; then your prayer has authenticity. It means, "Now what can I do? Everything that was possible for me I have done, and this is what I have attained to — great light, great benediction, great bliss, but still I feel that this is just the outermost part of your being. Now only you can help."

You can ask for help when you have done all that you can do, not before that. Prayer comes only after meditation.

That's why I don't teach prayer to you, I teach meditation, because I know only after meditation prayer is possible. And the beauty is that if you have meditated well prayer comes on its own accord, there is no need to teach it. Just as a flower opens and the fragrance is released, exactly like that when meditation is happening, the fragrance of prayer comes on its own accord, it simply happens. And then the prayer can be only one:

Reveal It, O Lord, For My Dharma Is To Know The Truth.

The word dharma is untranslatable, that's why the translator has left it as it is. Ordinarily dharma is translated as "religion" which is wrong, absolutely wrong. Religion is a very ordinary thing; religion means a creed, a theology, a theory, a hypothesis, a doctrine. dharma means your innermost nature, svabhava, your self-nature. dharma means your deepest longing for truth, your ultimate thirst for being. It is there in everybody's center. It is a seed; it can become a flower.

Two things have to be done. The first is the meditative part: it will help the plant to grow, it will help the buds to arrive. And then you have to pray; the second part is prayer. If you start forcibly opening the buds you will destroy the whole beauty; you will destroy the fragrance, even the possibility of fragrance. Then you have to pray:

Reveal It, O Lord, For My Dharma Is To Know The Truth.

My deepest longing is to know the truth, the ultimate truth, the naked truth and nothing else. I don't want this golden light, I cannot be contented with this. Your veil is beautiful — of course it is your veil, hence it is beautiful — and something of you is radiating out of the veil, but I want to see you in your absolute nudity, I want to see you unveiled. Hence reveal, unveil, O Lord, and this only you can do, I cannot do. I have come so far that I can see your veil, but more than that is beyond me.

Prayer is significant only when you have done all that you are capable of; then your prayer has a sincerity.

O Lord Of Light, The Knowing One, The Golden Guardian, Giver Of Life To All, Spread Apart Thy Rays, Gather Up Thy Brilliance, That I May Perceive Thy Finest And Most Splendrous Nature, That Cosmic Spirit Which Lies At Thy Heart. For I Myself Am That!

O Lord Of Light...

Remember, God is the lord of light but not light itself; he is also the God of darkness. He is the lord of this and that both. He is the lord of both the shores of life.

O Lord Of Light, The Knowing One, The Golden Guardian,

Giver Of Life To All, Spread Apart Thy Rays...

The prayer is now that: "Allow me to see you as you are spread apart thy rays. Give me little bits of windows, doors. spread apart thy rays, so I can have few spaces to enter within you; otherwise your rays are so beautiful they can prevent me. I can get allured by them, I can become hypnotized by them. I am in a danger: if you don't help me I will think I have come to the very end."

... Gather Up Thy Brilliance...

See the prayer: Gather up thy brilliance. Don't shine so much, because I cannot even open my eyes — how can I see you? Gather up thy brilliance. Help me — withdraw your brilliance. Gather up your rays so that I can see you, so that I can perceive thy finest and most splendrous nature. And I want to see you because I am not separate from you. Unless I know you I will not be able to know myself.

That Cosmic Spirit Which Lies At Thy Heart.
For I Myself Am That!

I am that. This is the ultimate statement of the Upanishads: I am that! This "I" does not mean the ego; this "I" simply means your pure existence, without any ego in it. It is more "amness" than "I-amness". There is no I in it; it is pure existence. One simply is.

And the moment you are without the ego, just utterly empty of the ego, without the self, just pure consciousness with no idea of any "I" at the center of it, then you are that, then there is no difference.

That's what Al-Hillaj Mansoor was crucified for. If he had been in India we would have loved and respected him as an Upanishadic seer, but he was killed. He declared: "Ana'l haq — I am the truth!" Mohammedans could not tolerate him; that was too much. Anybody declaring, "I am the truth!" seemed to them that it was sacrilegious, that it was against their religion, that it was egotism, that this man is saying that "I am God." Truth means God. "Ana'l haq — I am the truth, the ultimate truth!" But they could not understand, they could not see. They were unable to feel Mansoor's being.

He was not saying that Al-Hillaj Mansoor is the truth. He was saying Al-Hillaj Mansoor is no more and what is left now is the truth. When he was saying, "I am the truth," in fact he was saying, "I am no more, only the truth is."

The words of the mystics have to be very cautiously understood, otherwise there is every possibility of misunderstanding. Upanishads say: "Aham brahmasmi — I am God, I am absolute, I am the ultimate truth." But it has nothing to do with "I". In fact, they are trying to convey something which is not conveyable. They are saying, "I am not, now only God is. Hence I say I am God." Now God is speaking; they are no more speaking.

For I Myself Am That!
Let My Breath Merge With The Cosmic Breath...
This Is The Prayer; Only After Meditation It Is Possible.
Let My Breath Merge With The Cosmic Breath...

I should not be in any way separate from the whole. I should breathe with the whole, I should dance with the whole. This is ultimate let-go. Ordinarily we are continuously pushing the river, fighting the river, trying to go upstream. Hence we are miserable, because we cannot win, we are bound to fail.

You cannot win against the whole; you are just a part, such a tiny part, trying to win against the whole. It is sheer stupidity! But you can win — you can win with the whole, not against the whole. You can win if you merge with the whole. You can be a conqueror.

That's why we have called Mahavira the jina, the conqueror. Why we have called him the conqueror? — for the simple reason he dissolved himself with the whole, he merged with the whole. His breathing was no more separate, his heartbeat was no more separate. His heartbeat and the heartbeat of the universe were in deep rhythm, they were in tune; there was a great communion happening.

Let My Breath Merge With The Cosmic Breath,
May My Body Be As Dust.

Forget my body — I know I am no more in it. Please just think of me as consciousness. This is the prayer!

Remember, O Mind, Remember What Has Been Done.

This is a very significant sutra, hence the Isha Upanishad repeats it twice:

Remember, O Mind, Remember What Has Been Done.
Remember, O Mind, Remember What Has Been Done.

The first statement — Remember, O Mind, Remember What Has Been Done — means remember what has been done by others to you. They have made you identified with the body. As the child is born we start conditioning the child as if the child is nothing but the body. Hence we separate the boys from girls. We insist again and again that a girl has a feminine body and the boy has a masculine body. Directly, indirectly, we emphasize the fact so much that it becomes a conditioning. Anything repeated again and again becomes a conditioning. And the woman becomes identified with the body and the man becomes identified with the body.

And then we start emphasizing a new identity — with the mind, with the ambitions, desires. We go on and on stuffing our children with all kinds of nonsense. We want them to become great, famous, wealthy, powerful, presidents, prime ministers, this and that. Nobody seems to be concerned to tell them that, "You are neither the body nor the mind — that you are something transcending both." Our whole education is miseducation because of this and it is a long process. Almost one third of your life is wasted in education — twenty-five years. When you come back from the university as a Ph.D. your one-third life is gone down the drain. And they have conditioned you to be a body and to be a mind.

Remember, O Mind, Remember What Has Been Done.

Remember all that has been done to you by others so that you can uncondition yourself.

Remember, O Mind, Remember What Has Been Done.

Why this repetition? They both have different meanings. First meaning is: remember what has been done by others to you; and the second meaning is: remember what has been done by yourself to you. Only the others are not the culprits: you have done much to yourself too. You have participated, you have accepted, you have never rebelled, you were very obedient to all kinds of superstitions.

If your parents said, "You are a Hindu," you became a Hindu. You never said, "Why?" You never asked a question. Your parents said, "You are a Jain," and you became a Jain, without ever inquiring, without ever asking. You were ready to be a slave; slavery was very acceptable to you.

So remember that too, what you have done to yourself: you have betrayed yourself, you have not been true to yourself, you have been false. Even when you wanted to say no you have said yes, because it was comfortable, convenient. When you wanted to rebel you obeyed, because rebellion can lead you into danger, obedience is respectability. When you wanted to cry and weep you still smiled.

You have been false to yourself, you have not lived an authentic life. You have not been true. You have been wearing masks upon masks; you have never asserted your original face. You have never dared to be just yourself. You have never risked. You were always ready to bow down to authorities; they may be religious or political. You were always ready to be enslaved by the establishment; it may be Christian, it may be Hindu, it may be Buddhist; it does not matter.

Even people you respect very much are basically slaves.

Just the other day I was reading a letter from a Protestant Christian. He has written a letter to Mother Teresa of Calcutta, because now Mother Teresa is thought to be one of the great saints in the world; since she has won the Nobel Prize she has become one of the most respectable persons in the world. And this Protestant Christian went to Mother Teresa's orphanage where she collects children from beggars, abandoned children, poor children, and he wanted to adopt a child. That's what Mother Teresa has been doing her whole life: collecting orphans and then giving them to families, and she has been respected for that.

But he was asked whether he is Catholic or not. He said, "I am a Protestant." He was refused — then he cannot adopt a child. He has to be a Roman Catholic. He was very much puzzled. This woman is thought to be a great saint, one of the greatest servants of the society, but the whole service and the whole mission is basically a Catholic strategy to convert people into Catholicism. It is a trick, a political trick. All those orphan homes are not really for orphans, they are to increase the number of Roman Catholics. They have nothing to do with beggars; it is a political game. Even a Protestant — he is also a Christian — cannot be allowed to adopt a son. All those children are going to the Catholics, so Catholics go on becoming more and more, so they have larger numbers in the world. This is a way of converting, exploiting poor people, exploiting their poverty.

Even Mother Teresa is nothing but an agent of the Catholic Church. Your so-called saints, although they are thought to be saints, still belong to certain churches, religions, sects; they have not gone beyond. They cannot say, "I am just human." They cannot simply say that, "I belong to the universe — not to the Catholic Church or to the Protestant Church or to Hindus or to Buddhists — I belong to the cosmos." They are not in tune with the cosmic breath.

She is dancing according to the dictates of the Roman Catholic Church. She is dancing to the tune of the Vatican, of the Pope. And even in India people think she is a great saint. They write letters to me, "Why don't you do something like Mother Teresa?" Should I start converting people to Roman Catholic Church? But behind beautiful facades ugly things are hiding.

All these Christian missionaries serving poor people and the ill and the sick have nothing to do with poor people or sick people. Their whole effort is how to purchase people through bread, through butter, through medicine, through better hospitals — just how to purchase people through money, how to make more Catholics in the world.

Somebody makes people through the sword, somebody makes through money, and somebody simply goes on torturing their children, crippling, paralyzing their intelligence.

So remember, O mind, remember what has been done to you by others, and also remember what has been done to you by yourself, because others can do it to you only if you allow them to do it. I know small children cannot do anything, they cannot rebel, they are helpless. They have to depend on their parents, and because of their helplessness they are exploited...

Children are the most exploited people in the world, and the misery is their own parents are doing tremendous harm. They may be thinking that they are doing something good, something great; they may be thinking that they are helping their children to become good people. But what Christians, Hindus and Mohammedans have done to the world? The whole history is full of blood because of these religions! Man has not been able to become one, humanity has remained divided, and continuous wars, crusades... Kill each other in the name of God, in the name of religion! And when you kill anybody in the name of religion you are not a murderer. If you are killed in the name of religion your paradise is absolutely certain. People have been bribed to kill and to be killed.

If a parent really loves his children he will not condition the child in any way. He will help the child to inquire on his own, to become a seeker.

Upanishads don't belong to Hindus, remember. The same cannot be said about Koran; Koran belongs to the Mohammedans. The same cannot be said about Ramayana. Ramayana belongs to the Hindus. The same cannot be said about the Bible; the Bible belongs to the Christians. But about Upanishads one thing can be absolutely said, categorically said: they don't belong to Hindus, Mohammedans Christians — to anybody. Their whole approach is cosmic, it is holistic.

O Agni, show us the right path, lead us to eternal freedom, thou who knowest all.

May We Not Be Diverted From Our Goal,
For With All Devotion We Submit Ourselves To Thee.

O Agni...

Agni means fire. The translator has also left it untranslated for the simple reason because to translate it just as fire will give you a wrong impression, a wrong idea. Agni is a metaphor and metaphors become more difficult to be translated; they have something poetic in them. Literally it means fire, but the metaphor is of the fire within you, the fire of a deep, intense, passionate longing for truth, fire of longing to be with the beloved, to be one with the cosmos.

Buddha's last statement on the earth was: "Be a light unto yourself" — and this is the last sutra of the Isha Upanishad: "O fire, O my fire, my inner fire, my longing to be one with my beloved... show us the right path. Now nobody can lead me; only my inner passion for truth can guide me. No outer person can be of any help."

The Master can help you to get rid of the relative; there the function of the Master ends. Then you have to depend on your own inner insight, your own intuition, and that insight is called fire. It is fire because it burns and consumes you as a separate entity as an individual. It reduces you into nothingness. It is fire, but out of this fire a totally new life is born.

... Show Us The Right Path, Lead Us To Eternal Freedom.

Only this fire can lead you to the eternal freedom. When you are consumed completely, when you are free of yourself, then you are absolutely free. Remember these two expressions: freedom of the self and freedom from the self. The second is the meaning of absolute freedom, not the first. Freedom of the self again simply means the ego has come from the back door. Freedom from the self it self is total freedom, absolute freedom. When you are not, you are really free.

It is a paradox: when you are, you are in bondage, because your mind is a bondage, your ego is a bondage. When you are not, your imprisoned splendor is released.

Thou who knowest all.

May We Not Be Diverted From Our Goal.

Now this prayer has to be a constant fragrance to the seeker that, "My Lord, help me not to be diverted." because as you enter into the inner world, greater treasures are revealed and there is every possibility you may stop somewhere and you may think that this is the end. The danger becomes more and more as you go deeper, because greater richnesses, greater wealth, greater kingdoms become yours. And you have lived in such poverty that anything can enchant you.

There is a beautiful parable:

A mystic used to live under a tree, and he saw for years a woodcutter coming every day, an old man. The whole day he will cut wood and sell the wood, and then too it was difficult to feed himself, his wife and children.

One day the mystic asked the woodcutter, "Will you listen to me?"

The woodcutter used to respect the mystic. In the early morning when he will come he will bow down to the mystic, and when by the evening he will take the wood back home, he will again bow down to the mystic.

The mystic said, "Listen, don't waste your life cutting wood. Just go a little ahead and you will find a copper mine, and that will be enough. You do one day's work and for seven days it will be enough to keep your family perfectly comfortably, conveniently, and there will be no need for you to work every day."

The man did not believe. What this mystic can know about the copper and the mines? He had never seen him leave his tree. "Under the tree he is always sitting there with closed eyes — what can he know?" But then he thought, "What I am going to lose? Let me give it a try."

He went ahead and round a copper mine, and he was immensely pleased. Now he used to work only one day and for the remaining week there was no need to work. It was enough to feed his family, not only to feed but even invite guests, friends. And all were surprised that he has become suddenly rich.

One day the mystic said, "You are such a fool! Just go a little ahead and you will find a silver mine. — and one day's work, and for six months you need not work at all."

The woodcutter was perfectly happy with the copper mine and he did not believe this mystic — again! But he said, "For the first time he turned out to be right. Who knows? Let me give a try!"

And he found the silver mine, and he was immensely happy. And one day he will come and for six months he will not work at all.

One day he was coming, and the mystic said, "But you are just a fool! You just go ahead a little bit more and you will find a gold mine!"

Now this was too much! The woodcutter could not believe that this could be his fate — impossible! But again he was seduced by the idea — he went and found the gold mine. Now he became so rich that for years he will not come, and even if he comes he won't bother even to bow down to the mystic. 'Who cares about this fool? He just goes on sitting under the tree, and he knows where the gold mine is, still he has not bothered...'

One day the mystic called him and he said, "You don't come to see me any more, you don't bow down to me, but, still, I am now getting old and I cannot wait any more. Just a little ahead there is a diamond mine — and why you are wasting your time with gold? You can find diamonds!"

And the man found the diamonds; now for years he will not come. And one day the mystic sent a message that, "Come quickly, because I am on my deathbed and I have to reveal you the last secret."

He could not believe — what can be more than diamonds? That is the end! There can be nothing, there cannot be anything more. But he came. He asked, "What is the matter? Now you are again trying to tell me to go ahead?"

He said, "Yes, because if you go a little bit ahead you will find a treasure which is inexhaustible. This mine will be exhausted soon."

The woodcutter said, "I don't believe you any more. And I am perfectly happy — why should I go? And if you know that there is some inexhaustible treasure, why you go on sitting under this tree?"

The mystic said, "That inexhaustible treasure is within me, and that's what I have called you for, to tell you just go a little ahead. If you go a little ahead you will find yourself, and that's the real treasure."

But it was too much for the poor woodcutter even to understand. He laughed at the whole idea and he said, "You must have gone crazy! I am perfectly happy."

The mystic died. After many years the woodcutter thought — his death was also coming closer — "Maybe he was right, I should go a little further." He went a little further and he found such a beautiful forest that he wanted to sit under a tree. And it was so silent that he wanted to close his eyes. And it was so tremendously peaceful that he started sinking within himself... And he found the treasure the mystic was talking about, but it was found within himself.

The seer of the Isha Upanishad is saying:

May We Not Be Diverted Form Our Goal...

Unless you have found your ultimate being you have not found anything, remember. And go on praying to God that we should not be diverted.

For With All Devotion We Submit Ourselves To Thee...

Meditation is effort, prayer is surrender. Meditation is your doing, prayer is becoming available to God; whatsoever he wants to do with you, you are ready. It is submission, it is devotion, but devotion comes only after meditation.

Aum

Purnamadah
Purnamidam
Purnat Purnamudachyate
Purnasya Purnamadaya
Purnameva Vashishyate

Aum

That Is The Whole,
This Is The Whole.
From Wholeness Emerges Wholeness.
Wholeness Coming From Wholeness,
Wholeness Still Remains.

14

Without Women — No Buddhas

Question 1

OSHO,

I would like to fall in love, but I am afraid of beautiful women, and so afraid of love, and I don't know why.
Why is it so hard for me to fall in love?

— Prem Parivartan

Love is the hardest thing in the world, the most arduous. It needs really guts to be in love. That's why for thousands of years people have escaped from the world in the name of religion. They were not really escaping from the world, they were escaping from love. It was the fear of love that drove them away to the deserts, to the mountains, to the monasteries. But they were not even courageous enough to accept the fact that they are afraid of love; they covered it up with beautiful religious words. They condemned the world rather than condemning their own cowardliness.

And humanity has worshipped these people as saints — cowards have been worshipped! And naturally, if you worship cowards you will also become a coward. One should choose very carefully and cautiously whom to adore, because whomsoever you adore you start becoming like him — unconsciously, unknowingly. If a man escapes from the war we call him a coward, we condemn him — he has betrayed. But the people who escape from the battle of life are thought to be heroes, are thought to be doing something great. Their basic fear is of love — and why there is so much fear of love?

The first thing that love requires is dropping of the ego. It is easy to protect your ego in the name of religion, in the name of virtue, morality, puritanism, character — beautiful words to decorate the ego, to nourish and feed it. Hence your so-called saints are the most egoistic people in the world, and you can see it. The facts are so immense, so self-evident, that there is no way to deny them. Your saints have caused more bloodshed on the earth than anybody else, for the simple reason because wherever there is ego there is going to be bloodshed. But when you hide behind beautiful facades you not only deceive others, ultimately you yourself are deceived.

Love is one of the most dangerous phenomena. You have to put aside your ego, only then it can blossom. Love is real spirituality, but when I use the word "love" you can again misunderstand on the other extreme — you can start thinking in terms of lust. Love is not lust either. It is not the so-called religion and it is not the so-called worldly life. Love is different from both.

Love is a transcendence of lust and ego. Religious life gives you ego and destroys love, and the irreligious life gives you lust and destroys love. These are the two extremes: ego and lust. Exactly in the middle of the two is love; it is neither ego nor lust, it is transcendence of both.

Lust means you are trying to exploit the other, and naturally there will be fear. The fear will be that the other may exploit you. To get into a relationship means getting into a space where you are thinking to exploit and the other is also thinking to exploit. Both are going to use the other as a means. Hence there is great attraction — the opportunity to exploit the other — and great fear because you may be exploited.

Lust can never be free of fear, the ego can never be free of fear. Hence the people who have escaped into the deserts, into the mountains, into the monasteries, are still afraid, trembling, because you can escape from the world but how you will escape from your nature?

Love is a basic need. You can escape from the world, but you will still need food. You can escape from the world; that doesn't mean that now there is no need for food. And love is food for the soul, just as food is food for the body. One cannot avoid love. If one avoids love one is avoiding life. To avoid love means to commit suicide.

Your saints have committed suicide, your sinners have committed suicide. In a way they both are same because they exist on the polar opposites.

My sannyasin has to transcend the polarity, the opposition. He has to go beyond both. Beyond lust means never be cunning, never try to use the other. That is ugly, that is inhuman, that is irreligious. That is violence, pure violence. To respect the other as an end unto himself or herself is the way of the sannyasin. Avoid being cunning.

A fellow who had won the first prize in a state lottery was suddenly besieged by relatives and friends who had previously ignored him. But he refused to give or lend them any money.

"You now have more money than you will ever spend," said one. "Why are you so unkind?" I have two good reasons," explained the lucky winner. "First, I hate my relatives, and second, I love my money!"

To love somebody means to respect; it means not to exploit. To love somebody means to give love and all that you have without any idea of getting anything in return. If there is even a slight idea, a slight motivation, it is cunningness, it is lust. Even to ask for gratitude is wrong. Love is possible only when you love for love's sake.

A rich widower invited his three sons and their wives to a birthday dinner at his house. As they sat down at the table he explained why he had brought them all together.

"This is my fifty-eighth birthday, as you know, and I am about to change my will. Because of my disappointment at not being a grandfather, I am going to give $250,000 to my first grandchild." Then he bowed his head and said grace.

When he looked up he found himself alone at the table.

This is how people are behaving with each other! Their minds are full of lust, greed a thousand and one motives and they go on calling all this love.

Prem Parivartan, it is not anything personal to you to be afraid of love or to feel, "Why it is so hard?" It is everybody's problem, but it has been created by a long, stupid conditioning. Instead of helping you to become clear about what love is, instead of helping you to love without any motivation, you have been taught to love with motivation. You have been taught to love in an artificial way.

The mother says to you, "Love me because I am your mother," as if love is a logical proposition: "Because I am your mother, therefore you have to love me." And the poor child feels at a loss; he cannot understand — how to love? You may be the mother or the father; that does not mean that love will arise inevitably. If it was arising inevitably towards the mother and towards the father and the brothers and the sisters and the relatives, then there would have been no need to tell anybody to love your mother, your father! It does not arise naturally; it has to be cultivated.

And the child is certainly helpless; he starts pretending. He becomes a politician from the very beginning — he starts learning diplomacy. He becomes a follower of Machiavelli. He starts pretending to love the mother because he needs the mother; he cannot survive without the mother. He smiles at the father. That smile is false; it is not coming from his heart. But this is how from the very beginning his love is poisoned.

Later on we say, "Love — it is your wife. Love — this is your husband." We go saying this stupid thing to everybody: "Love — because... therefore..."

Love is not a logical proposition; either it is there or it is not there. If it is there, help to grow it; if it is not there, accept it. There is no other way. But don't create an artificial phenomenon.

But the mother has lived without love; she has not been loved by the husband. He was loving her because she was his wife, because he had to love; it was a social duty that he had to perform, it was a formality. So she is hankering for love; she starts exploiting the child.

Many women are interested in children not because they want to be mothers but just because it is easier to exploit the child for love than anybody else, because he will be absolutely dependent on you. To be a mother is a rare phenomenon. To hanker for children is a totally different thing; it has nothing to do with being a mother. That hankering comes from a totally different source.

To be a father is even more difficult than to be a mother, because to be a mother is at least instinctive, biological. Father is a social invention, a social institution. A father has been created, he does not exist in nature; hence it is even more difficult to be an authentic father. But everybody wants to be a father — to prove his manhood, to prove that he loves his wife, to prove that he is reproductive, that he is really a man. But these are not things that have anything to do with love.

And then there is the need to dominate the children. He cannot dominate the wife — the wife dominates him. The wife allows him to show to the world that he is the master; she allows it because she is so self-confident about her mastery over him that she does not bother. At the outside he can play the game of being the husband. He knows, she knows, everybody else knows, who is the real master.

The father is hankering to be a master; he wants to dominate somebody. He cannot dominate the wife, he cannot dominate the boss in the office, he cannot dominate anybody. Children are needed; it is a desire to dominate. And then he starts asking the children, "Love me — I am your father. You have to love!" As if love can be managed. Everything goes false. By the time you are young your love is almost plastic, it has lost all spontaneity. It has become very cunning, very calculating.

Two women met for the first time since graduating from high

school. Asked the first one, "Have you managed to live a well-planned life?"

"Oh yes!" said her friend. "First I married a millionaire, then an actor. My third marriage was to a preacher and now I am married to an undertaker."

"What do all these marriages have to do with a well planned life?"

"One for the money, two for the show, three to make ready and four to go!"

This is a well-planned life! Remember this sutra:

"One for the money, two for the show, three to make ready, and four to go!"

This is how people are living!

You ask me, Parivartan: I would like to fall in love...

It is not a question of liking. One simply falls or one does not fall! You would like to fall in love — then it is not going to happen. Falls don't happen through liking — you simply stumble and you fall! You are trying to manage a fall. You can manage, but it will not be a real fall — no fracture, nothing! You can put a Dunlop mattress and you fall on it, but you will simply look stupid and nothing else. A little bit embarrassed, that's all.

You ask: I would like to fall in love, but I am afraid of beautiful women...

Only that thing seems to be a little bit intelligent! Beautiful women are dangerous, ugly women are good — they have to be good. Fall in love with an ugly woman... This is one of the observations of thousands of years... whenever a woman is beautiful she need not care about being nice. It is enough to be beautiful, why she should be nice too? She will be nasty! Ugly women are very nice, they have to, otherwise who is going to fall in love with them? Their faces, their bodies make you feel like running away to the very end of the world and never look back

— they have to compensate. They compensate by being nice, by being very loving. They become your mamas; they take care as if you are a small child, they breastfeed you. They become absolutely necessary, they make you utterly dependent, so that you can tolerate their ugliness.

Parivartan, that thing you are certainly saying with some intelligence. And when you are thinking and planning a well planned life, then fall in love with an ugly woman. It will be difficult in the beginning, but then it is sweet all the way! And always think of the future — that's how calculating people do. What it is? Just a bitter pill in the beginning, it's okay, but then it is very health-giving. Ugly women are medicinal, but beautiful women are sweet in the beginning and very bitter in the end.

And this is not my advice to you; Gautam Buddha also says the same thing — in a different context, of course. He cannot be so truthful as I am. He says: The world is sweet in the beginning but very bitter in the end, and the other world is very bitter in the beginning but very sweet in the end. It is a totally different context, but it is significant — in your context too.

The beautiful woman looks beautiful and you are tempted, but remember the great philosophers who say that beauty is illusory; it is nothing but just on the surface. When you see a beautiful woman always remember the great philosophers: that inside she is nothing but bones, blood, pus, et cetera, et cetera. Keep in your bedroom a skeleton, meditate over it, and whenever you see a beautiful woman project the skeleton. That will scare you! And whenever you see an ugly woman feel compassion — compassion is good, it is great service. In fact it is conquering the world! To fall in love with an ugly woman is to be a saint, and your rewards will be great. She will be nice to you, and always nice to you.

The only problem is, Parivartan, here you will not find an ugly woman. Somehow ugly women don't fall in love with me, that's the trouble! So you are in a wrong place.

A traveling salesman once found himself in a howling storm near a washed-out bridge somewhere in the hinter-lands. Since he could drive no further he got out of his car and went to the nearest farmhouse. An old man answered the door.

"Can you put me up for the night?" asked the salesman.

"Yes, you can stay here," said the farmer, "but you will have to sleep with my son."

"Your son?"

"That's right."

"Excuse me, said the salesman, "I must be in the wrong joke!"

Parivartan, you are here in a wrong joke; you will have to find the right joke for yourself. Here you will not find an ugly woman; that will be difficult.

You say: I would like to fall in love, but I am afraid of beautiful women, and so afraid of love, and I don't know why.

There is not much to know in it; it is very simple and obvious. It is not something great to contemplate upon.

He: "Have you ever loved anyone as much as you love me, Mary?"

She: "No, John. I have sometimes admired men for their looks or intelligence or money. But with you, John, it is all love — nothing else."

At lunch one woman said to her friend, "I don't know what to do. The other night I dreamed that John was having lunch with some blonde, and they were laughing together."

"Oh, for God's sake, Helen!" protested her friend. "It was only a silly dream."

"Only a dream," repeated the other. "But if he does such things in my dreams, can you imagine what he must do in his?"

Fear is natural because the woman means the beginning of the world; the woman means the beginning of the trouble. Before the woman there is no world and after the woman is no world. Before the woman there is all darkness, after the woman there is all light. But between the two is the problem, and everybody has to pass through it.

The aggressive wife was raking her husband over the coals for having said something tactless when some friends called. "And don't sit there," she continued sharply, "making fists at me in your pockets, either!"

Among the objects displayed in the Vatican Library are two Bibles close together: a huge one about two feet thick, the other a tiny one less than one inch square.

One of the guides tells visitors: "This big Bible contains everything Eve said to Adam, and this little one contains everything Adam said to Eve."

I can't see why you don't understand — it is so obvious! People have always been afraid of the woman for the simple reason that man functions through the head and the woman functions intuitively. They can't agree on anything; there is no possibility of agreement. The woman jumps on conclusions, and the trouble is she is almost always right! And the man goes through a very long, arduous, logical process to reach a conclusion, and, again, almost always he is wrong.

So to fight with a woman — that means to love a woman — you are doomed, you are bound to fail. You cannot win a single argument because her ways of arguing are so puzzling. You want her to sit down calmly at the table and discuss, and she starts crying and throwing things. Now you don't know what to do! It is your money she is destroying so you cannot throw other things because that will be simply foolish. And the whole day you come home tortured by the world, you want some moments of peace, and the whole day she has been getting ready, exercising. She is ready for a fight! You come home completely defeated, and she is fresh and ready to fight. Now how can you win? And you don't want to fight at all, you want to be left alone to read your newspaper, and she throws your newspaper.

She cannot tolerate anything that you do — except Dynamic

Meditation. That comes very close — that makes women afraid. I invented the Dynamic Meditation for poor men: at least one defense! You can simply shout and jump and start hoo-hooing, and that she will understand. She will calm down and she will start agreeing with you; otherwise she is going to create trouble. That is one of the ancient feminine methods — of course she has never called it meditation. I call it meditation, to give it a religious color!

Prem Parivartan, so these are a few clues for you. If you want a peaceful life, find a homely woman and your life will be peaceful — of course without joy. You can't have both together. It will be peaceful, completely peaceful, but there will be no ecstasy in it. It will be as if you are already dead; there will be no excitement. It will be flat, like a flat tyre, stuck in one place, sitting silently doing nothing, the spring comes and the grass does not grow by itself. How can the grass grow under a flat tyre? It is impossible! You can go on sitting and waiting, springs will come and go... That is the first possibility.

The second is: take the risk, fall in love with a beautiful woman. There will be great excitement, ecstasy, but there will be trouble too. Heaven and hell come in the same package. You will have a few heavenly moments, but they are worth — for all the hell that will follow, they are worth. And they will teach you a lesson. That's how one finally becomes a Buddha. Without the women there would have been no Buddhas; about that I am absolutely certain. There would have been no religion, no Buddhas, no Mahaviras. It is because of the woman.

Many women ask me the question, "Why women have not become enlightened?" How they can become enlightened? Who will drive them to become enlightened? That is the point. They drive men to become enlightened. Finding no other way in life, he becomes enlightened. It is simple! I have not answered it yet, but today I thought better to say it and settle it forever. Never ask me again, "Why women don't become enlightened?" There is no need! Their function is to make people enlightened — to drive them crazy — so sooner or later they start meditating, sooner or later they want to be left alone. They are finished! Their dreams are shattered, they are disillusioned. It is the great work of woman; the whole credit goes to women.

The Buddha, the Mahavira, Lao Tzu and Chuang Tzu, they were possible only because the woman was continuously forcing them: either become enlightened or go crazy! And they decided to become enlightened. they said, "It is better to become enlightened." It is good to pass through the experience.

So, Parivartan, choose a beautiful woman and fall wholeheartedly... don't hold anything back. The deeper you love, the sooner you will get free of it. The more passionately you go in, the more quickly you come out.

Question 2

OSHO,

In lecture yesterday you spoke about the Master's work: Keeping his disciples from settling for less than "freedom from the self".

In the west, much is made of the experience that "this is it," that nothing can be different than it is — right now!

Is this a copper mine experience?

How can there be anything else?

— Deva Sambuddha

I also say this is it, but when I say this is it, it has a totally different meaning. It is not the same statement as it is being made in the West. The statement in itself has no meaning of its own; the meaning comes through your experience.

Man can live on different planes. When Gautam the Buddha says "This is it!" he is using the same words as you use. The words are exactly the same and the dictionary meaning is the same, but the existential meaning is totally different; it may be even diametrically opposed to your meaning.

In the West it has become fashionable to say that this is all, to live right now is all there is. But the people who are saying it have no idea of meditativeness, have no idea of absolute silence, thoughtless awareness, they have not experienced witnessing. Hence what they are saying — "This is it" — is nothing more significant than their mind.

So if your mind is full of lust, your "this is it" will be only lust and nothing else. If your mind is full of greed, full of anger, full of jealousy, then how it can have the same meaning as it has when Chuang Tzu says "This is it"? It is not possible to have the same meaning. Meaning comes from the person, his presence, his realization.

The West has got cliches from the East. Now Zen has become very fashionable in the West, not that the West is capable yet to understand Zen. Zen, the very word "Zen", comes from dhyana. Buddha himself never used Sanskrit language; he was the first enlightened person in India who used the language of the people. That was one of the things that made the priesthood, the brahmins of India, to be antagonistic to Buddha. Amongst many things that was one of the major, because the priests of India have always used Sanskrit as their language, it was their property. And only the scholarly people could understand it; the masses were absolutely ignorant about it. Hence what was written in the scriptures was known only to the few priests, and of course through that knowledge they were powerful. And they never wanted it to be known by the masses, otherwise their power will be lost, their vested interests will be destroyed.

Buddha was the first man who dynamited their whole establishment. He used the language of the people; the language of the people in Buddha's time was Pali. In Pali, dhyana is pronounced as jhana. Because Buddha used the word jhana it changed its color. When it reached China through Bodhidharma it became ch'an, because in Chinese jhana cannot be written; in Chinese there is no alphabet. The Chinese is a pictorial language, so the closest picture that they had which could express the word jhana was ch'an or ch'ana.

And from China it reached Japan. They use the same pictorial language, but their pronunciations are different. In Japan it became

Zen; in a way it came back to the original place. It came closer to Buddha's jhana; it became Zen.

Now the West has not yet understood what it is all about, but Zen has an appeal for the simple reason because it is very absurd, illogical, paradoxical. And the West has become fed up with logical philosophies — with Kant, Hegel, Fichte, Bertrand Russell, Wittgenstein — it has become fed up. From Aristotle to Wittgenstein, two thousand years of logical thinking has not led anywhere except to a point where West feels that life is absolutely meaningless and accidental. Now this is the right situation for any illogical philosophy to become fashionable.

The western painting has become illogical. You can see it in Picasso, Dali, Cezanne and other painters: the painting has become absolutely illogical, absurd. The poetry has become illogical — Ezra Pound and others. You can read it, but you will not find any meaning in it. The novels, the plays, all other art forms have taken a turn; they have become very illogical. This illogicalness is the outcome of two thousand years of logical effort which has completely failed: it has not provided any significance and meaning to man's life.

In the same flood of illogicalness, Zen also has become influential, but the reasons for its influence are totally different. It is not that the West has experienced meditation — it is simply a reaction against logic that Zen has become a great appeal. The absurd anecdotes the absurd lives of the Zen Masters — seems to be appealing because it has no logical construction.

A great Zen Master, Ryokan, is known in Japan as the Great Fool — a great Master, of the same caliber as Buddha, is known as the Great Fool for the simple reason because his whole life was absurd, unpredictable. If you ask him a question he may hit you on the head; if you don't ask him a question he may hit you on the head. He used to say, "Ask me a question and I will beat you; don't ask me a question and I will beat you!" He used to throw his disciples...

Once he cut one of his disciples' finger with a knife, and when the finger was cut and the disciple was in deep agony, he said, "This is it!" And in that moment the disciple became enlightened — because he was meditating for twenty years. Don't forget those twenty years! In the West those twenty years are completely forgotten. Those twenty years have brought this climax. At the right moment the Master gave the last push. He wanted to bring him to the present, and cutting the finger is so painful that you cannot think of the past, you cannot think of the future, you cannot fantasize any more. For a moment everything stops. It is like an electric shock — you are suddenly herenow. But those twenty years of meditation had created a different quality: the shock became a satori. Just by cutting somebody's finger, you cannot make him enlightened, but Ryokan did the miracle.

Ryokan lived in such a way that anybody will call him a fool, an idiot, and he enjoyed the word "idiot" very much; he himself used to call himself an idiot. He will forget his robe, will reach to the marketplace naked — with his shoes on! He will forget about everything.

He had written a list of things that he has to take when he goes out, and he has pasted the list on the door so that he can look at the list, of what things he had to carry: his staff, his robes, the shoes, the cap. And even this was written: "Where you have to put the cap — on the head." Otherwise he will forget, he may put the shoes on the head! But still the same thing continued — because he will forget to read the list.

This Ryokan helped many people to become enlightened. His illogical ways, his absurd methods proved of tremendous help. Now in the West people will love Ryokan; they will feel at ease with him. They are fed up with Aristotle. Aristotle has become "Aristotlitis" — a great disease! They don't want to do anything with Aristotle; they want something more alive, something more paradoxical because life is paradox; it is not logic.

Remember it, that life is not logical and cannot be understood by just logic. Life is far more than logic, far bigger than logic. It is not arithmetic. So there are planes to understand.

The West is not yet capable of being herenow; he has only heard the word. And there are different motives why the western youth, particularly the new generation, has become infatuated with Zen-like things. The Third World War is gathering around. Life seems to be very fragile; it had never been so before. Wars have always been there — in three thousand years we have fought five thousand wars — so war is not a new thing, but something new has happened. The Third World War will be the last war, it will be a total war. It will destroy not only humanity but all life from the earth. And the clouds are becoming darker and coming closer every day. It is creating a great fear. The western new generation is freaking out.

And now because the world can end, the whole future Zen seems to be appealing: Live here and live now because there is no future. Tomorrow may never arrive. This is a totally different reason why West has become interested in right now.

Sambuddha, this has to be remembered: the motive is different. The eastern mystics, from Buddha to Ryokan, were talking about the beauty of now-here for totally different reasons. Not that there is no future — there is infinite future, eternity — but the future never comes. All that comes is now; now is the only reality. When future comes, it also comes in the form of now. When tomorrow comes it will come as today, so you have to learn the art of being here, living today, because tomorrow will come but it will also be another today. And if you know how to live this day you will know how to live that day which will be coming. This was a totally different vision.

These are the four planes which have to be understood. First is the body. On the bodily plane, the man who lives identified with the body, if he says, "This is it," he will only mean food and sex and nothing else. His "this is it" will contain only of two things, food and sex, which are not very different either. Food is nourishment for you; you cannot survive without food. And sex is nourishment for the coming generations; they cannot survive without sex. Your parents' sex has created you, your sex will create your children. The society needs sex as food; it is food, it is survival for the society, just as food is your survival.

Food and sex are deeply connected. Hence it always happens if somebody starts controlling sex, becomes a celibate, he will start eating more; he will substitute his sexuality by food. It almost always happens when women get married they start becoming fatter, for the simple reason that before marriage they are interested in sex, after marriage they become fed up with it. They start feeling as if the man is exploiting their bodies. Reluctantly they go into it, but they are fed up. Then their interest changes towards food.

And the people who starve themselves for any reason — maybe naturopathy, dieting, or some religious reason, fasting — the people who will starve themselves will become full of sexual fantasies. Hence Jain monks are more full of sexual fantasies than anybody else, because of the fasting. It is a natural change: their energy starts moving from one pole to another.

Sambuddha, anybody who knows only his body, his "this is it" simply means food and sex. That's what is happening in institutes like Esalen — food and sex. That's what is happening all over America. Sambuddha comes from America.

The second plane is mind. With food and sex you can have pleasure and pain. On the body level, if your body is satisfied, you will have a pleasant feeling; if it is not satisfied you will feel pain. The second phenomenon above the body is mind. Mind goes a little higher than pleasure; it starts experiencing happiness and unhappiness. With body there is only duality, food and sex, only two dimensions; with mind there are many dimensions. Mind opens up a greater world: music, poetry, painting, dance, et cetera, et cetera. It opens up many dimensions; you can enjoy more.

With the first you are just like an animal; your "this is it" will be nothing but animalistic. With the second, if you know that you are more than the body, higher than the body, you will have many dimensions, more richness. You become human, you rise above animals. When you say, "This is it," now it will be music, poetry, painting, dance; it will have a totally different meaning.

On the third plane is the soul, the self. With the body the duality; with the mind, manyness, multitude; with soul only oneness, and that is meditation. You will know the real meaning of "this is it" only when you arrive at the third point.

And with the fourth... In the East we have called it the fourth, simply "the fourth", turiya; we have not given it any name because no name is possible, it is inexpressible. With the fourth, turiya, there is neither two nor many nor one. You can call it either wholeness or nothingness. Buddha used the word "nothingness", Isha Upanishad uses the word "wholeness"; they mean the same thing. The zero symbolizes both, nothing and the whole. This is the state of bliss, ecstasy.

On the body level pleasure is opposed by pain; on the mind level happiness is opposed by unhappiness; on the soul level joy is opposed by misery. But on the fourth, bliss is not opposed by anything; bliss has no polar opposite to it.

Where you are on these four planes will make the difference. When I say, "This is it," I am talking from the fourth plane. And when in America, in the institutes like Esalen, people are talking about "this is it," they are talking about the first plane, the body.

You ask me, in the west, much is made of the experience that "this is it," that nothing can be different than it is — right now!

Yes, nothing can be different than it is, but you can be different. The world is the same — to the Buddha, to the enlightened, to the unenlightened — but you are different and that makes the difference. That's the difference that makes the difference. The world is the same — Buddha moves here, you move here, gods live here, dogs live here — it is the same world. But because their awareness is different, their depth and height is different, their "this is it" will be different too, their now will also be different.

So when I am talking about now, my "now" contains this and that both. When in the West people are talking about now, their now only contains "this".

Remember what the Isha Upanishad says: This is whole. That is whole. The whole comes from the whole, still the whole remains behind.

This is the fourth state, turiya, the ultimate state beyond which nothing happens. Unless you have reached to it, Sambuddha, you are living at the copper mine. You have to move to the silver mine, then to the gold mine, and then to the diamond mine, and then to the beyond.

Question 3

OSHO,

What would be the best thing to do if you were mad?

— *Virendra*

Change your mind!

Question 4

OSHO,

I have taken the vow to remain a celibate my whole life, but why do I still suffer from sexual thoughts, fantasies and dreams?

— *Swami Nityananda Giri*

It is natural — it is because of your vow. Nobody can change one's life by force. The vow simply is a violent act against yourself. It will only repress your sex, and the repressed will take revenge; it will come on again and again and again. You will push it from one door, it will enter from another door. You cannot get rid of it so easily, so cheaply.

Just the other day, Morarji Desai revealed that when he was the prime minister he had visited a nightclub in Canada, just to find out what was going on there. Now, why he should be interested in a nightclub? And whatsoever is going on there, why he is interested in it? At the age of eighty-two! And he had kept it a secret up to now; he never revealed it before.

A repressed sexuality will haunt you to the very end of your life. Even when you will be dying you will be having sexual fantasies.

Swami Nityananda Giri, it is still time — beware! Life is never changed by vows, life is changed by awareness. Never take a vow; the vow simply means that you are forcing something upon yourself. Try to understand. When there is understanding there is no need to take a vow; your understanding is enough. You see something is wrong and it drops.

Seeing is enough, understanding is enough; no other discipline is ever needed. Whenever you need some other discipline it means your understanding is lacking, something is missing in your understanding. You are trying to compensate your understanding by taking a vow, but the very taking of the vow shows that you are afraid of your sexuality. Then it will come, then it is bound to come.

And now you are asking me: Why do I still suffer from sexual thoughts, fantasies and dreams?

You must be hoping that by taking a vow all this will stop. It is your vow that is causing it! If you have lived a natural life, if you have gone through the world and all its experiences of good and bad, pleasure and pain, you would have learned something; you would have come out of the world with understanding.

But for centuries the so-called saints have depended on violence. They talk about non-violence, but they go on doing violence to themselves.

"I am sick and tired of being left alone every weekend," growled the golf widow at breakfast one Saturday. "If you think you are going out to play today..."

"Nonsense, dear," the husband interrupted, reaching for the toast. "Golf is the furthest thing from my mind. Please pass the putter."

If you just force things they will erupt, they will come back.

A seventy year-old man went to see the doctor.

Without Women – No Buddhas

"I have been in practice for twenty-five years," the doctor told him, "and I have never heard of such a complaint What do you mean, your virility is too high?"

The septuagenarian sighed. Pointing to his head, he said, "It is all in my mind."

"The virility has gone too high — it's all in my mind."

Now, Nityananda Giri, you have taken a vow. Your sexuality is repressed at its natural center: it has reached in your head, and that is far more dangerous because it will poison your head. Now in dreams, in thoughts, in fantasies it will come.

Just go for a fast one day and you will see what I mean — you will think of food the whole day. Ordinarily you don't think about the food at all; the food is not a problem. When you feel hungry you eat, and then all is forgotten. But go for a fast, and suddenly food becomes your obsession. It is a simple psychological fact.

But religious people have been really stupid: simple facts they go on denying, and they can always rationalize. They will say, "It is because of your past lives' bad karmas that, Nityananda Giri, you are still suffering from sexual thoughts." They will tell you to practice yoga, stand on your head, and all kinds of nonsense.

Just the last week I was reading about one yogi, Dhirendra Brahmachari, who goes on showing his yoga postures on the television. And he was telling the last week to his audience that, "Do you know how I remain so healthy? I am pulling my anus upwards right now, but you cannot see it because I am wearing clothes." And then he told that his disciple, one girl who sits by his side to show yoga postures, "She is also holding her anus upwards, but you cannot see because she is wearing the clothes."

The girl must have gone red! It is good that India has not yet gone for color TV — in black and white you cannot see whether the girl is blushing or not. But then you have to do all kinds of nonsense things. Now pulling your anus upwards will simply force your sexual energy to go into your head; that's what its purpose is.

It is trying to bring the sexuality towards the head, and you will be more in a danger.

And that's the purpose of sirshasana, headstand. Standing on your head, the basic purpose is to force your sexual energy to go towards your head. Because of gravitation, if you stand on your head naturally your sexual energy starts moving towards the head. But how long you can stand on your head? Sooner or later you will have to stand on your feet.

And this messing around with centers is one of the problems all the religions have been facing.

Gurdjieff, one of the great Masters of this age, used to say that man has become so ugly for the simple reason because none of his centers is functioning in a natural way; every center is being interfered with by other centers, they have all become entangled. His whole effort was how to disentangle them, how to bring the energy to each center that belongs to it.

And that's my effort here too: to bring the energy to the right center, where it belongs. When all your centers are functioning naturally you will have a deep silence in you, you will have a subtle harmony in your being; a joy will surround you.

Nityananda Giri, you must have lived according to the old, traditional way; your name shows that. Giri is one of the most ancient traditions of Hindu sannyasins; you will have to come out of it. You will have to come out of your orthodoxy, out of your superstitions.

An elderly spinster went to see her doctor and complained that her sleep was being disturbed by dreams of a young man who was constantly following her and flirting with her.

The doctor prescribed some pills, but a couple of weeks later she was back.

"What is the matter now?" he asked gently. "You are sleeping better now, aren't you?"

"No," she said, "Now I can't sleep because I miss that young man so much!"

Life cannot be avoided easily. The only way to go beyond is to go through. Life is an opportunity to grow — don't avoid it. If you avoid it you will remain retarded.

Now what is happening to you cannot happen to any of my sannyasins, it is impossible — because my sannyasins are living naturally, accepting whatsoever God has given. He knows better than you. If he has given you a sexuality, then it means that there is something to be learned through it. It is your creative energy — don't repress it. Refine it, certainly, make it as pure as possible, because it is your sexual energy which will create many things in your life.

This is a well known fact, that great poets naturally find that they are transcending their sexuality. Great painters, great dancers, great musicians have always found it to go beyond sex very easily — but not the so-called monks and the saints. They have found just the opposite: the more they have tried, the more they were disillusioned, the more they got deeper into the mess.

This fact has to be meditated upon. A musician creates music, hence his sexual energy is used in a non-sexual way. A dancer creates dance, he need not create children. He becomes a creator of something higher — what is the need to create the lower? Even animals can create children; that is nothing special to man. In fact, animals are far more productive — even mosquitoes can defeat you! That is nothing special to you.

Now there are two ways: either repress sex — as has been done by all the so-called religious traditions of the world — or transform it.

I am for transformation, hence I teach my sannyasins to be creative. Create music, create poetry, create painting, create pottery, sculpture — create something! Whatsoever you do, do it with great creativeness, bring something new into existence, and your sex will be fulfilled on a higher plane and there will be no repression. Let your sex become more and more love and less and less lust. And then finally let your love also become a little higher — that is prayer. Lust is the lowest form of sex, love higher than sex, and prayer is the ultimate transformation.

The meditative person can transform his sexuality without any antagonism without any conflict. He is in deep friendship with all his energies, sexual or others; he is not in any fight. Why fight with your own energies? Love them, rejoice in them, and help them to transcend the lower forms, the animal forms. Let them move from the body towards the turiya, the fourth.

This is a totally different process. That's why I am so much opposed, because I am against all the repressive traditions, all the so-called moral, puritanistic stupidities. I simply call them stupid. I am not a polite person. If a spade is there I call it a spade — in fact, a fucking spade! I want to be clear and straightforward. Two plus two is four to me, neither more nor less.

A Rajneesh sannyasin went to visit an old friend living in a big town. The only lodging he could find was in a very dilapidated hotel. The receptionist told him he would have to share a double bed and take his breakfast — toast, jam and coffee — upstairs with him that night.

He entered the room and was surprised to find a gorgeous blonde lying naked on the bed, fast asleep. He prepared himself for bed, said his prayers and lay down to sleep.

Fifteen minutes later, he turned over and looked in the direction of the beautiful girl. "Should I or shouldn't I? No! I must not!" he said to himself, and turned over and tried to sleep.

Half an hour later he turned around again, looked towards the girl and said to himself, "No, I must not! I won't! It is not proper!" So he turned over again and went back to sleep.

But after half an hour he sat up and said out loud, "I just can't resist any more. I don't care whether I am breaking any rules or not." So he got up, walked over to the foot of the bed, then poured his coffee, buttered his toast... and ate his breakfast!

This is possible only to a Rajneesh sannyasin.

Nityananda Giri, to you it will be very difficult, impossible!

Once a Zen Master was asked, "What sort of sex life do monks get?"

The Zen Master said, "Nun!"

Don't repress, try to understand your sexual energy. And you will be surprised, immensely surprised, that it is not your enemy, it is your friend. It is not a curse, it is a blessing, because it is the source of all your creativity. Have you known any impotent person to be creative? Have you known any impotent person to create great music, painting poetry? And why the so-called monks down the ages have not been creative? They have not contributed anything to the earth, they have not enriched the earth. They have not been a blessing; on the contrary, they have proved a curse. Why? — because being repressive of their sexuality they became uncreative, they cannot create.

Creativity is sexual, basically sexual. When the painter gets lost into his painting it is the same orgasmic joy that two lovers have when they meet and merge into each other; for a moment they are no more separate. The painter gets the same joy, longer, deeper, far more profound, when he is lost with the painting. A dancer comes to the highest point...

Hence my emphasis on dance and music here in my commune. I want everybody to be a dancer, a singer, for the simple reason because that is the most natural, spontaneous way of transforming your sex. When the dancer is completely lost, when there is only dance and no dancer left, he experiences the greatest orgasm, more total than any sexual orgasm can ever be.

Nityananda Giri, if you accept your sexuality, if you embrace it with deep love and gratitude towards God, knowing that its his gift so that there must be something in it which has to be discovered... it is not to be rejected. Rejecting it will make you uncreative, and the uncreative person remains a miserable life.

That's why your saints look so sad, with such long faces, almost dead and stinking.

Look again — look again into your own being, into your own existence, and you are in for a great surprise.

A man was asked by his wife to bring home a live chicken for a special meal she was going to prepare. He bought the chicken after work and was on his way home when he realized that he had forgotten his front door key. He knew his wife would not be home for a few more hours, so he decided to pass the time by going to the cinema.

He could not carry the chicken inside so he stuffed it down the front of his trousers, then bought a ticket and went in. He sat down towards the front of the cinema, next to two old ladies. He soon became very engrossed in the film and did not notice that the chicken had poked its head through his fly buttons.

"Winifred," whispered one of the old ladies, nudging her friend. "Look at that big thing poking through this guy's fly!"

Winifred grunted, "Ah, Millie, when you've seen one, you've seen them all!"

"I know that," replied Millie, "but have you ever seen one that eats popcorn?"

15

Everybody Has His Uniqueness

Question 1
OSHO,

You have been speaking on several occasions against socialism, and yet I feel that in this commune the first experiment of an alive socialism is happening. Is this another of your contradictions?

— Swatantra Sarjano

The real socialism can only be the fragrance of a commune deep in meditation. It has nothing to do with the social structure or the economy. Real socialism is not a revolution in the society, it is not social: it is the revolution in the individual consciousness.

If many people who are going through an inner revolution live together, then there is bound to be a new quality. You can call it socialism; the better word will be "communism", out of "commune". Only a commune can have communism, but a commune exists only once in a while. When Buddha was alive a commune grew around him; he called it sangha, another name for commune. The meaning of sangha is: where the initiates have dropped their egos and are no more functioning like islands but have become one with each other, where a communion is happening. Communication is between the heads; communion is between the hearts.

Whenever so many hearts open, become flowers, a great fragrance is released. That fragrance surrounds a Buddha, you can call it a Buddhafield. The energy is totally different: there is no politics involved in it.

Politics belongs to the world of the ego. The game of politics is an ego number: how to be more powerful than the other. It is ambition in its ugliest form. It is sheer cunningness, exploitation. It is an effort to enslave others. It is not possible at all to the meditators, because for meditation the basic requirement is to drop the ego. You cannot play the games of the ego any more. There is no question of being higher, more powerful than the others. In fact, there is no question of "the other".

The moment "I" disappears, instantly the "thou" also disappears. I and thou exist together; they are like two sides of the same coin. Drop other your "I" and you will be surprised that for you there is nobody who is other than you; the reality appears as one organic whole. But it is possible only with a center.

When Buddha died his commune existed at least for five hundred years, but slowly died; slowly it withered away. It remained alive till... few people continued to become enlightened and went on replacing the Buddha. When there was nobody enlightened any more, when there was not the center, the whole field disappeared. When there is no sun, how can there be rays? It is an individual phenomenon.

If Buddha is there, the commune is bound to happen; it cannot be prevented. It is inevitable. The real seekers will start moving towards the Buddha from the farthest corners of the world. It is just like when a fragrant flower opens, bees start queuing from faraway places. Suddenly the fragrance becomes a magnetic pull — but only for the bees, not for everybody. The dogs will pass by the flower without ever looking at the flower; it does not exist for them, they are not sensitive towards it.

The Buddha exists only for those who have the sensitivity, the perception, the availability, the openness, the search. Many came across Buddha and missed him. Millions of people encountered him, but could not recognize him. To them he was just another learned man, just another saint. And India has always been full of saints. There was nothing special for them in him. They listened to him, they gathered a little bit of knowledge from him and went on their way.

But those who had the sensibility, who had the heart which can dance with this fragile energy of a Buddha, this delicate perfume, were lost, completely lost and dissolved, merged. Out of these merged individuals the commune arises, the Buddhafield, the sangha.

It happened with Jesus, of course on a smaller scale, because Jews have never been much interested in the interiority of man. They are extrovert people; their whole religion has remained extrovert. Jesus was recognized only by very few people; those few people can be counted on fingers.

It happened again and again around these precious diamonds — Lao Tzu, Chuang Tzu, Lieh Tzu, Lin Chi, Baso, Bahauddin, Jalaluddin, Kabir, Nanak — again and again. But the problem is: when the Master dies, the commune starts withering away. Maybe for a time being a sequence of Masters continues...

For example, after Nanak nine other Masters followed. After Adinatha, the first Jain Master, twenty-four teerthankaras followed — from Adinatha to Mahavira, a long span of time, almost of three thousand years. But it is very rare. It cannot be enforced by the government, by any outside agency; then it will be plastic.

Sarjano, you are right — it is one of my contradictions. I am against socialism which is imposed as an economic, political ideology on people, because then it destroys something which is very precious: it destroys the individual. Rather than destroying the ego it destroys the individual; it enhances the ego. The ego is represented by personality.

These two words have to be understood very clearly: the personality is that which is given to you by the society, and the individuality is that which you have brought with you from the beyond; it is a God's gift. The individuality has no ego in it, it is egolessness. The personality is nothing but ego.

The society imposes a certain structure, a certain pattern around every individual the society is very much afraid of authentic individuals. It creates a false personality, because the false personality can easily be manipulated, enslaved, dominated. The personality is very obedient, the personality is very dependent on the society, because the society has created it.

If you go against your personality that the society has created, you will lose all respect; your ego will start collapsing. And that creates great fear in you, so you go on fulfilling the demands of the parents, of the teachers, of the priests, of the politicians, of all kinds of people who surround you and are trying to exploit you in every possible way. They depend on personality, and they go on enforcing the personality against the individuality. The individuality has to be repressed, completely forgotten, so that you start living in the false and the phony.

Socialism destroys individuality more than any other kind of political ideology, because socialism means society is the goal, not the individual. The individual has to be sacrificed for the society, not vice versa; the society cannot be sacrificed for the individual. And in fact "society" is a beautiful word; behind that beautiful word is hiding the ugly state. It is really the state that dominates in socialism, and the state does not want any kind of individuality in people. It effaces all individuality, it creates robots. It wants everybody to be just an efficient machine, nothing more.

This kind of socialism I am certainly against, but there is certainly a different kind of socialism which I am absolutely for. But the process is totally different, just diametrically opposite: the individuality has to be saved and the personality has to be dissolved.

That is the meaning of surrendering to a Master: you surrender the ego, not the individuality; individuality cannot be surrendered. When you surrender on your own, when you are not forced to surrender, when it is not a question of submission... out of your love and joy, out of your understanding you surrender — it is your choice and your decision. When you surrender, of course you surrender the false; the true cannot be surrendered. You are the truth! You simply put aside all that has been imposed on you, conditioned upon you. In the presence of a Master only the false disappears, and the true comes in its absolute flowering.

Everybody Has His Uniqueness

In a commune of a Buddha everyone has individuality, nobody has any personality. Nobody is egoistic, but everybody has his uniqueness; he contributes to the commune in his own unique way. And everybody is respected for whatsoever he is doing; there is immense respect for the individual.

You can see it happening here. The well-trained psychoanalyst who could have earned thousands of dollars per month in the West, may be having a Ph.D. or a D.Litt. and other educational qualifications, is respected in the same way as the toilet cleaner; there is no difference. The toilet cleaner has the same respect, the same individuality; he is contributing in his own way.

And many times it is happening here that a Ph.D. decides to drop all that he has learned and he wants to become a cleaner. There are few Ph.D.s who are toilet cleaners. This may be the only place in the world where Ph.D.s have found the right work! There are M.D.s who are cleaning the toilets. They have been told, "You are M.D.s, why don't you work in the Medical Center?" They say, "Cleaning is so beautiful, so relaxed! We don't want to bother with the Medical Center any more."

There are poets, painters — famous, well-known — authors who have published much, and they may be making shoes or just working in the carpentry or doing some manual work in the garden, because one thing is absolutely clear: that your job makes no difference, your individuality is intact everywhere. Your job does not give you any higher position, it does not create any hierarchy. Everybody else is doing in his own way, wholeheartedly.

The commune can happen only in the presence of a Master: otherwise, your awareness is such you will start fighting, quarreling, and your ego games will come in. That happens each time a Master dies. I there is a chain of Masters then it is okay, otherwise very difficult.

For example, Jesus could not create a chain; he was not given time enough. He worked only three years, from the age thirty to thirty-three. There was not enough time for him — he was crucified at thirty-three — he had no time to work.

Buddha worked for forty-two years; he created a great line. He triggered many people, from Mahakashyap to Manjushri, Sariputra, Modgalyayan, Purnakashyapa... and many others became enlightened while he was alive and they carried the torch.

If a chain is created then the commune goes on living, but it is a very fragile phenomenon, very unpredictable; it may happen, it may not happen. Even if it happens, then too it cannot be a permanent phenomenon. One cannot conceive that it will go on and on forever; it can stop anywhere. The world is such a desert, and the stream that Buddhas create is such a small stream; it can be lost in the desert anywhere.

But the only true commune exists while the Master is alive. I am all for that kind of commune.

But the communism that exists in Soviet Russia or China is not my cup of tea! It is really exactly the opposite of what I am trying to do here. Communism should arise spontaneously, and differences are many. For example, Karl Marx, Friederich Engels, V.I. Lenin — the communist unholy trinity — these people were talking of the dictatorship of the proletariat; that means dictatorship of the lowest.

In the commune of a Buddha, in the first place there is no dictatorship, although for the outsiders it may seem that there is a dictatorship. For the outsider, if he comes here, he will think this is my dictatorship, although I never order anybody. I never have even visited the office once in these six years! I don't know who is living where, how many people are living in the commune. I have not visited the other houses of the commune. I simply know the way to my room! I cannot find even in my own house where I live, Lao Tzu House, the rooms of other sannyasins who are living with me Vivek has been telling me that, "One day give us a surprise — come to the kitchen!" I have never been there; I really don't know where it is. So in fact I will not be able to find it unless I am guided by somebody. I have some idea where it should be, but it is very vague.

But anybody from the outside will think that I am the dictator;

that is absolutely wrong. People are here working out of their love, nobody is ordered. And if they ask me and I say something, it is always a suggestion, never an order. They are free to accept it or not accept it. They always accept it — the credit goes to them; it has nothing to do with me. If they don't accept it they are perfectly free to do that way.

In a real commune, the commune of my vision, the highest becomes the center. In the communism of Karl Marx, the lowest dominates; it is the dictatorship of the proletariat. Naturally, these are two different things, polar opposites.

When the highest... and by "highest" I simply mean one who is no more, one who has become one with the whole, one who has no more any separate existence, one who is no more pushing the river, one who is flowing with the been, one who is in a deep let-go, one who is just a vehicle, a hollow bamboo on the lips of God. And if God sings, of course the hollow bamboo becomes a flute, but it all depends on God. The song does not belong to the flute, it belongs to the singer.

Through the Buddha, through the enlightened person, God starts flowing. It is the highest, the suprememost that creates a real commune. The communism that exists in Russia and China is dominated by the lowest. Joseph Stalin and Mao Tse-tung belong to the lowest type, the most violent, murderous people that have ever existed on the earth.

The name of Joseph Stalin means a man of steel; that was not his real name. Stalin means a man of steel; it is not his real name, it is because of his hardness.

A Buddha is represented by a lotus flower, not by steel. The lotus flower has been in the East the symbol of all the Buddhas — very fragile, very delicate, with a subtle perfume, not aggressive at all.

If you surrender to a Buddha it is your decision, it is your freedom; you are not made to surrender. And when many people surrender to a Buddha they are really surrendering to their own future, to their own ultimate potential. Buddha simply represents what can happen to them. He is just a reflection of their ultimate flowering.

When you surrender to a Buddha you are really surrendering your lower reality to your own higher reality; the Buddha is just an excuse. Then a real commune comes into existence. It is out of love, out of meditation and prayer. It is not based on violence; it is not rooted in the lower qualities, animal qualities of man.

Sarjano, in that sense you are right, that a real commune is happening here, but it is not the first experiment, remember it. The experiment has happened many times before. But it always looks like that. When you fall in love you think, "Such kind of love has never happened before; it is something unique." And in a way it is — for you it is a new experience. You have never been in love with a Buddha, so to you it is a new experiment. Otherwise, for thousands of years humanity has existed, and many times small oases in the desert have arisen. But the desert is vast and hard...

And remember one fundamental law: whenever the lower comes in conflict with the higher, the higher is destroyed, not the lower. If you clash a rock with a lotus flower, don't hope that the rock will be destroyed by the lotus flower; the lotus flower will be destroyed. The higher is more fragile.

That's why I say the woman is a higher sex than man: she is more fragile, she is more flowerlike. Man is harder, a little bit of rock is still in him. Man is more closer to the animal than the woman. Man is more aggressive than the woman; the woman is receptive. And because of this higher quality of the woman she has been destroyed by man. The rock is always going to win against the flower.

Such communes have existed again and again. They cannot be totally destroyed because God has a tremendous investment in these communes. They cannot be destroyed, they will go on coming again and again, but the vast world is desertlike. The greater humanity has not yet been transformed, although the possibility of such communes is becoming more and more.

Man has evolved, has matured, and particularly today. The time has come when thousands of such communes can erupt, explode all over the world. And that's what I am intending to do by creating so many sannyasins and then sending them back to their countries so that thousands of communes start functioning.

I would like to create a chain of communes all around the world, so this commune does not remain only one oasis in the vast desert but becomes interlinked with many communes. That type of interlinking has never been done before; that will be new. Communes have always existed, but many communes functioning all around the world was not possible before; it is possible only today. Science has made it possible. The world is now so small, it is almost like a village, a global village. Man has come so close that now this possibility exists.

I have got two hundred thousand sannyasins working all around the world, two hundred communes slowly growing. Soon there will be thousands of communes all around the world, and this will be the first chain of communes surrounding the whole globe! And the possibility of their success is becoming more and more than it was ever before, for the simple reason that science has come to such a growth that unless religion also reaches to the same point, humanity is doomed. Everything has become lopsided. It was never so before, in fact just the opposite was the case.

Buddha's commune was far more advanced than the technology and the science of Buddha's day. Mahavira's commune was far more advanced, far ahead than the society, than the inner growth of man; there was a big gap. Now the gap is there, but it is a totally different gap. The society, science, technology, have gone far ahead than man's inner growth. Now the society and the science and the technology have prepared the ground; we can use this opportunity. We can help man come to the same growth, and that will be a balancing thing. All those communes in the past created an imbalance; they were out of tune. They were far ahead of their time, hence they were doomed to fail.

But this time we can hope we may succeed, for the simple

reason that we are not going against or too ahead of time. Time is ready and ripe and we are in tune with it. Only we are in tune with it; the whole society is falling behind — the modern technology, the modern science. All your so-called churches, religions are far behind modern science.

What I am doing here is a very balancing phenomenon. Now religion can exist on a far higher level than it has ever existed, because science has provided the right background. And moreover, science has created a tremendous fear in the world that science can destroy the whole humanity. And now the only hope is that religion can save it. And when it is a question of survival, millions of people are bound to become interested in meditation because only meditation can save them; nothing else can save. If man remains the same and science goes on developing, then the very developing science will become a mountainous burden on man.

It is a well-known fact that somewhere in the past, one hundred thousand years back, there were huge animals, far bigger than elephants, ten times bigger than elephants. What happened to those huge animals? They suddenly disappeared from the earth; only their skeletons are discovered. What calamity happened? No calamity from the outside, but they became too huge. The burden of their bodies became so much that they could not carry it; they became incapable from inside. Their inner being remained very small and their outer body became too big; it lost balance.

The same is happening today with man: his inner soul is too small and his outer technology, his science, has become too huge. It can bring a Third World War, a total war, because it is a question of life and death; it has never been such a question before. There is a hope that religion can explode, and millions of authentic seekers are searching for it.

We can create a chain around the world of such communes, and the whole world can be transformed into a Buddhafield. Then only there is a possibility of a communism arising out of love and arising from the highest sources, from the Everests — not a dictatorship of the proletariat, but a trust, a surrender to a Buddha. And out of that trust and surrender a totally new kind of communism can be given birth.

In that sense I am for communism — but communists will be very much against me because if my type of communism succeeds then their type of communism is bound to fail.

Question 2

OSHO,

Your talks are very logical, but on the other hand your way of working is so illogical.
What is this mystery? please explain.

— *Prem Vinod*

My talks are logical because when you come to me you come obsessed with logic. I can start communicating with you only through logic. But as you start relaxing with me, feeling that your mind is not in danger, then I start working illogically — because life is bigger than logic, far bigger than logic. The working has to be illogical because working means I will be creating a situation for a transformation of your total being; it cannot be logical.

My talks are logical only for this simple reason that: if I start talking illogically you will escape, you will not be able to connect with me. So I come to the valley of your darkness to hold your hand, and then slowly I persuade you, seduce you to come towards my heights.

A clever college student had lost a textbook and put up a notice on the students' bulletin board. But instead of the customary lost heading he captioned his notice sex.

Below it he wrote: "Now that I have your attention..."

Who bothers to read the bulletin board? There are so many notices. And who bothers to read the notices with the captions "Lost"? But if the caption is "Sex", then it is very difficult — difficult for the students, difficult for the professors difficult for the vice-chancellor, difficult for the chancellor to miss. He has to read it.

I am logical only so that "Now I have your attention..."

Life is not logical, it is supra-logical; logic is only a small fragment of it. Watch, and you will see what I am saying. Watch yourself — are you logical in your life? Have you fallen in love with a woman logically? Can you give any proofs why you have fallen in love with a certain woman and not with somebody else? In fact, you cannot argue even that love is existential, you cannot even prove love's existence. It is one of the most difficult things to prove, that love has any existence. Science cannot give any support.

You can go full of love to the cardiologist and ask him, "Just check my heart — it is throbbing with love! Just look at your diagram on your graph, whether something is there or I am just befooling myself." And he will say, "There is nothing wrong with your heart — you are perfectly normal."

Even your heart can be dissected and no love will be found there. That's why science cannot prove love — love is not matter. Science cannot prove your soul; the soul is not matter. The word "matter" is significant: it comes from meter; it means measurable, that which can be measured. Matter is that which can be measured. But there is something in you which is immeasurable, that is beyond the scope of science, mathematics, logic, physics, chemistry.

If you go to the chemist he will find all that is chemical in you, but he will not find the formula for love. If you go to the biologist he will find everything about your hormones, et cetera, but he will not find anything like love in you. He will say, "It is just a hormonal thing. You are deluded, you are hallucinating."

Diogenes was watching an archer at practice who was so clumsy that Diogenes went and sat down next to the target. "This is the safest place to be," he explained.

A couple of American sailors had been shipwrecked in the mid-Pacific and had been living on a desert island for several years. One day one of them found a bottle washed ashore — a king-size Coca-Cola bottle he had never seen before. He examined it, then a sudden hysterical shock overcame him.

"Joe!" he cried in terror. "Look at this Coca-Cola bottle — we have shrunk!"

This is logical. The Coca-Cola bottle has become so big, the only logical conclusion is: "We have shrunk!"

Diogenes went into a theater on one occasion just as the audience was crowding out. Upon being asked why, he explained, "I have been opposing people all my life!"

A burglar broke into a small factory and noticed a sign on the safe: "Don't waste dynamite. This safe is open. Just turn the knob."

He did so. At once the place was flooded with light and a bell rang loudly.

As he was taken to the police station he said, "My faith in human nature has been shattered!"

"Why do you look so sad?" Johnny asks his friend.

"Well," his friend replies, "my wife drove herself over a cliff!"

"That's horrible!" exclaims Johnny.

"But that's not the worst of it," continues the friend. "It was a brand new Mercedes!"

He was despondent. "The woman I love has just turned me down," he told his friend. "She won't marry me."

"Don't be so disheartened," said his friend, trying to ease his misery. "Don't you realize a woman's no often means yes?"

"But she didn't say no," he answered. "She said phooey!"

Life is strange! If the woman says no you can understand yes, but if she says phooey, then what you are going to understand?

Mulla Nasruddin was in hospital. A lady doctor knocked on the door. "Come in," said the Mulla.

"Take your clothes off, please," said the doctor.

"All of them?" inquired Nasruddin.

"Yes, all of them."

After taking off all his clothes, the lady doctor gave him a thorough examination. When she was finished, Nasruddin said, "I want to ask you one thing."

"Yes?" she said.

"Why did you bother knocking?"

Just watch all around, and you will find life is not logical — it is the most illogical thing.

She was looking for a parking place and found one near a sign reading, "No Parking On This Street."

A policeman was standing nearby, so she called to him, "Can I park here?"

"No," he said.

"Why not?"

"Can't you read that sign? It says 'No Parking'."

"But what about all those cars parked here?"

"Listen, lady," the policeman said, "they didn't ask me!"

Prem Vinod, watch life and you will see its illogicalness. It is so apparent that if you really want to change life you have to take account of all its illogicality.

I can talk logically because language belongs to logic, but I cannot work logically; existence does not belong to logic. Language is created by logic, it is very logical. The grammar and the language, the mathematics, everything that has been invented by man is logical. Mathematics is very much logical, but life is not.

And mystics have always known it; physicists have come to know it only recently, just within these fifty years. After Albert Einstein's discovery of the theory of relativity they had to encounter the illogical world, the illogical existence. And then they realized that for three hundred years science has been living only in a very small place lighted by human logic. It is just like a candle lighting a small place, and the whole existence is dark, very dark.

If you study Albert Einstein's theory of relativity you will be very much puzzled; you will not believe that these are the words of a scientist. Albert Einstein's theory proposes that if a man leaves on an air spaceship with the same speed as light he will never grow old. For example, if you leave today on a spaceship with the same speed as light, that is one hundred eighty-six thousand miles per second, and after fifty years you come back, all your friends will be in their graves or maybe very old, and you will be exactly the same, of the same age, because time stops at that speed.

Now this is very illogical! Why time should stop at such a speed? And Einstein was asked again and again, "Where is the logic?" He said, "What can I do? If existence functions that way, I can only say how it functions."

When the atom was broken, split, and electrons were found, a new experience physicists had to go through. It was very crazy, because electrons suddenly disappear from one point and appear at another point; in between the two points they are not.

For example, I disappear here and appear into my room — that is very illogical, but that's how electrons have been doing forever; just we were not aware of it!

When this phenomenon was known it was very puzzling. Eddington said that physics is becoming mysticism. Even mystics cannot do such miracles; no mystic has been known to do it. They have walked on water and they have raised the dead, but even Buddha has to walk from one village to another — not just appearing in one village, disappearing, appearing into another. Then in forty years time he would have done at least the work of four thousand years!

But when physicists were asked, "How do you explain it?" they said, "we cannot explain it. This is how it is." They were asked, "It does not fit with logic." So they said, "we have to change logic!" Logic will have to fit with it; existence has no obligation to fit with logic. Why it should fit with your logic? Logic is man's invention, existence is not. Man himself is part of existence, and then man invents logic, just a part of man. And the whole existence is vast, immense; you cannot hope that it should fit with your logic.

Hence many things have changed. Although in the schools and colleges and universities we still go on reading Newton, Edison, Eddington, but modern science has gone far away from the ordinary logic.

The ancient Euclidean geometry is replaced by non-Euclidean geometry. Non-Euclidean geometry is absolutely illogical; Euclidean geometry was logical. Euclidean geometry says, "The shortest distance between two points is a straight line." Non-Euclidean geometry says, "There can be no straight line ever. Straight lines don't exist at all, they cannot." And you will be puzzled — why? If you ask them why, they say, "Because the earth is round whatsoever you draw is just a part of a big circle. It is a small piece so it looks straight, but nothing is straight."

For example, this floor you are sitting on is just straight, but it cannot be; it only appears. You go on expanding this Buddha Hall and then you will come to know that it becomes round, because it will go around the earth. So even this small Buddha Hall is part of that big earth, and the earth is round.

No straight line exists, cannot exist, because in existence everything is spherical. All stars are spheres, all planets are spheres. You cannot find a place where you can draw a straight line. Wherever you draw it will be just an arc, of course so small that you cannot see; for you it seems straight, but it is not straight.

Ordinarily we are trained for mathematics with ten digits, from one to ten. The reason why there are ten digits has no mathematical reasoning behind it — the only reason is that man has ten fingers. Because the primitive man started counting on his fingers, hence the ten digits. What kind of logic is this? And mathematics have tried...

One of the greatest mathematicians, Leibnitz, tried only with three digits — one, two, three, that's all. After three comes ten, eleven, twelve, thirteen, twenty. So in Euclidean geometry the world is a totally different world; in non-Euclidean geometry it is totally different. If you understand Leibnitz, then two plus two is not four, it is twenty, because four does not exist at all.

Albert Einstein tried with two digits, one and two. He said, "Even three is unessential. Science should go only with the essential, one and two." And then comes ten... and that way, Einstein says, everything can be worked out. Yes, less than two won't do; at least two digits will be needed. So that is the most essential; all non-essential is dropped.

Even science is no more logical, cannot be. It has come to a point where logic has fallen far behind.

Mystics have never been logical. I am not a logical person, but just to persuade you, just to attract your attention, I start with logic. But I always end in some illogical thing!

Question 3

OSHO,

I am an ex-Catholic monk I am leaving for my country tomorrow will you tell me few jokes for my other Catholic friends?

— *John*

The first:

A Catholic, a communist and a black Southern Baptist arrived at the Pearly Gates on the same day. Saint Peter came out and the Catholic threw himself face down in front of him and cried, "Oh, Saint Peter, great have been my sins! I don't deserve to enter Paradise!"

"Have faith," said Saint Peter, "for our Lord is both great and forgiving. Spell God!"

The Catholic was taken aback, but waveringly said, "G-o-d." Trumpets sounded, an angelic choir began to sing, and the Pearly Gates swung open. The Catholic got up amazed and walked into heaven.

The communist, watching all this, quickly fell to his knees and started to cry, "Oh, Saint Peter, I have been a communist all my life. I have not been in a church all these years — surely I don't deserve to get into heaven!"

Saint Peter smiled and said, "Brother, all men are the same in the eyes of God. He is great and forgiving. Just spell God!"

The communist took a deep breath and quickly said, "G-o-d." No sooner had he finished than once again the trumpets sounded and the great choir of angels sang out. The Pearly Gates opened and the communist happily entered heaven.

The black Southern Baptist immediately threw himself on the ground, started crying and beating his chest: "Oh, Saint Peter, it is no good! I've been a wicked man, drinkin' and runnin' with loose women. But I've been to church every Sunday and I reads the good book!"

Saint Peter looked at the black man and smiled, "All right, brother, God is great and forgiving. To enter through these gates all you have to do is spell Engelbert Humperdinck!"

Second:

A monk from a Catholic monastery wrote to his mother, "On cold mornings I often miss the old pot under the bed."

She wrote back, "On cold mornings you often missed it at home too!"

Third, and the last:

Sister Mary was taking tea to Mother Superior. When she reached Mother Superior's room she bumped the tray and spilt the tea.

"Oh, shit!" Sister Mary said. "I spilt the tea... oh damn, I said shit... oh Christ, I said damn... oh fuck, I said Christ!"

16

It Is Already The Best

Question 1

OSHO,

I am feeling helpless. I don't know what I can do any more. It is as if everything I do won't change this, it only makes things worse. But also doing nothing does not make things better. You say that emptiness is bliss. For me it seems to be dull and boring; it is like being dead. When there is nothing I cannot see any beauty in it. I am fed up with it, I want to get out out. Please answer me, but please don't answer me like this: That taking sannyas would change everything and make everything beautiful. Thank you.

— Alexander

The first thing is to understand that life remains the same whatsoever you do. It is already perfect; it cannot be improved upon. The very idea of improving it is egoistic; it is the cause of our misery. It is the way it is — there is no need to improve it. Enjoy it! Don't waste your time in improving it. If you try to improve it you will feel helpless, obviously, because you will be failing again and again, falling short. And your desire can never be fulfilled — it isn't in the very nature of things.

Ais Dhammo Sanantano, Gautam the Buddha has said: This is the way things are. Whenever people used to ask him, "How can we improve upon things?" he will always say, "Ais Dhammo Sanantano." There is no need to improve, there is no way to improve.

And in this Isha Upanishad we have come across this truth again and again: aum. That is perfect, that is whole. This is perfect, this is whole. The whole comes from the whole, the perfect comes from the perfect. How it can be imperfect? The whole comes from the whole, yet the whole remains behind. Everything is as it should be.

Unless this is understood... Buddha calls it tathata, suchness. The rose is rose, the marigold is marigold. The effort to make a marigold a rose is doomed to fail. Then there is helplessness, misery, failure. The ego feels hurt, wounded.

This is the first thing: a deep, total acceptance of things as they are. Then life enters into a different dimension — the dimension of joy, celebration — because then the whole energy is available to dance, sing, to be.

Now the whole energy is engaged into improving, into changing, into making things better.

You say: I am feeling helpless.

You are causing this helplessness yourself.

You say: I don't know what I can do any more.

You have done already enough; that's why you are feeling helpless. Stop doing! And when I say stop doing it does not mean do nothing. That is the second thing to be understood: when I say stop doing, don't misunderstand me — I am not saying do nothing. "Stop doing" simply means stop pushing the river, flow with the river. It is already going towards the ocean. It will take you to your destiny, whatsoever it is — xyz, it is unpredictable. Where the river will enter the ocean nobody knows, when and where, and it is good that nobody knows. It is good because life remains a mystery, a constant surprise. One feels wonder on every step; a great awe surrounds one.

But misunderstanding is always possible. Because I say, "Don't try to improve, doing nothing is the best." that does not mean that you become inactive. It simply means you don't make any effort to improve upon things, you relax. You will be still doing things, but now there will be no effort in your doing, there will be no doer in your doing; they will be simply happening.

It Is Already The Best

When you will feel hungry you will eat; that is not doing. When you are not feeling hungry and you force yourself to eat, that is doing. Forcing is doing. When you feel sleepy you sleep; that is not doing. But when you are not feeling sleepy and you force yourself to go to sleep, that is doing. When you are feeling fast asleep, then trying to wake up is doing. When the sleep is over of its own accord and your eyes open up, that is not doing.

Eat when hungry, drink when thirsty, sleep when sleepy. Let go! Don't try to struggle, don't make life a conflict. Enjoy it! And then each moment is precious and you will never feel helpless and you will never feel that nothing is getting better, because you are not expecting it to get better.

It is already the best world that can be, the most perfect existence that ever can be. But your ego wants to improve upon things. You think you know better than existence itself? You are just a small part of it, you are just a small ripple in the infinite ocean — and you want to improve upon the ocean? That is just being foolish! Relax! Dance in the sun while you are! Sing a song! It is beautiful to be and it is also beautiful not to be. When the wave rises, good. For a moment enjoy the sky, the air, the wind, the sun, the rain. And when the wave disappears, good; go into deep rest.

Nothing is ever born and nothing ever dies. Things only move between manifestation and unmanifestation. They become visible, they become invisible. To become invisible is a resting place. Just as after each day you need deep sleep in the night to rejuvenate you, to make you again young and fresh, in the same way after each life you need death. Death is a deeper sleep and nothing else. After each life your body is so tired, you need a new body, a new manifestation. The old wave disappears, but the water in that wave remains in the ocean; it will come again in a new wave. The old is continuously becoming new — allow it. You simply allow life and go with it in deep trust.

This is what I call religiousness — this trust. It is not a belief. Belief is always in dogmas, creeds, theories, philosophies, ideologies. This is not belief, this is simply trusting existence. We have come from it, it is our source. We are not outsiders, we are insiders. And we will go back to the source — it is our source. Coming out of it is good, going back into it is good. All is good! To feel it brings rejoicing — all is good. That's the meaning of trusting in God: that all is good.

You are unnecessarily getting into trouble; you are trying something absurd. You are trying to pull yourself by your own shoestrings. You will feel helpless — you cannot do it. You are like a dog chasing its own tail; it is not possible. The faster the dog will jump, the faster the tail will also move away. It will drive the dog crazy!

It is said that if you want a philosopher to remain engaged, just give him a piece of paper and on both the sides write P.T.O., so he will look on this side and then turn it over, and then P.T.O. again is there, so he will turn it over... and he will go crazy — but he will remain occupied!

You are being too much philosophical. You ask me:

You say that emptiness is bliss...

I don't say — it is so! Ais Dhammo Sanantano. And what you are saying, you are saying. I am not saying, "Emptiness is bliss." What can I do? It is! It is my experience, and what you are saying is simply a statement without any experience. You have not experienced emptiness, but now see what a great problem you have made out of something which you have not experienced.

You say: For me it seems to be dull and boring.

As if you have experienced it! Think over the matter again. Have you ever experienced emptiness? And in emptiness how can there be boredom? If there is boredom it is not empty — it is full of boredom! If there is dullness it is not empty; the mind is there feeling dull, feeling bored. Emptiness cannot be boring, it cannot be dull. Emptiness is simply empty — of everything. You cannot say anything about it. But you have not experienced it, you have just thought about it.

It Is Already The Best

Yes, if you think about emptiness it will look boring, it will look dull, it will look dead. But the people who have experienced it — Buddha, Jesus, Zarathustra, Lao Tzu, Chuang Tzu, Mahavira, Bodhidharma, Bahauddin, Nanak, Kabir — not a single person has said that it is boring. You are really an exception! If you have experienced it then you are denying all the awakened people — but you have not experienced it at all. I can say it because I know what emptiness is.

When I say emptiness is bliss I am not saying that emptiness is full of bliss — don't misunderstand me. "Emptiness is bliss" is simply making you aware of their synonymousness. You can call it empty or you can call it bliss; both the words are synonymous. Emptiness is bliss because there is nothing which can bore you, which can make you feel dull, which can create anxiety, which can make you afraid, which can create anguish. There is nothing at all! Because there is nothing, the whole mind has gone, that state is called bliss. One can call it emptiness, one can call it bliss; these are just two expressions for the same phenomenon.

And, Alexander, don't be a coward. You have such a great name — Alexander — don't be a coward! But Alexander himself was a coward in this sense. He was told by Diogenes, one of the greatest mystics of his time that, "Stop this foolish effort to conquer the world. Look at me! Without conquering the world I have conquered!"

And Alexander looked at Diogenes and felt the beauty of the man, the grace of the man. He was lying naked on the bank of a small river, taking a morning sunbath. The place was absolutely silent, and Diogenes looked so beautiful that Alexander felt jealous for the first time in his life. Alexander had everything, he had almost conquered the whole world. Just India was left out, so he was coming towards India and was certain that he will conquer India too. But he felt jealous of Diogenes, a naked fakir with nothing, not even a begging bowl. Buddha at least used to carry a begging bowl, but Diogenes has thrown the begging bowl also because one day he saw a dog drinking water from the river, and he immediately threw the begging bowl in the river, saying to the dog, "Master, you have taught me a great lesson! If you can manage without a begging bowl, why cannot I?"

He had nothing, and yet he had something which was missing in Alexander. Alexander immediately said that, "If next time God will ask me to come back to the world, I would like to be Diogenes rather than Alexander." But, mind you, he said "next time" — postponing for the next life.

Alexander laughed because he has said something great. He thought Diogenes will appreciate — but Diogenes said, "Don't be a fool! Don't try to deceive me! What do you mean, 'next time'? If you are so much interested in being Diogenes, why not now? Now or never! And who is preventing you? God is not preventing you. This bank is big enough for both of us. Throw the clothes in the river, lie down, take the sunbath! And you need not even bother about food, because I go to beg, and I will bring enough for you too. You simply rest here, forget all about the world. Be Diogenes right now!"

Alexander said, "That is difficult. Right now I cannot do it, but I will come one day. First I have to finish my conquest — I have to conquer the whole world!"

And Diogenes said, "Two things I have to say. One: remember, if you have conquered the whole world, then what you will do?" And Alexander was only thirty-two at that time. "What you will do when you have conquered the whole world? Do you know? There is no other world! You will be at a loss! At least right now you are occupied, busy, without business, but if you conquer the whole world then the real problem will arise: what to do next? — because there is no other world."

And it is said, Alexander felt sad even listening to the idea that there is no other world. He was shocked. He felt immediately a great sadness descend on him and he said, "Don't talk such sad things to me. First let me conquer this and then I will see. And I will come to see you when I have conquered the whole world."

Diogenes said, "Nobody comes back — you will not be able to come back. Don't be so certain about the future. One can be certain only about this moment."

And actually it happened that way: Alexander died on the way; he never reached back home. He was only thirty-three when he died, and he really died for the same reason that Diogenes has pointed to him. The moment he conquered India he became very much depressed, so much so that he became an alcoholic; he started drinking too much. What to do now? He died of too much drinking, he died as an alcoholic. He killed himself — it was suicide. Otherwise he was perfectly healthy, but he was continuously drinking day and night.

Your name is Alexander — be a little aware! Don't do the same foolishness again. You have come the next time, and still you don't want to become a sannyasin! And I am nobody else but Diogenes asking you: Take the jump, become a sannyasin! Nothing will change, but everything will become beautiful. Thank you!

Buddha insists on calling it emptiness, shunyata, and the Upanishads emphasize on calling it bliss — and they are talking about the same phenomenon. Buddha's insistence is far better because it is more applicable to you. You are bound to misunderstand the Upanishad because the Upanishad's way of telling is positive. It says it is bliss, and in you certainly it creates greed; you start searching for bliss. You are miserable and you want bliss, you desire bliss; you start making every effort to improve things so that you can be blissful. You go astray because of the word "bliss" and its positivity.

Buddha became aware of this phenomenon. Twenty-five centuries had passed between Buddha and Isha Upanishad. Isha Upanishad is perfectly right — it is bliss — but to say it to you is not right because you are bound to misunderstand it. Hence Buddha changed the whole expression; he said it is emptiness.

Calling it emptiness is of tremendous importance because nobody wants emptiness — Alexander does not want emptiness. It does not create greed in you. Who will be greedy for emptiness?

The very negativity of it destroys greed, desire, ambition and ego.

And again and again Buddha was asked, "What happens when one becomes empty?" and he will remain silent. He will say, "Don't ask me. You become empty and see what happens." He will never say, "Bliss happens," for the simple reason because you will immediately jump upon the idea of bliss. And to you bliss will mean only pleasure, at the most happiness — something of the mind, something of the body — but it will not be exactly what bliss is.

It is neither of the body nor of the mind. It is a transcendence — a transcendence of all that you know, of all that you have experienced, of all that you are. It is better to call it emptiness; it cuts you from the very roots.

But twenty-five centuries have passed since Buddha again, and people are so stupid that they will misunderstand everything. They misunderstood the Isha Upanishad which talks about bliss. Buddha tried to move to the other extreme, started calling the ultimate state emptiness, shunyata, just zero, pure zero and nothing. It worked for a time being, while he was alive. It always works when the Master is alive — it works. Any method becomes magical when the Master is alive, any word becomes significant when the Master is alive. It is the charisma, it is the presence of the Master that makes things work. It is his magic.

Once Buddha was gone, the same people who have misused the word "bliss" started misusing the word "emptiness". People like Alexander, they started thinking emptiness is boring, emptiness is dull, emptiness is nothing but death. What is the point of attaining emptiness? Without knowing anything about emptiness they start condemning it.

Buddhism was uprooted from India for the simple reason that Buddha has used total negative terms, and India has become accustomed of positive, affirmative terminology. Buddha seemed very strange, not belonging to the tradition, antagonistic to tradition. He was trying to help.

It Is Already The Best

Now I am trying to do both the things together. I am saying bliss is emptiness — another effort. Upanishads said it is bliss, Buddha said it is nothingness. You have escaped from both; I am trying to catch hold of you from both the sides. I say emptiness is bliss, bliss is emptiness.

You are saying things which you have not experienced at all. You say:

When there is nothing I cannot see any beauty in it.

When there is nothing, do you think you will be there? When there is nothing you will not be there! There will be something which cannot be called "I", which cannot be identified with the ego. So who will be there to see beauty? There will not be beauty and there will not be the seer, there will be just silence: no I, no thou, no subject, no object — no duality... a pure oneness, an utter silence.

But you got caught, you got caught in your own words.

You say: I am fed up with it.

As if you are living in it — you are fed up with it. You have not even tasted a single drop of nothingness, emptiness, and you are fed up with it. How tricky is the mind! How cunning is the mind! And how politically it finds ways to avoid certain things. How it rationalizes!

Just one month before one friend, Ajai Krishn Lakhanpal, has asked me — he had written a letter — "Osho, I am ready to take sannyas today. If you give me sannyas today I am willing, I am ready to surrender. But my own choice will be," he said, "that I would like to take sannyas after one month, on 25th October, because that is my birthday."

Seeing his "but"... because I don't like "buts". Otherwise, when somebody asks for sannyas I insist now. What can be said about tomorrow? You cannot be sure of tomorrow. Tomorrow may come, may not come. Even if it comes your mind is constantly changing. How can you be sure of tomorrow? Tomorrow your mind may give you some other ideas.

Seeing his "but"... it was the first time I allowed him, the first person I have allowed — just for a change, to see what happens. I said, "Okay, 25th October, settled. You take sannyas 25th October." Yesterday was 25th October. I told Sheela to call Ajai Krishn and ask him, "What happened? 25th has come!" Now he has found rationalizations. I was expecting; that "but" was enough to show me. He has found rationalizations.

Now he says — he wrote a letter again — "I know that I had promised you to take sannyas on 25th..." And that time he had written that, "It is because of my birthday. And secondly, I would like to ask my mother's permission. I know she will say yes, so there is no problem about that." And now he says, "My mother has said yes, but she says she will not be very happy about it. She says, 'Yes, if you want to take sannyas you can, but I will not be very happy about it.' And I don't want to hurt her feelings." And moreover, one of his gurus, Kammu Baba, had told him few years before — he is dead, he is no more alive — that "Never hurt the feelings of your parents." "... so I cannot hurt her feelings."

Mind goes on finding rationalizations. It never sees things directly; it tries to evade. Now if Kammu Baba is right then Buddha was wrong. He hurt very much the feelings of his parents, his wife, his child. Then Mahavira was wrong, then Jesus was wrong, then Nanak was wrong. Then except Kammu Baba... and I don't know whether Kammu Baba has said it to Ajai Krishn or he has invented it, or he has thought that he had said it. Then the whole spiritual tradition will be wrong.

Jesus says to his disciples, "Unless you hate your parents you cannot follow me." And that is nothing...

Once it happened that a great king, Presenjit, came to see Gautam Buddha. When he was sitting in front of Buddha, a man came, touched Buddha's feet — a very old man, one of his disciples, a sannyasin — and he said that, "I am going now on a long journey to spread your message. Bless me."

It Is Already The Best

Buddha looked at Presenjit and said, "This man is the answer to your question."

Presenjit was asking that, "I would like to become a sannyasin, but my old mother may feel hurt — she is too old."

Buddha said, "Look at this man. He has killed his father and mother both!"

Presenjit was very much disturbed: Killed? Father and mother? And Buddha is appreciating the man! When the man left Presenjit said, "I don't understand! You praised that man and you said he has killed his father and mother!"

Buddha said, "Yes, psychologically. Not really, not physically, but deep inside he has dropped the clinging with the father and the mother?"

Ajai Krishn is forty-five years old and still clinging with the apron of the mother! Now when he is going to become mature? It is time. One should kill... not the mother on the outside, but the clinging in your inner world.

That's what Jesus means when he says, "Unless you hate your father and mother..." He does not mean that hate your father and mother: he means deep down you have to uproot the whole conditioning, the whole clinging, the whole attachment. Only then you can become mature, centered, grounded. Only then you can be an individual in your own right. But mind goes on finding subtle strategies to avoid reality.

Now, Alexander, you are saying that, "I am fed up with nothingness, emptiness. I want to get out of it."

And you must have believed what you are writing. You have no idea of nothingness and you are fed up with it, and you want to get out of it! The real thing is how to get into it!

And you ask me: Please answer me, but please don't answer me like this, that taking sannyas would change everything and make everything beautiful.

No, taking sannyas will not change anything but it will certainly make everything beautiful! The world remains the same, just the vision, the attitude, the approach changes.

Question 2

OSHO,

Pope John Paul has stated recently that if a man looked lustfully even at the woman who is his wife he could likewise commit adultery in his heart. What do you say about it?

— *Gayatri*

What can be said about it? A Polack is a Polack! Pope or no pope, a Polack remains a Polack. Now this is the ultimate in stupidity, one cannot surpass it: even to look at your own wife with desire is adultery! Then why in the first place one should get married? Just to commit adultery?

In a way he has made a very difficult thing simple. One of Milan's newspapers seems to be far more wiser. The newspaper writes: "Life is hard for the adulterer — an endless round of cover-ups, tricks, juggling of the daily calendar and the need to buy useless and expensive presents for two women at once. Now the Pope has removed all these vows, because you can have infidelity in your own house!" This seems to be far more intelligent. It is really beautiful and juicy to have adultery with your own wife. A great idea!

But these repressed people are bound to do such things.

I have come to know that for the whole year, the whole past year, in his every weekly sermon he has been talking about sex — for the whole year condemning, condemning... Now why he should be so much concerned about sex, for one year continuously condemning? There must be something inside him, some wound which has not healed.

At the marriage counselor's the husband accused his wife of being frigid.

It Is Already The Best

"That's not true!" she said. "I don't disapprove of sex relations." Then turning from her husband to the counselor she continued, "But this sex fiend expects it every month!"

The woman must have been a Catholic! The Catholics have done one of the greatest harms to humanity. Christianity has been one of the most repressive religions; what has happened out of this repressiveness is just the opposite of it. It was bound to happen, it was inevitable. The pendulum has moved to the other extreme in the West, and the responsibility wholly and solely rests on the shoulders of the church. People have become indulgent, people have become really too much obsessed with sex.

For two thousand years Christianity particularly the Catholic Church, has been repressing, condemning. But now a point has come when the volcano has erupted. What you see now in the West is sheer indulgence, ugly.

Sex is beautiful, but it can become ugly in two ways: either you become repressive — it becomes ugly; or you become indulgent — it becomes ugly. Sex is beautiful if it is accepted naturally, as part of life there is no need to condemn it, there is no need to praise it either. When humanity is going to accept things easily, in a relaxed way?

But these people have not learned any lesson, and they go on interpreting scriptures according to their own inner turmoil.

What the Polack Pope was doing was simply making a commentary on one of the statements of Jesus. The statement is totally different, but just a jugglery of words, just a little change, and the whole thing has gone wrong.

This is the original statement of Jesus. Jesus says: "You have heard it was said, 'You shall not commit adultery.' But I say to you that everyone who looks at a woman lustfully has already committed adultery with her in his heart."

Now the woman is one thing and wife is totally another. The Polack has read "wife" instead of "woman" — your own wife!

And of course he can play with words. He can say, "Of course your wife is also a woman." True, but what is the meaning of her being your wife? why one gets married? To live a natural, untroubled sexual life. But to change the word "woman" into "wife" is really ugly; it is against Jesus, it is not true to his message. But you cannot expect anything better from the Polacks.

How do you recognize a Polack in a busy shoe store?

He is the one who tries to put on the shoe boxes.

Now trying to change woman into wife is exactly like that — trying to put on the shoe boxes instead of the shoes!

Two Polacks are driving a lorry which is three meters high. They drive past a road-sign indicating a tunnel up ahead two meters high. "Just ignore the sign, Sol. I know that at this time of the day the police are not going to be there!"

Wykowsky, the window washer, was called in by a homeowner to give an estimate. "How much to clean the windows on the ground floor?"

Wykowsky pulled out a pad, scribbled a minute and replied, "Two dollars a window."

"On the second floor?" asked the homeowner.

Again Wykowsky wrote on the pad and answered, "One dollar fifty cents a window."

"And the basement?"

"Five dollars a window," said Wykowsky.

"Wait a minute!" said the homeowner. "How come two dollars for the windows on the first floor, a buck and a half for the second floor, and you want five dollars for each of the basement windows?"

"Mister," said the Polack, "don't you realize the size of the hole I have to dig to put the ladder in?"

It Is Already The Best

At a Polish wedding:

The ceremony had taken place in the ballroom of the town hotel. The newly married husband came down from the bridal suite and said to a buddy, "My best friend he upstairs in bed with my wife!"

"What do you... what you going to do about it?" asked his pal.

"Nothing," replied the Polack. "He is so drunk he thinks he be me."

The Polack was on his honeymoon, but he was too inexperienced to know the difference between love and nymphomania, because he had just escaped from a Catholic monastery.

The first morning after the wedding he rose, walked over to the window of the hotel, and raised the shade. The day was dark and gloomy and the rain was falling in torrents. Disgusted, he lowered the shade and climbed back in bed.

The next morning the young man rose again and lifted the shade. It was still raining. Once more he lowered it and crawled back into bed.

The third morning he staggered out of bed, tottered over to raise the shade — and went up with it.

All that I can say: that one cannot expect anything better from the Pope — he is a pure Polack! What he has said is absolutely absurd — mental adultery with one's own wife? But in a way this is one of the oldest ideas in the Catholic Church. Sexual pleasure is suspect. In fact, all pleasure is suspect. These so-called religious people are afraid of pleasure, they are against all pleasure. They want your life to become so utterly depressed, gloomy, sad that you are bound to start looking for some other life — life beyond death. Their whole effort is to destroy your life herenow so totally that the only shelter for you left is in the life after death. Then you become available to the priests to be exploited.

If you are happy, if you are enjoying life, if you are living each moment with pleasure, a dance in the heart and a song on the lips, if your life is a sheer festivity, you will not bother much about the churches and the temples. If your life is a ceremony, who cares about the life beyond? This very moment, if you are living totally, all concern for the future disappears.

And these churches, these priests, all depend on your desire for a future life their whole strategy is to destroy your pleasure here so that you become interested in pleasure of heavenly life. And do you see? — what they deny here they supply there.

Here they say that to love a woman is sin. And in heaven? — you will be provided with beautiful women. In some religions even beautiful boys will be made available to you, so homosexuals need not be worried! Here they condemn wine and there streams of wine are flowing, in paradise. Here they insist for prohibition and there all that is denied and prohibited will be made available in a thousandfold way.

Hindus say that all the pleasures are wrong, but in heaven you will be sitting under wish-fulfilling trees — kalpavrishkas — and whatsoever you wish will be immediately fulfilled, instantly, not even a single moment's distance between the desire and its fulfillment. Naturally they have to destroy all possibilities here so you become focused on the future. And then they can exploit you, because they have the keys of the future.

If you are a Catholic only then you can be saved; or if you are a Mohammedan only then you can be saved; or if you are a Hindu only then you can be saved. The strategy is the same, the trick is the same. All the priests have been using the same trade secret: destroy pleasure in people's life, make them as much miserable as possible — once they are miserable they are bound to fall unto your feet and ask for your advice and guidance.

There is nothing wrong in pleasure. Even in physical pleasure there is nothing wrong; it is a God's gift. If God was against the body he would not give you the body in the first place; if he was against sex he would not give you sexual energy, sexual desire and longing. If all these things are given by nature to you, they are natural. Yes, one thing is certain: don't remain clinging to the physical pleasure only because there are higher possibilities greater potential in you.

So I say physical pleasure is beautiful in its own place, but that is not the end of life. You can have psychological pleasures; psychological pleasures are called happiness. Listening to beautiful music — Beethoven or Mozart or Ravi Shankar — listening to great poetry — Kalidas, Balbhuti Shakespeare, Milton — listening to the nature — the birds, the wind passing through the trees, the dance of the trees in the sun, or looking at the beautiful paintings, great sculpture, architecture — these are pleasures of the mind.

The physical pleasures are two: food and sex. Nothing is wrong in them, so don't repress them, because repression will bring indulgence. Accept them in a simple, innocent way, and then move ahead. That is not the end, that is only the beginning of the journey.

And even the pleasures of the mind are not the end; then there are joys of the spirit. Meditation, silence, prayer, these are the joys of meditation, joys of the soul. And still there is the ultimate, the turiya, the fourth — even to go beyond the self. That's what Buddha calls attaining the zero, nothingness: just being, without any idea of "I". That is inexpressible; it is called bliss.

These are the four planes: pleasure, happiness, joy bliss. And the higher you go, richer you become. But remember, the higher contains the lower. The ultimate, the fourth, is fourth only because it contains all the three. It is not against the three: those three are its foundations, steppingstones the ladder. The higher contains the lower; the lower does not contain the higher. Once this is understood, then the lower is good as far as it goes, although it does not go far enough.

So go as far as it goes, but don't stop there. There is still more to life. Explore! Move from the body to the mind, from the mind to the self, and from the self to no-self, anatta, nothingness. Then only you will know the ultimate unfoldment of your being. That is bliss, the one-thousand-petaled lotus blossoming.

And lastly: what the Polack Pope has said is male chauvinistic.

He talks about men lusting after women but not the reverse. Women are not considered at all — they are not worth consideration. Nobody bothers about them. He is talking about men, that man should not lust after women, but not about women. What about women? Nothing has to be said. They are not counted as human beings; they are commodities, far lower. They don't have any future, they don't belong to the spiritual world.

For centuries this male chauvinistic attitude has prevailed. In India the so-called saints go on saying that the woman is the door of hell, but they don't say the same thing about men. They go on condemning the women, but they never say anything about the men. If the woman infatuates man, then the man infatuates the woman.

But even your saints are not true sages — they are male chauvinistic pigs! Otherwise man and woman are two aspects of the same humanity; they require the same respect. But the whole past has been condemnatory about women. It only shows one thing, nothing else: that your saints were deep down afraid of women, hence they were creating all kinds of barriers around themselves, that "the woman is the door to hell." They were trying to convince themselves that the woman consists only of bones and blood and pus and mucus. And what they consist of? — gold, silver, diamonds?

It is very strange! Not a single saint says what he consists of — and he comes from the woman. From the woman's womb he comes, brings all the blood and the bone and the pus and the mucus from the woman, and he condemns the woman. He is really afraid, afraid of his own sexuality; afraid because he has been told that sex is sin. And of course to him the woman symbolizes sex.

Nobody bothers about the woman, what is her situation. In fact, women are very non-aggressive as far as sexuality is concerned. No woman can rape a man, only a man can rape a woman. Man's sexuality is aggressive, woman's sexuality is receptive. Woman can live without sex far more easily than man, hence nuns are far more true than the monks — the monks are hypocrites. But the poor woman is condemned continuously.

I would like to change this whole ugly tradition. The woman will be respected only when sex is also respected, remember it. The woman will be accepted only when sex is also accepted as natural.

These popes, these shankaracharyas, these imams, these so-called saints have created a very ugly situation. It has to be completely destroyed and a new beginning has to be made in which man and woman are no more separate, are no more thought separately, in which man and woman are considered equally because they are two aspects of the same sex, two sides of the same coin.

Question 3

OSHO,

Is this world insane?

— Siddhartha

It seems so. At least up to now it has been insane. Man is not born insane but is driven towards insanity by the priests, by the politicians, by the parents, by your whole educational system, by your morality, by all that is enforced upon you, by all the conditionings. You are driven insane.

Man need not be insane, but it has not been possible yet to accept man in his naturalness. We create a structure around him, we prune him, we go on and on giving a certain form and pattern to him, we don't allow him to be himself

And that's my whole effort here: to accept humanity with deep respect, love, trust, so that man can regain his sanity. And the problem is that man is driven insane by your so-called well-wishers. The people who are trying to help you are the people who are poisoning you. Great mischief is being done by public servants, missionaries, by the so-called saints. They are the most mischievous people in the world — not intentionally, not consciously, but that's the ultimate result of whatsoever *they* have been doing. they have been driven insane by other saints and *they* are driving you insane.

And if you don't follow them you feel guilty; if you follow them you become hypocrites. They don't leave you any other alternative, only two alternatives: either be insane like them or feel guilty. And both the alternatives are ill, sickening.

Siddhartha, watch life all around you and you will find in every possible way that man is insane.

When the seven-year-old started for school his mother suggested softly, "Son, put a smile on your face and have a happy time!"

But when the lad returned home his face was a big frown.

"What happened?" his mother asked. "I thought you were going to smile and have a happy time at school."

"It didn't work, Mom," he said. "I tried to keep smiling, but the teacher thought I was up to something and was always giving me dirty looks!"

Nobody wants you to be happy. If you are happy, everybody will become suspicious of you: "you are up to something. Why you are looking so happy?" If you are sad you are accepted — you are part of the crowd. Everybody is sad and you are also sad; it fits. But if you are dancing and rejoicing then you are crazy, mad. Then you have to be put into a hospital, you have to be treated, given electric shocks or something, because how you can be happy? How you can be so blissful? When the whole humanity is suffering, you have to suffer.

And the crowd has always been against the people who were blissful. They crucified Jesus, they poisoned Socrates, they murdered Mansoor; and their only sin was that they were trying to be blissful, that they were not part of the mob, the sad, sick society. They were trying to be individuals.

The marriage counselor was asking a woman some questions about her disposition. "Did you wake up grumpy this morning?"

"No," she answered. "I let him sleep."

It Is Already The Best

A woman driver passed a red light and collided with another car. Jumping out of her car, she snapped at the other driver, "Why don't you watch where you're going? You are the third car I hit this morning!"

When a customer was told he could no longer buy his favorite patent medicine, he angrily berated the druggist.

"But I tell you, it has now been banned," the druggist insisted. "Now you need a doctor's prescription because it is habit-forming."

"It is not habit-forming!" the customer cried. "I know it's not because I've been taking it every day for twenty years!"

A client was complaining to a marriage counselor that his wife's immaturity was causing his marriage to go on the rocks. "She is so immature," he charged, "that every time I take a bath she comes in and sinks my boats!"

The elderly millionaire emerged from his exclusive club feeling despondent and hopeless, and slowly climbed into his limousine.

"Where to, sir?" asked his chauffeur.

"Drive off a cliff, James," was the reply. "I am committing suicide!"

A leading sexologist interviewed on television was asked, "What do you think of the view that impotence is on the rise?"

"I think the question is self-contradictory!" he replied.

It is an insane world!

In old age Diogenes stopped a veteran and asked, "What were you in the last war?"

"Oh, I was only a private," replied the veteran.

Diogenes rocked as if about to fall. "Ye gods!" he gasped. "At last!" Then after catching his breath he blew out his lantern and went home.

You think over it — it is a little difficult.

Question 4

OSHO,

You sure make a great sit-down comic! what would happen if you stood up?

— *Vivek*

I don't know... but I can try!

About Osho

Osho defies categorization, reflecting everything from the individual quest for meaning to the most urgent social and political issues facing society today. His books are not written but are transcribed from recordings of extemporaneous talks given over a period of thirty-five years. Osho has been described by *The Sunday Times* in London as one of the "1000 Makers of the 20th Century" and by *Sunday Mid-Day* in India as one of the ten people – along with Gandhi, Nehru and Buddha – who have changed the destiny of India.

Osho has a stated aim of helping to create the conditions for the birth of a new kind of human being, characterized as "Zorba the Buddha" – one whose feet are firmly on the ground, yet whose hands can touch the stars. Running like a thread through all aspects of Osho is a vision that encompasses both the timeless wisdom of the East and the highest potential of Western science and technology.

He is synonymous with a revolutionary contribution to the science of inner transformation and an approach to meditation which specifically addresses the accelerated pace of contemporary life. The unique OSHO Active Meditations™ are designed to allow the release of accumulated stress in the body and mind so that it is easier to be still and experience the thought-free state of meditation.

Osho International Meditation Resort

Every year the OSHO International Meditation Resort welcomes thousands of people from over 100 countries who come to enjoy and participate in its unique atmosphere of meditation and celebration. The 40-acre meditation resort is located about 100 miles southeast of Mumbai (Bombay), in Pune, India, in a tree-lined residential area set against a backdrop of bamboo groves and wild jasmine, peacocks and waterfalls.

The basic approach of the meditation resort is that of Zorba the Buddha: living in awareness, with a capacity to celebrate everything in life. Many visitors come to just be, to allow themselves the luxury of doing nothing. Others choose to participate in a wide variety of courses and sessions that support moving toward a more joyous and less stressful life by combining methods of self-understanding with awareness techniques. These courses are offered through OSHO Multiversity and take place in a pyramid complex next to the famous OSHO Teerth Park.

You can choose to practice various meditation methods, both active and passive, from a daily schedule that begins at six o'clock in the morning. Each evening there is a meditation event that moves from dance to silent sitting, using Osho's recorded talks as an opportunity to experience inner silence without effort.

Facilities include tennis courts, a gym, sauna, Jacuzzi, a nature-shaped Olympic-sized swimming pool, classes in zen archery, tai chi, chi gong, yoga and a multitude of bodywork sessions.

The kitchen serves international gourmet vegetarian meals, made with organically grown produce. The nightlife is alive with friends dining under the stars, with music and dancing.

Make online bookings for accommodation at the new OSHO Guesthouse inside the meditation resort through the website below or drop us an email at guesthouse@osho.com

Take an online tour of the meditation resort, and access travel and program information at: www.osho.com/resort

Books by Osho in English Language

Early Discourses and Writings
A Cup of Tea
Dimensions Beyond The Known
From Sex to Super-consciousness
The Great Challenge
Hidden Mysteries
I Am The Gate
The Inner Journey
Psychology of the Esoteric
Seeds of Wisdom

Meditation
The Voice of Silence
And Now and Here (Vol 1 & 2)
In Search of the Miraculous (Vol 1 &.2)
Meditation: The Art of Ecstasy
Meditation: The First and Last Freedom
The Path of Meditation
The Perfect Way
Yaa-Hoo! The Mystic Rose

Buddha and Buddhist Masters
The Book of Wisdom
The Dhammapada: The Way of the Buddha (Vol 1-12)
The Diamond Sutra
The Discipline of Transcendence (Vol 1-4)
The Heart Sutra

Indian Mystics
Enlightenment: The Only Revolution (Ashtavakra)
Showering Without Clouds (Sahajo)

The Last Morning Star (Daya)
The Song of Ecstasy (Adi Shankara)

Baul Mystics
The Beloved (Vol 1 & 2)
Kabir
The Divine Melody
Ecstasy: The Forgotten Language
The Fish in the Sea is Not Thirsty
The Great Secret
The Guest
The Path of Love
The Revolution

Jesus and Christian Mystics
Come Follow to You (Vol 1-4)
I Say Unto You (Vol 1 & 2)
The Mustard Seed
Theologia Mystica

Jewish Mystics
The Art of Dying
The True Sage

Western Mystics
Guida Spirituale (Desiderata)
The Hidden Harmony
(Heraclitus)
The Messiah (Vol 1 & 2) (Commentaries on Khalil Gibran's The Prophet)
The New Alchemy: To Turn You On (Commentaries on Mabel Collins' Light on the Path)
Philosophia Perennis (Vol 1 & 2) (The Golden Verses of Pythagoras)
Zarathustra: A God That Can Dance
Zarathustra: The Laughing Prophet (Commentaries on Nietzsche's Thus Spake Zarathustra)

Sufism
Just Like That
Journey to the Heart
The Perfect Master (Vol 1 & 2)
The Secret
Sufis: The People of the Path (Vol 1 & 2)
Unio Mystica (Vol 1 & 2)
The Wisdom of the Sands (Vol 1 & 2)

Tantra
Tantra: The Supreme Understanding
The Tantra Experience
 The Royal Song of Saraha
 (same as Tantra Vision, Vol 1)
The Tantric Transformation
 The Royal Song of Saraha
 (same as Tantra Vision, Vol 2)
The Book of Secrets: Vigyan Bhairav Tantra

The Upanishads
Behind a Thousand Names
(Nirvana Upanishad)
Heartbeat of the Absolute
(Ishavasya Upanishad)
I Am That (Isa Upanishad)
The Message Beyond Words
(Kathopanishad)
Philosophia Ultima (Mandukya Upanishad)
The Supreme Doctrine (Kenopanishad)
Finger Pointing to the Moon
(Adhyatma Upanishad)
That Art Thou (Sarvasar Upanishad, Kaivalya Upanishad, Adhyatma Upanishad)
The Ultimate Alchemy, Vol 1&2
 (Atma Pooja Upanishad Vol 1 & 2)
Vedanta: Seven Steps to Samadhi (Akshaya Upanishad)
Flight of the Alone to the Alone

Books by Osho in English Language

(Kaivalya Upanishad)

Tao
The Empty Boat
The Secret of Secrets
Tao:The Golden Gate (Vol 1&2)
Tao:The Pathless Path (Vol 1&2)
Tao: The Three Treasures (Vol 1-4)
When the Shoe Fits

Yoga
The Path of Yoga (previously Yoga: The Alpha and the Omega Vol 1)
Yoga: The Alpha and the Omega (Vol 2-10)

Zen and Zen Masters
Ah, This!
Ancient Music in the Pines
And the Flowers Showered
A Bird on the Wing
Bodhidharma: The Greatest Zen Master
Communism and Zen Fire, Zen Wind
Dang Dang Doko Dang
The First Principle
God is Dead: Now Zen is the Only Living Truth
The Grass Grows By Itself
The Great Zen Master Ta Hui
Hsin Hsin Ming: The Book of Nothing
I Celebrate Myself: God is No Where, Life is Now Here
Kyozan: A True Man of Zen
Nirvana: The Last Nightmare
No Mind: The Flowers of Eternity
No Water, No Moon
One Seed Makes the Whole Earth Green
Returning to the Source
The Search: Talks on the 10 Bulls of Zen
A Sudden Clash of Thunder

The Sun Rises in the Evening
Take it Easy (Vol 1 & 2)
This Very Body the Buddha
Walking in Zen, Sitting in Zen
The White Lotus
Yakusan: Straight to the Point of Enlightenment
Zen Manifesto : Freedom From Oneself
Zen: The Mystery and the Poetry of the Beyond
Zen: The Path of Paradox (Vol 1, 2 & 3)
Zen: The Special Transmission
Zen Boxed Sets
The World of Zen (5 vol.)
Live Zen
This. This. A Thousand Times This
Zen: The Diamond Thunderbolt
Zen: The Quantum Leap from Mind to No-Mind

Zen: The Solitary Bird, Cuckoo
of the Forest
Zen: All The Colors Of The Rainbow (5 vol.)
The Buddha: The Emptiness of the Heart
The Language of Existence
The Miracle
The Original Man
Turning In

Osho: On the Ancient Masters of Zen (7 volumes)*
Dogen: The Zen Master
Hyakujo: The Everest of Zen–
With Basho's haikus
Isan: No Footprints in the Blue Sky
Joshu: The Lion's Roar
Ma Tzu: The Empty Mirror
Nansen: The Point Of Departure
Rinzai: Master of the Irrational
*Each volume is also available individually.

Responses to Questions
Be Still and Know
Come, Come, Yet Again Come
The Goose is Out
The Great Pilgrimage: From Here to Here
The Invitation
My Way: The Way of the White Clouds
Nowhere to Go But In
The Razor's Edge
Walk Without Feet, Fly Without Wings and Think Without Mind
The Wild Geese and the Water
Zen: Zest, Zip, Zap and Zing

Talks in America
From Bondage To Freedom
From Darkness to Light
From Death To Deathlessness
From the False to the Truth
From Unconsciousness to Consciousness
The Rajneesh Bible (Vol 2-4)

The World Tour
Beyond Enlightenment (Talks in Bombay)
Beyond Psychology (Talks in Uruguay)
Light on the Path (Talks in the Himalayas)
The Path of the Mystic (Talks in Uruguay)
Sermons in Stones (Talks in Bombay)
Socrates Poisoned Again After 25 Centuries (Talks in Greece)
The Sword and the Lotus
(Talks in the Himalayas)
The Transmission of the Lamp
(Talks in Uruguay)

Osho's Vision for the World
The Golden Future
The Hidden Splendor
The New Dawn

The Rebel
The Rebellious Spirit

The Mantra Series
Hari Om Tat Sat
Om Mani Padme Hum
Om Shantih Shantih Shantih
Sat-Chit-Anand
Satyam-Shivam-Sundram

Personal Glimpses
Books I Have Loved
Glimpses of a Golden Childhood
Notes of a Madman

Interviews with the World Press
The Last Testament (Vol 1)

Intimate Talks between
Master and Disciple – Darshan Diaries
A Rose is a Rose is a Rose
Be Realistic: Plan for a Miracle
Believing the Impossible Before Breakfast
Beloved of My Heart
Blessed are the Ignorant
Dance Your Way to God
Don't Just Do Something, Sit There
Far Beyond the Stars
For Madmen Only
The Further Shore
Get Out of Your Own Way
God's Got A Thing about You
God is Not for Sale
The Great Nothing
Hallelujah!
Let Go!
The 99 Names of Nothingness

No Book, No Buddha, No Teaching, No Disciple
Nothing to Lose but Your Head
Only Losers Can Win in This Game
Open Door
Open Secret
The Shadow of the Whip
The Sound of One Hand Clapping
The Sun Behind the Sun Behind the Sun
The Tongue-Tip Taste of Tao
This Is It
Turn On, Tune In and Drop the Lot
What Is, Is, What Ain't, Ain't
Won't You Join The Dance?

Compilations
After Middle Age: A Limitless Sky
At the Feet of the Master
Bhagwan Shree Rajneesh: On Basic Human Rights
Jesus Crucified Again, This Time in Ronald Reagan's America
Priests and Politicians: The Mafia of the Soul
Take it Really Seriously

Gift Books of Osho Quotations
A Must for Contemplation Before Sleep
A Must for Morning

Contemplation
India My Love

Photobooks
Shree Rajneesh: A Man of Many Climates,
  Seasons and Rainbows
through the eye of the camera
Impressions... Osho Commune International Photobook

Books about Osho
Bhagwan: The Buddha for the Future by Juliet Forman

Bhagwan Shree Rajneesh: The Most Dangerous Man Since Jesus Christ by Sue Appleton

Bhagwan: The Most Godless Yet the Most Godly Man by Dr. George Meredith
Bhagwan: One Man Against the Whole Ugly Past of Humanity by Juliet Forman
Bhagwan: Twelve Days That Shook the World by Juliet Forman
Was Bhagwan Shree Rajneesh Poisoned by Ronald Reagan's America? by Sue Appleton.
Diamond Days With Osho by Ma Prem Shunyo

For More Information

www.OSHO.com

A comprehensive multi-language website including OSHO Books, talks (audio and video), a magazine, the OSHO Library text archive in English and Hindi with a searchable facility, and extensive information about OSHO Meditation techniques.

You will also find the program schedule of the OSHO Multiversity and information about the OSHO International Meditation Resort.

The original recordings of the talks/interviews in this book can be downloaded from osho.com\audiobooks.

To contact:

Osho International Foundation

go to: www.osho.com/oshointernational

Osho International Meditation Resort

17 Koregaon Park,
Pune 411001 MS, India
resortinfo@osho.net